Autism in History

The Case of Hugh Blair of Borgue

Alexander Carse. 'The arrival of the country relations' (1812).
Visiting was a central part of sociability in eighteenth century Scotland, both
between kin and friends. Hugh Blair's visits were often awkward, being both
unannounced and conducted in silence. When people visited his family home
he was generally kept out of the way. In the early and mid-eighteenth century
it is unlikely that the dress and material comforts of rural lairds would have
been as different from those of the fashionable urban set as this later picture
shows.
Source: Scottish National Portrait Gallery, B987. In the collection of the Duke of
Buccleuch and Queensberry KT.

Autism in History

The Case of Hugh Blair of Borgue

Rab Houston and Uta Frith

BLACKWELL
Publishers

The right of Rab Houston and Uta Frith to be identified as authors of this work has been asserted in accordance with the Copyright, Designs and Patents Act 1988.

ABJ4704
03/15/2001
LAN
‡22.95

First published 2000

2 4 6 8 10 9 7 5 3 1

Blackwell Publishers Ltd
108 Cowley Road
Oxford OX4 1JF
UK

Blackwell Publishers Inc.
350 Main Street
Malden, MA 02148
USA

British Library Cataloguing in Publication Data

A CIP catalogue record for this book is available from the British Library.

Library of Congress Cataloging-in-Publication Data has been applied for

Frith, Uta.
    Autism in history : the case of Hugh Blair of Borgue [c. 1708–1765] / Rab Houston and Uta Frith.
        p. cm.
    Includes bibliographical references and index.
    ISBN 0–631–22088–7 (alk. paper) — ISBN 0–631–22089–5 (alk. paper)
    1. Blair, Hugh 1708–1765. 2. Autism—Patients—Scotland—Biography. I. Houston, R. A. (Robert Allan), 1954– II. Title.

RC553.A88 F75 2000
616.89′82′0092—dc21
[B]   00–036033

Typeset in 11 on 13.5 pt Bembo
by Ace Filmsetting Ltd, Frome, Somerset
Printed in Great Britain by T.J. International, Padstow, Cornwall

This book is printed on acid-free paper.

Table of Contents

List of Plates

List of Plates

Acknowledgements

It was the late Dr Leah Leneman, formerly of the Department of Economic and Social History, University of Edinburgh, who first brought the Hugh Blair case to my attention while I was working on a related project funded by a fellowship from the Leverhulme Trust. Funding from the Carnegie Trust made possible additional archival research in Kirkcudbrightshire. Writing of the book was concluded thanks to a sabbatical leave funded by the Arts and Humanities Research Board. Dr Ian Donnachie and Professor Roy Campbell commented on earlier drafts of this book and provided information on the economy and society of southwest Scotland. Dr David Sellar gave advice about earlier drafts of the sections on the law of marriage and mental incapacity. Dr John Shaw of the National Archives of Scotland provided helpful references. Marion Stewart, of Dumfries and Galloway Archives, furnished background material. I should also like to thank the archivists of the Stewartry Museum and Broughton House, both in Kirkcudbright. Margaret Torrance, Adam Gray, David Devereux, Betty Watson and Jean Stoddart offered valuable local knowledge and references. Greta Arnott, Professor Gavin and Dr Maureen Reid, and Dr Veena O'Halloran provided insightful comments. Veena also prepared the family tree. Margaret Dewey made valuable suggestions for the final revisions of the draft manuscript. Finally, I should like to thank Dr Evelyn McGregor, who first alerted me to the work of Uta Frith.

RAH

Acknowledgements

I too would like to thank Evelyn McGregor for having set in motion the events which made this historical-psychological collaboration in sleuthing possible. I am deeply indebted to Chris Frith and to Francesca Happé, with whom I was able to discuss the evidence about Hugh Blair from a scientific and clinical point of view. With their help and encouragement it was exciting to apply contemporary ideas about autism to the historical evidence. As always, Francesca Happé has clarified numerous points of fact, theory and style.

I owe a huge debt to Margaret Dewey who has been the guiding spirit in my endeavour. Snowbound over one very cold month in Ann Arbor, she read and revised drafts of chapters that were still very rough. Her incisiveness and her wisdom shaped and sometimes changed what I wanted to say. Her down-to-earth examples have happily replaced dense and abstract passages. But her help went far beyond wording. Margaret Dewey's long-standing personal experience with autism has played a vital role in interpreting the witnesses' evidence. It was a critical moment for me when she was able to confirm that in her view too Hugh Blair suffered from autism, and that the family members reacted just as similar families would react today. Above all, Margaret encouraged me to see the signs of gradual learning and genuine affection that people with autism can experience. If readers can empathize with, rather than censor, the members of the Blair family, then this is very much due to her insight into the impact of autism on the sufferer, the family and society.

I should also like to thank Fulvia Castelli for her help with producing the photos of test materials and Laure Coates, Sarah Griffiths and Lauren Stewart for their assistance with proofreading and indexing.

UF

Chapter 1

The Background to the Study

We cannot talk to the people of the distant past. Yet, sometimes they can speak to us. Occasionally documents come to light which reanimate the lives of families who once lived where now only stones remain. The drama of the Blairs of Borgue in Kirkudbrightshire unrolled in a document that was found in the National Archives of Scotland. In the year 1747, an Edinburgh court had to decide on the mental capacity of Hugh Blair, the family's eldest son, and thus to confirm or dissolve a marriage he entered into in 1746. John, his younger brother, claimed that Hugh was unfit to enter into any contract, and that consequently his marriage should be annulled. The court considered the weighty evidence from 29 witnesses and decided against Hugh, concluding that he was a 'natural fool' and 'void of common sense'.

However, the story is more than a family feud. It is the story of a particularly intriguing kind of mental incapacity and how it affected people's lives in the eighteenth century. One of Hugh's lawyers spoke of his condition as a silent madness. In fact, the evidence suggests that Hugh suffered from autism. The unravelling of the court case and its implications for modern-day theories of autism has led to this book.

We are not the first to write about the Blair family. One account was written by a Victorian amateur collecting the folklore and genealogy of his region. In his *History of the lands and their owners in Galloway*, another name for the area embracing Kirkcudbrightshire, the Reverend McKerlie wrote that David Blair and his wife Grizell Blair had two sons, Hugh and John. McKerlie states: 'When David Blair died we do not know, and we

1

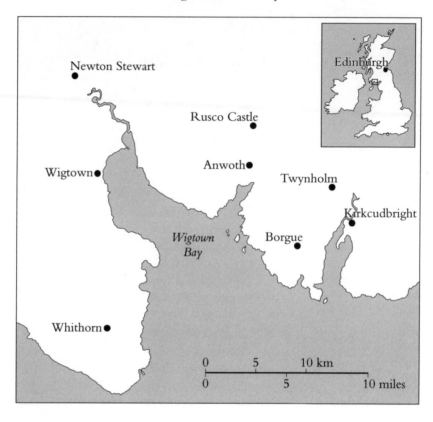

Map of Kirkcudbrightshire (with insert of Great Britain) showing principal places mentioned in the text

are in the same position in regard to his eldest son Hugh, only that we know he was unmarried'.[1] Having discovered archives of relevant legal papers, we can now fill in the missing facts. David Blair died in 1716, Hugh, his son, in the mid-1760s. Hugh died indeed unmarried, at least in the eyes of the law, and the line was carried on by John's offspring. However, this is not the whole story.

What led to the court case that concluded in the annulment of Hugh's marriage? As the documents reveal, the Blairs of Borgue were a typical family of their place and time. But they were also an extraordinary family. Just as today, the impact of autism on the family was formidable. It split the family apart and caused financial ruin. Just as in many modern-

2

Plate 1: Borgue Old House, 1999
This ivy-covered shell is all that remains of Hugh Blair's family home. Built in the 1690s and later added to, it was occupied until the mid-nineteenth century.
Source: Professor R. A. Houston.

day cases, the mother had a key role. It was she who had arranged the marriage. If she perhaps first neglected Hugh, she later defended him and cared for him at the expense of John. She was thwarted in her scheme, but not entirely so. Ultimately, Hugh's condition did not preclude him from attaining a reasonably happy life.

An Interdisciplinary Case Study

This book offers more than painstaking historical or clinical analysis of a particular case. It is a product of the collaboration between a historian and a scientist. As we worked on separate chapters, we continually discussed the implications of the evidence from our two disciplines. This markedly influenced us as we considered the central question that the court debated: What if anything was lacking in Hugh Blair's mental abilities? Rab Houston's chapters focus on how people of the time understood what 'was wrong' with Hugh Blair and why the court came to the conclusion that he could not be legally married. These chapters also provide examples of other cases of mental incapacity in eighteenth-century Scotland. Uta Frith's chapters focus on theories of autism and examine the court papers for the clinical evidence they contain.

The records of this case offer a wealth of detail about Hugh Blair's life and times through the eyes of ordinary witnesses. It is therefore possible to obtain an account of the family and community in which Hugh lived and of the way his mental capacity was understood. The life of any extraordinary person tells us much about the lives of ordinary people. From a historian's point of view, it is necessary to accept the judgement of Hugh's contemporaries that he was (in their words) an idiot. From a clinician's point of view, it is necessary to analyse this judgement in the light of present-day knowledge of psychopathology. The initial reading of the case suggested the hypothesis of autism. This hypothesis was confirmed by detailed reading of the materials and comparison with modern cases. The systematic resemblance of features over time and space constitutes evidence that autism existed long before it was identified and named as a disorder.

We believe that it is important to separate the existence of labels and explanatory theories from the existence of pathological conditions. The syndrome now called autism was not categorized until the 1940s. Similarly, the term schizophrenia was not coined until the early years of the twentieth century. However, that does not mean that these conditions did not exist before then – just as there were presumably germs around before germ theory was promulgated to explain disease.[2]

Historical cases are valuable for the researcher who wants to find out about the enduring core of a pathological condition. Conversely, it is important to find out what historical changes in everyday social life have an impact on mental disorder. Cultural values of the time might either aggravate or reduce the handicap. Through studying Hugh Blair's condition in its historical context we hope to be able to expose the unchanging core of autism. By the same method we hope to be able to identify some ways in which different societies understand normal and abnormal mental conditions.

Our challenge is to reconstruct the mind of an unusual person from fragments of information salvaged from ancient legal papers. The reconstruction of archaeological objects from fragments has been achieved often. The reconstruction of a mind from legal fragments has scarcely been tried.[3] In this sense we are embarking on a bold new enterprise. The reason we can embark on it at all is that the information which has survived is so exquisitely detailed and alive that it can bear comparison with modern-day clinical case studies. To understand the clinical facts of this case, we have to look through layers of potentially obscuring information. Fortunately, most of these problems can be solved by historical methods: ordinary and extraordinary behaviour can be distinguished by comparative study; meanings of key words can be elucidated by related contemporary materials; biases in the lawyers and witnesses can be exposed by comparing testimonies and by collating the court evidence with independent evidence from other sources. Thus, the clinical examination of the case can use material that has been cleansed, metaphorically speaking, in a way which is as transparent as possible.

The case might be treated as a story to be interpreted in its own historical context. But we are not merely engaged in a narrative, elaborating another narrative. As we argue below, the papers about Hugh Blair are more than a source of biographical material and can lead to insights beyond the actual case.

The Nature of the Evidence

The papers of the Blair v Blair trial were not recorded and preserved with the purpose of flattering or denigrating a person. They had their function within the system of law at the time. The court was interested in fact finding with the purpose of establishing whether Hugh Blair had a mental incapacity. The evidence served this function, and further use was not envisaged. Unlike biographical accounts, this material was not intended for posterity. It was intended only to be looked at by lawyers interested in an appeal or in any legal precedents set by the case. We believe that by examining this unique bundle of evidence with the hindsight of current knowledge, it is possible to go beyond the conclusions reached by the court.

The documentation on which this study relies is decidedly non-clinical. It was generated in a civil court case raised to challenge the

> March 14. 1748.
>
> # INFORMATION
>
> FOR
>
> *Hugh Blair* of *Borgue*, and *Grisel Blair* his Mother and Tutrix, and *Nicolas Mitchel*, Daughter to *Archibald Mitchel* Surgeon in *Kirkcudbright*, Spouse to the said *Hugh Blair*, and the said *Archibald Mitchel* for his Interest, Defenders;
>
> AGAINST
>
> *John Blair* Brother-german to the said *Hugh Blair*, and the Procurator-fiscals of the Commissary-court of *Edinburgh*, for their Interest, Pursuers.
>
> *D*AVID BLAIR Heretor of the small Estate of *Borgue*, of about 100 *l.* Sterl. of yearly Rent, happened to provide the same, in his Contract of Marriage with the said *Grisel Blair*, to the Children of the Marriage, and deceased, leaving Issue the said *Hugh* and *John Blairs*, *Jean* and *Grisel Blairs*, who were all served Heirs-portioners of Provision to him.

Plate 2: Information for Hugh Blair, 14 March 1748
This is the title and first lines of a printed submission or 'Information' presented by lawyers for Hugh Blair to the courts. The document summarizes the evidence and the legal arguments for pronouncing Hugh Blair mentally capable. It is one of several lengthy printed and manuscript sources for the case.
Source: Broughton House (National Trust for Scotland), Kirkcudbright.

validity of Hugh Blair's marriage. Put simply, those who had personal knowledge of the parties in the case and the circumstances surrounding it gave testimonies in response to questions set by the 'pursuer' (initiator of the suit), and the 'defender' or their legal representatives. These questions were known in legal language as 'interrogatories' and at least 15 different ones were asked of witnesses in the case. Social historians of medicine often rely on such apparently unpromising sources when trying to understand the experience of illness and the ways in which medical conditions were understood outside medical circles. For example, some of the more interesting advances in the study of forensic medicine during the eighteenth century come from analysing criminal trials, notably those of mothers alleged to have killed their new-born babies.[4] Of course, doctors' 'case notes' do survive in the records of early infirmaries like Edinburgh Royal,[5] or public asylums such as Glasgow (opened in 1814),[6] or for earlier periods among the personal papers of prominent physicians such as William Cullen or James Gregory.[7]

The papers we use here are the testimonies of lay people about the mental capacity of an individual. We need not necessarily regard such sources as inferior to clinical investigations, however. In some respects the procedure adopted in courts concerned with mental capacity then was similar to what some psychiatrists today regard as a good compromise. They combine clinical diagnosis with questionnaires to detect and measure mental incapacity. Carstairs and Kapur call it the 'structured interview', which marries flexibility with standardization:

> This is similar to a questionnaire in providing a standard check list of symptoms and of questions designed to elicit these symptoms, but differs from the latter in that a cross-examination is permitted to clarify doubts and in that the decision about the presence or absence of psychopathology is made by the investigator, guided by a set of standard definitions for the various symptoms.[8]

The other advantage of lay testimonials is that behaviour is reflected through the eyes of many different people. It all adds up, and is mostly consistent. None of the testimony in this case comes from a medical professional. The only medical man involved is a surgeon who was the father of the woman to whom Hugh Blair was married. It was not until the early nineteenth century that the opinion of a doctor was necessary to confine an insane person, and most courts continued until much later to rely on common sense lay testimony when seeking to define mental incapacity. If there was professional input, it came from lawyers and clergymen. Thus, the documentation which survives was created to answer the question: 'Does this man possess sufficient intellect to make an informed judgement?'. Courts and the witnesses before them wanted to discover what, if anything, was wrong with the way a person thought. However, the outcome which was sought was not to place a medical label on the person. Those who brought the case, gave evidence in it, and provided a legal judgement were interested not in whether Hugh Blair had 'autism' or some other syndrome, but whether he had the mental capacity to deal with life's decisions in the same way as other ordinary people. Causation was not relevant.

How Did the Courts Establish Mental Incapacity?

The same was true of any contemporary legal procedure to assess the ability of individuals to manage their own affairs. Civil courts could judge whether a person was *compos mentis* (also known as *capax*) or whether they were likely to dissipate their resources to the detriment of themselves and their kin. This process was knowing as 'cognoscing' or 'cognition'. Yet, even here, the legal categories into which a court placed someone found incapable were simple in the extreme. A man or woman could be found 'fatuous' (stupid or idiotic) or 'furious' (mad or lunatic) or, sometimes, a combination of the two. The classifications were legal ones. The same is true of those rare cases before the nineteenth century when an insanity defence was entered on behalf of someone alleged to be insane. Eighteenth-century courts were interested in the duration of mental incapacity, its depth, and the possibilities of recovery. They had little concern with clinical labels or psychological theories. Thus, the case we analyse below bears directly on Hugh Blair's intellectual abilities, but only indirectly on the reasons behind the court case. Hugh found a bride late in life. Most contemporaries, and indeed modern readers of the story which follows, would have been glad for him. Why did his nearest kin seek to dissolve his union and deny him the formalized companionship to which the vast majority of eighteenth century people aspired? We can only speculate on the motives of John Blair, Hugh's younger brother. We shall piece together some of the indirect evidence that hints at venal motives and indicates a dramatic rift between John and his mother.

A major problem, of course, is that the historian cannot interview the principals or witnesses in a case, or formulate the questions asked of them. While broadly similar questions were posed throughout our period to meet the legal definitions of mental incapacity, each case had its own particular quirks arising from the specific circumstances of an individual's behaviour and the knowledge which others had of it. Hugh Blair's is no different. Generally, the questions compartmentalized and broke up any story witnesses had to tell, resulting in a fragmented and partial account which might trace the person's mental condition from inception to the date of the case, but more commonly touched only on certain key portions known to the witness or deponent.

The Whole Truth?

Testimonies cannot be read literally as whole and truthful accounts. But neither is it appropriate to try to expose fiction in the archives because that implies that it is possible to know the truth about historical events. Better to look at the interpretation which prevailed rather than to try to identify the 'true' one, because truth itself is contingent. Perhaps all deponents were 'telling the truth' in describing behaviour and drawing conclusions, but we should recognize that truth was far from free of factual or ethical ambiguity. This does not mean that each testimony is independent and that each text is autonomous. We are not simply dealing with multiple narratives or constructed representations in competition with each other. In the sources we use, contemporaries faced by allegedly mad or mentally disabled individuals came to a decision about whether the subject was *incompos mentis* and they gave their reasons. Ambiguity and uncertainty there surely was, but these gave way to decisions on which we shall focus.

Truth was relative then as now. What created a standard in a case was the accumulation of overlapping fact and opinion about the behaviour of an individual and what this told people about his or her mental capacities. Narratives were separate and opinions more or less subjective, but judges and/or jurors had the opportunity to disregard a testimony which did not fit the pattern of other depositions and of their own eyes and ears. Each case was different but between cases what matters is the considerable overlap in the criteria used to judge mental incapacity. That uniformity may have been created by an existing awareness of legal requirements or the immediate needs of the case. However, it will not do to create an artificial distinction between law and society, or to reify the former. Indeed, what is striking about all the cases, civil and criminal, is the diversity of the social contexts and personal detail contained, rather than the uniformity imposed by legal proceedings. This makes the existence of a clearly identifiable general idiom in the Blair case all the more remarkable.

How do Modern-day Clinicians Diagnose Mental Incapacity?

The diagnostic approach is in many ways opposed to the legalistic approach. Diagnosis implies a judgement and a search for pathological causes, but not a search for guilt. However, there are also surprising similarities. Both procedures, for instance, rely on informants/witnesses, and both use direct observation and questioning of the patient/defendant. In both cases the judgement is arrived at by looking at the balance of probabilities.

How does one establish that a person suffers from autism? There is no single physical or behavioural sign which would uniquely secure the diagnosis. The whole history of the patient has to be considered from birth, the nature of the impairments, their severity, and their change over time.[9] In this clinicians, just as lawyers, have to rely on what they are told. To facilitate the work, a standardized interview procedure is used, so that leading questions are avoided and so that alternative diagnoses are covered.[10]

Good practice would ensure that the person, usually a young child, would be observed directly by more than one professional, including at least a psychiatrist and clinical psychologist, and would be given a range of psychological tests. Some of these tests would assess intellectual ability relative to the child's age. So, for instance, it is possible to find out whether or not a child has a vocabulary that is within the range of normally developing children of the same age. Certain tests would assess specific problems commonly found in cases of autism. The child in question may be said to pass or fail these tests relative to normally developing children of the same age. Like the lawyer, the clinician would then collate the evidence – which can sometimes be contradictory – and discuss it with learned colleagues. Comparisons would be made with other known cases, so that unique features can be highlighted as well as those that are typical for the condition.

It has been said that a good diagnostician relies as much on experience and intuition as on textbook knowledge. Nevertheless, clinicians need objective procedures, or else their conclusions fail to convince. There are two instruments that have made a big difference to diagnostic practice and have ensured that clinicians will be identifying the same condition even if they work in different countries: the *International Classification of*

Diseases (ICD) and the *Diagnostic and Statistical Manual of Mental Disorders* (DSM).[11] These handbooks contain the currently agreed diagnostic criteria in the form of lists. They are updated from time to time in the light of increasing knowledge. This underlines the fact that a complete set of scientifically objective criteria for the diagnosis of mental disorders has not yet been established.

The differences between a modern-day clinical diagnosis of mental disorder and an eighteenth-century court judgement about mental capacity are not as large as might be presumed. They lie in the instruments used for assessment and in the accumulated scientific knowledge. Remarkably, in the courts of eighteenth-century Scotland, semi-standardized interviews were conducted, and even some psychological tests were given. None of these would, however, yield data that could compare an individual's performance with that of the population at large. This results in differences of precision, but not necessarily differences in the soundness of the judgement. More important are the differences in accumulated professional knowledge. Over the last 200 years slow progress has been made, punctuated by occasional breakthroughs. In the case of autism, the idea of a neurological cause has been empirically substantiated, and this has transformed the approach to diagnosis and treatment.

The Structure of the Book

Between the introduction and the conclusion, the book falls into two sections. The first, chapters 2 and 3, sets the historical context for understanding the accounts of Hugh Blair given by 29 witnesses in his court case. It explains the social and economic situation of south-west Scotland in the eighteenth century and explores who the witnesses in the case were. An explanation is given of the law of mental incapacity and guardianship on the one hand, and of marriage and divorce on the other. By picking out the specific and the general pointers which Hugh Blair's neighbours and acquaintances used to support their interpretation of his mental capacity, it is possible to expound a sort of standard for understanding this apparently protean phenomenon. Issues such as humour, appropriate behaviour, literacy and learning, and the significance of appearance are highlighted. Throughout, we learn much about the values of family and community in historic Scotland, including the role of the church and the central importance of both social hierarchy and social conventions.

From the extensive source of materials we chose transcripts of two examples of witnesses' depositions, one by William Taggart speaking on behalf of the 'pursuer', John Blair; the other by Mr John Gordon on behalf of the defender, Hugh Blair. They give a flavour of the source materials which altogether amount to approximately 100,000 words, some 15,000 of which are depositions. The examples are particularly rich in detail and representative of the content of the depositions in general. Also included, and of central importance to the case study, is the transcript of Hugh Blair's interrogation by the judges on 16 July 1747. In the transcripts reproduced here, the grammar and punctuation have been modernized and, with some exceptions, the spelling standardized in modern English. Had this not been done, the sense of the evidence would have been difficult to follow for those not conversant with the archaic stylistic forms. Little has been changed in the language and the tone of the depositions. The terms used in everyday life to describe mental defects may be blunt and insensitive to most modern ears. Yet, they were acceptable in the context of the social and cultural values in which these words were spoken.

The second section, chapters 4 and 5, offers a clinical interpretation of the case. Here, the court evidence is used to test the hypothesis that Hugh Blair had autism. The development of the scientific understanding of autism is summarized to set the context of the clinical interpretation. The scientific analysis relies on the case papers and relates the contents with up-to-date knowledge of the condition. Far from prejudging the issue of Hugh Blair's mental capacity, the autism hypothesis allows a systematic and principled treatment of the evidence. Thus information can be classified according to signs that provide positive diagnostic indicators, signs that are neutral or ambiguous, and signs that are incompatible with autism. Just as in modern-day diagnostic procedure, the available data have to be rigorously checked for consistency. The main difference to a modern case study is that the papers do not report statements by the family members themselves and that they lack psychometric and neuropsychological test data.

In the final chapter we discuss the interdisciplinary questions that we set out to explore. We ask what contribution cognitive science can make to the social history of mental disorder and what cognitive scientists can learn from historical cases. We will discuss how studying this case in its historical context has furthered our understanding of the essence of autism. We will also discuss how culture-specific context may modify the impact of mental disorder. Finally, we will address differences and similarities between the understanding of the nature of mental incapacity then and now.

The interpretation of the case material draws on current research both in modern history and in cognitive neuroscience. References to relevant work will be given in the notes. To make these sections accessible to those readers who have little prior knowledge, there will be occasional excursions into basic methods in our respective fields. In addition, we provide glossaries for the more technical or archaic terms used in our different disciplines. Further reading lists have been added.

The historian's view is that mental disorder is largely defined by the social context of its time. The neuroscientist's view is that mental disorder is also a brain disorder and therefore largely independent of the historical context. In our collaborative enterprise we have tried to reconcile these views. The key was to understand the merits of defining a disorder at both the biological and the social levels. One without the other would lead to a very poor definition. The case of Hugh Blair challenges our notions of mental disorder. Mental disorder is not only in the eye of the beholder, not only in the mind and not only in the brain, but it is in all of these.

Chapter 2

The Life and Times of Hugh Blair

An Outline of the Case

Hugh Blair was born in 1708 or 1709, the son of Grizell and David Blair of Borgue in Kirkcudbrightshire, south-west Scotland. David Blair died in February 1716.[1] In March 1737, Hugh's younger brother John became the guardian or 'curator' of both Hugh and his sister Jean on the grounds that they had been deaf and dumb from infancy, and were therefore incapable of managing their own affairs.[2] Sometime in late 1746 Hugh's elderly mother organized a marriage between her son and Nicholas Mitchell, daughter to Archibald Mitchell, a 'chirurgeon' or surgeon who lived in the town of Kirkcudbright.[3] Brother John disapproved and began a civil suit to have the marriage annulled on the grounds of Hugh's mental incapacity: he claimed Hugh was an idiot. It is the subsequent court case, brought before the Commissary Court of Edinburgh, which generated the documentation on which this book is principally based.

Scottish Commissary Courts dealt primarily with debt litigation and testamentary matters. Edinburgh was Scotland's chief Commissary Court, dealing with the same range of issues as the other 12 such tribunals but having a special jurisdiction over questions of defamation of character, and of marriage and divorce. This branch of the Commissary Court was called the Consistory Court.[4] The Court of Session was the supreme civil court in the land and the sole appellate jurisdiction for the Commissary Courts. Hugh Blair's marriage was annulled by the Commissaries (judges

14

Plate 3: The last sitting of the old Court of Session, 1808
Hugh Blair's case was appealed to the supreme civil court in Scotland, the
Court of Session. Like the Commissary Court before which his marriage was
initially questioned, this relied on a panel of eminent judges. While the
representation of the seating is compressed, the setting must have been daunting
for litigants and witnesses alike.
Source: John Kay, *A series of original portraits and caricature etchings, by the late John Kay,*
miniature painter, Edinburgh; with biographical sketches and illustrative anecdotes, 2 vols
(Edinburgh, 1838), vol. 2, p. 380.

of the Commissary Court) on 29 March 1748, a decision upheld at
appeal before the Court of Session in June of that year.[5]

The Historical Background

The Blair family were landowners in the parish of Borgue, which lies
about three miles to the west and south of the market town and royal
burgh of Kirkcudbright, on the Solway coast at the southern edge of
Scotland.[6] Kirkcudbright itself lies approximately 25 miles south-west of
Dumfries, the major town in south-west Scotland at that time. In the

Map of Kirkcudbrightshire, *c.*1754/5
A series of maps covering the whole of Scotland was completed between 1747
and 1755 under the supervision of William Roy. The scale of the original is
one inch to 1,000 yards. Compiled for military purposes, the maps are
particularly good on features concerned with communication. However, they
also gives approximate locations of arable ground and of houses.
Source: British Library.

Plate 4: View of Kirkcudbright, 1792
This small royal burgh, which was a port and a market town for the area,
features prominently in the story of Hugh Blair and his wife, Nicholas
Mitchell. Nicholas's father was a surgeon there.
Source: The Stewartry Museum, Kirkcudbright.

eighteenth century, Borgue parish was about 40 square miles in area but
was sparsely populated with just 697 souls at the time of an ecclesiastical
'census' in 1755. The Rev. Andrew Sympson, a local minister, wrote a
description of Galloway in the 1680s which included mentions of Borgue:
'This parish abounds with plenty of corne, wherewith it furnishes many
other places in the Stewartrie, supplying them both with meal and malt.'[7]

The estate of Borgue was a modest one which brought in approximately £100 sterling a year in rents. It comprised lands then known as
High and Low Borgue, Boreland, Blackcraig, and the mill and mill lands
of Borgue. William McGuffog or McGuffock of Rusco acquired these
and other lands from Sir David Dunbar of Baldoon in January 1699.[8] They
comprised a strip of land approximately one mile wide from east to west
and four miles from south to north. The estate's southern boundary lay to
the east and slightly south of the village of Borgue. While Hugh Blair was
in his early teens, this part of the region was convulsed by protests against

17

the enclosure of land by walls or 'dykes' and the ejection of small farmers: the famous Galloway 'Levellers' riots of the early 1720s. Indeed, much of the modern landscape of south-west Scotland was created by the agrarian changes which occurred during Hugh Blair's lifetime. The largely subsistence agriculture of the region was transformed for cattle breeding and raising to meet the demands of the growing towns of Scotland's more economically developed neighbour south of the Border. In the parish of Kirkinner, Sir David Dunbar himself had a cattle park two and a half miles long by one and a half miles wide as early as the 1680s.[9] Hugh Blair's paternal grandmother was a daughter of this prominent landowner.

Nationwide, this was a period of both stability and profound political and economic change. After the flight of the last Stuart monarch, James VII of Scotland and II of England, William and Mary ruled Britain from 1689 to 1702, when Queen Anne ascended to the throne. The 1689 settlement re-established Presbyterian church government in Scotland, though a Toleration Act late in Anne's reign effectively allowed all Protestants rights of worship and laid the ground for the developing religious pluralism of the eighteenth and nineteenth centuries. The dynasty changed again in 1714 with the arrival of the Hanoverians. George I reigned between 1714 and 1727, and George II had been on the throne for two decades when the Blair case came to court. George III, who became king in 1760, was, of course, 'mad'. Without an independent parliament since 1707, Scotland was managed politically by powerful nobles such as the Duke of Argyll. The Earls of Galloway were the most politically powerful nobles in the south west in the early and mid-eighteenth century.

The Union of the Parliaments had nevertheless left some aspects of day-to-day life like currency and weights and measures unchanged. Scotland's separate legal system also remained intact. The institutional and legal context of the Hugh Blair case would have been very different in England. Among the important events of the decade of our case, the second and last Jacobite rising had been defeated at Culloden near Inverness only months before the Commissary Court began its deliberations. The Blair family were no Jacobites and indeed had a long history of association with the Williamites. Hugh's grandfather had signed a letter of congratulation to King William in 1689. Hugh's maternal grandfather had been accused of 'converse with Rebells and Traitors' in 1686, these being Covenanters who opposed James VII and II.[10]

Madness, Marriage, and Property

This case can tell us a great deal about the way ordinary people understood mental incapacity. To appreciate why, we need more than factual information about the geography and population of the parish or the political setting. The social and legal context of the struggle to dissolve a marriage involves familial relationships, community norms, and bonds and divisions based on social status and wealth. Such everyday matters as dress, speech, behaviour, religious observance, literacy, friendship, and work are no less significant. The laws of inheritance, marriage, and mental incapacity took account of all these subtle social factors. Our aim is to show how eighteenth-century people defined the nature and boundaries of mental ability. However, we shall also examine in detail the contingencies which caused the case to be brought.

The documents we use are legal rather than clinical ones and we should therefore begin by explaining the civil law and procedures relating to mental incapacity. When John Blair wanted to 'cognosce' (the word could mean judicially to investigate, or to pronounce a person insane after judicial investigation) his brother and sister, he purchased a 'brieve' or writ from the king's chapel or Chancery containing an order to a Sheriff or other judge to try his claim by inquest of a jury of 15 men. In the words of the actual document, the judge was to 'cause diligent and faithful inquest to be made by worthy and faithful men of the country by whom the truth of the matter can be better known'.[11] According to the noted seventeenth-century lawyer, James Dalrymple, Viscount of Stair: 'those of the neighbourhood were fittest [whatever their status], because . . . inquests are in the middle, betwixt Judges and witnesses, partaking part of them both'.[12] Jurors were adult males with sufficient property to make them independent of judgement.[13] This type of legal process existed from the late sixteenth century until 1847.

Brieves were purchased from Chancery and directed to any relevant judge, usually of the jurisdiction in which the allegedly insane person resided or held property.[14] The brieve was proclaimed at the market cross or at some other much frequented place, after which it was served. Anyone could purchase such brieves, though in his seminal text of the sixteenth century the noted lawyer Sir James Balfour opined that they should come from the next of kin ('nearest friends') on both the father's and mother's side.[15] Those who bought the brieve entered a petition to the court where they wanted to try the case. This petition, endorsed by the Sheriff or some other relevant judge, asked him to summon a jury, and call witnesses. The inquest was required to cognosce the capacities of the brieve's subject: the process was known as 'cognition'. Whoever purchased the brieve usually also put in a claim to be the tutor or curator of the brieve's subject (the allegedly incapable person). Thus, the jury which sat in judgement on Hugh and Jean Blair on 29 March 1737 comprised Kirkcudbright craftsmen and tradesmen. They found the siblings '*muti et surdi et tales quibus bonorum administratio seu alienatio de jure interdicuntur sic quod per curatorem sibi subvenire debeant ne propter fragilitatem consilii in egestatem reducantur*'.[16] They confirmed that John was the nearest competent male agnate and that he was aged at least 25 years, as the law required for tutors and curators.[17]

This procedure was not simply used for the deaf and dumb, or for the very young. The same sequence of brieve, petition, claim, inquest and verdict was employed by any relative – in practice, nearly always a male relative – who thought their kin mentally incapable of managing their own affairs. In this case the brother, uncle, cousin or nephew bought a brieve of 'idiotry' – asking the jury to investigate whether the subject was stupid – or 'furiosity', in which case the contention was that the subject was mad. John Blair did *not* buy this type of brieve, although he later claimed that he should have. However, hundreds of Scots families of the eighteenth century did so and the resulting court cases have been analysed in a major historical monograph.[18]

If successful, the procedure gave the person appointed as curator rights over the brieve's subject which were effectively those of a father over a teenager. In some senses the mentally incapable were treated like children. Simply locking allegedly insane people up might deprive them of certain freedoms of action, but an inquest was required to turn them into legal children. Those below a certain age were held to be incapable of informed consent. The very young required a tutor to guide them, protect their person, and manage their property; those in their teens were held to need a curator. Pupillarity lasted until 14 years of age for boys, 12 for girls. From then to the age of 21 everyone, regardless of mental state, was termed a minor. Legal majority came at 21 years for both sexes.[19] Tutors and curators had different legal relationships to their under-age charges. Tutors had control of pupils, 'as pupils are incapable of consent, they have no *person* capable of acting, which defect the tutor supplies . . . but in a curatory, it is the minor who subscribes as the proper party; the curator does no more than consent'.[20] Having a tutor implied that an individual had no legal capacity, whereas having a curator meant that he or she needed guidance in matters which had legal or financial significance. In short, a curator acted *with* his charge, a tutor acted *for* him or her. Minors under curatory nevertheless had the power to enter into legal obligations themselves. Hugh Blair and his sister Jean were under curatorship as a result of the inquest of 1737.

Hugh and Jean lost a number of legal rights in March 1737. Modern readers may be curious, even aghast, that someone deaf and dumb would be treated as a child. Yet, once again, we must examine eighteenth-century ideas of freedom and consent. The whole institution of tutorships and curatorships – and indeed many other relationships such as that between master and servant or husband and wife – shows that eighteenth-century Scots were comfortable with the idea that a person's legal capacity could reside wholly or partly in someone else. If the deaf and dumb or mentally incapable person lost some rights, most others could be transferred to the tutor or curator – a fiction which also applied to the political and other rights of minors and women. In other words, the law assumed that the person had not been deprived of most rights, for they simply resided in someone else who, by dint of close relationship, could be held to be the one best suited to exercise them. Husbands, masters, and tutors or curators had rights but also responsibilities over those beneath them in the hierarchy. This concept of representation extended into political life. Even at the end of the eighteenth century, Scotland had less than 3,000 parliamentary electors in a population of more than one and a half million. The point is that applying modern ideas of freedom and consent to a society with a wholly different political ideology is anachronistic. Attempts to do so tell us much about western societies in the late twentieth century, but little about social and political relationships in the eighteenth.

The purpose of civil court cognitions was to secure the material interests of those who had difficulty thinking or communicating correctly. They also prevented the patrimony from being heedlessly squandered, thus protecting the property interests of the wider family and of subsequent generations. Any system whereby minors, pupils and lunatics could be placed under curators or guardians was open to abuse. The law was not blind to baser motives and sought to ensure that even extremely disadvantaged people were not treated arbitrarily. Acts of the Scottish Parliament in 1672 and 1681 instituted safeguards by requiring full inventories and accounts to be prepared of the management of the dependant's affairs. The guardian had to provide a bond to that effect. The compilation of the curatorial inventory was to be overseen by two relatives on the father's side and two on the mother's side. Three copies were to be lodged: with the tutor, a kinsman on the father's side, and one on the mother's.[21] As it turned out, Hugh Blair needed these safeguards.

The Context of the Case

In the spring of 1737, John Blair took effective control of the entire inheritance of his siblings, including the house and estate. While John was the legal guardian, the documents make it clear that their mother was the focus of Hugh's life. Grizell Blair's situation is not specified in her husband's will, but she had been well provided for as a result of their marriage contract. Grizell was the daughter of John Blair of Dunskey in the nearby parish of Portpatrick and her marriage contract was drawn up in September 1705.[22] Hugh's paternal grandfather was Hugh McGuffock, third son of Rev. James Blair of Dunskey, known as McGuffock of Rusco or Blair of Borgue. His grandmother was Margaret Dunbar.[23] Grizell and David were cousins. Conventionally, the material interests of married women of her social class were protected by pre-nuptial agreements which specified what would happen in the event of her husband's death. Registers of Deeds and family papers contain thousands of these contracts from all over Scotland. It was not only the landed classes who entered into them but a wide spectrum of urban professionals, merchants and craftsmen including writers (legal clerks), ministers, apothecaries, tailors, brewers, shoemakers, fleshers, wrights, and masons.[24] Their aim was to protect the interests of both parties to a marriage, their existing kin, and their future lineage. Such contracts have been extensively and imaginatively studied in some European countries: for example, those mentioned in the document can be seen as the approximate equivalent of a modern wedding photograph.[25]

Plate 5: Catherine Denham of Westshiels, wife of Robert Welwood of Garvock, *c*.1740

We have no clue as to the physical appearance of any of the principal women in Hugh Blair's life. However, this portrait is from the correct period and social milieu. It may represent the style of clothing worn by women like Hugh's sister-in-law, Helen Lamont, or even his wife, Nicholas Mitchell.

Source: Scottish National Portrait Gallery, H720: from a private collection.

Plate 6: Catherine Bruce of Newton (*c*.1701–*c*.1796), wife of Henry Bruce of Clackmannan, *c*.1780

As with the younger women in the story, we do not know what Grizell Blair looked like. This is a portrait of a woman who would have been slightly older than Grizell at the time of the court cases, and it is taken from slightly later in the eighteenth century. Head-dress was the norm for matrons of the period. *Source*: Scottish National Portrait Gallery, H1661: from a private collection.

Marriage contracts set out the amount each person was to bring to the union by way of joint stock – a pool to be administered by the husband during his lifetime. The division of this stock after the couple's death was also specified. Different scenarios were envisioned, such as the portions to be received by interested parties in the event of the husband, wife, or both dying, with or without issue, or with only female children. In the case of David Blair and his wife, the estate was to pass to any children of the marriage and Grizell was to receive an annuity of 500 merks Scots a year (approximately £28 sterling).[26] As late as 1734 £12 sterling still remained to be paid of the 'tocher' or dowry which John Blair of Dunskey had agreed to settle on his daughter Grizell.[27] For comparison, the marriage contract of Hugh's sister-in-law, Helen Lamont, specified, among other things, that she should be provided with an annuity of 900 merks Scots (£50 sterling) net of all local dues and taxes if her husband predeceased her.[28] If she remarried, her annuity was to be reduced to 600 merks.[29] Grizell's mother-in-law's marriage contract specified that she was due £1,000 Scots of annual jointure.[30]

Such contracts were essential since all moveable property brought to and accumulated during a marriage belonged to the husband.[31] Widows commonly received a certain sum as an annuity, along with the 'liferent' interest on their husband's property once the needs of the children had been settled. One indicator of the separate lineage and interests of husband and wife is that in Scotland it was conventional for married women to retain their paternal surname. Thus, Hugh's mother had been born a Blair and had not changed her name on marriage. David Blair's father Hugh took the name of McGuffock at the time of his marriage to his first wife Elizabeth McGuffock, heiress to the estate of Rusco. This was again unremarkable by the standards of the day. Surnames were not fixed at this period and occasionally heirship to particular landholdings came with the condition that the successor should change his or her name to that of the onetime owner.

The Blairs' domestic circumstances changed in other ways in 1737. John Blair married Helen Lamont, sister to Mr John Lamont, minister of Kelton, and the daughter of John Lamont of Pyston. The couple moved in to the family seat at Borgue. The extended family of Mistress Blair, Jean, Hugh, and the newly-weds lived in what is now called Borgue Old House. In common with many landowners, the Blairs also spent a good deal of time in the county town, Kirkcudbright in this instance. Grizell

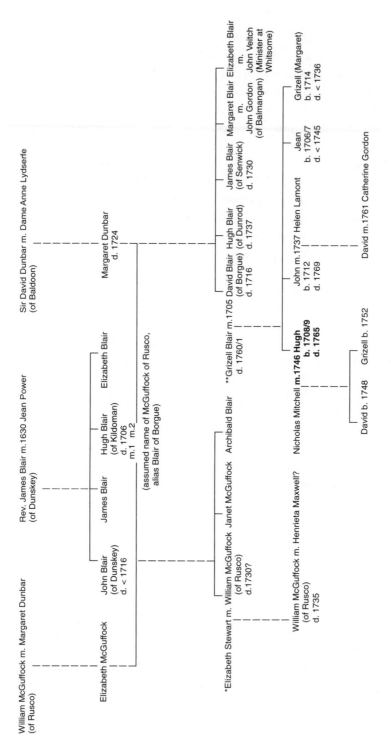

Family tree. Prepared by Dr Veena O'Halloran.

* Elizabeth Stewart (daughter of Robert Stewart, brother of the Earl of Galloway, and Elizabeth, daughter of Sir David Dunbar of Baldoon)
was a niece of Margaret Dunbar, second wife of Hugh Blair alias McGuffock.
** Grizell Blair was a daughter of John Blair of Dunskey and therefore a cousin of her husband.

Blair had a house there. Grizell Blair generally styled herself 'Lady Borgue', though she was not the wife of a baronet or knight. She may have been imitating her late mother-in-law, Margaret Dunbar, whose testament or will states that she used this style.[32] At certain periods prior to the court case both Hugh and his mother seem to have lodged somewhere other than in Borgue Old House. For example, we know from his deposition that around 1745 they stayed with Andrew Taggart, a weaver in Borgue.

The house in which Hugh was brought up was probably that built by Hugh McGuffock of Rusco in 1696. In the spring of that year, Rusco entered into a contract with two masons to build a house at lower Borgue.[33] It was to measure 45 feet long and 17 feet wide with end walls three feet thick and side walls two feet six inches. He wanted two chimneys in each gable and specified that they were to 'vent smoke exactly'; the downstairs rooms were to have ceilings of nine feet and the upstairs six feet. Rusco agreed to pay the men £300 Scots for the job in three instalments, the last only if they completed the house by 1 November. The formal registration of such contracts was unusual. Hugh clearly had a low opinion of builders. Now a roofless shell, albeit with its walls intact, this building reached its final, E- or Y-shaped form in the early eighteenth century.[34] Built of rubble, it had two storeys and an attic, which is where Hugh had a room. The house probably had three rooms on each of the main part's ground and first floors, and one room on each of the storeys of the wings.[35] This would have been a comfortable and spacious house by the standards of the day. It is an imposing building, even today when it rests next to its nineteenth-century replacement. In the early eighteenth century, it would have been one of the largest houses for miles around in the irregular rural landscape of the area.

A Dramatic Incident in the Family

Hugh McGuffock surely built 'the place of Borgue' to show that he was an important man. He had been known as Hugh Blair until he married his first wife, the heiress Elizabeth McGuffock, only known child of William McGuffock of Rusco. His eldest son by the first marriage, William, inherited Rusco. David Blair, the eldest son of Hugh's second marriage to Margaret Dunbar, took Borgue. For all that, Borgue Old House was no castle or mansion. Given that servants had to be accommodated (in cold weather they refused to sleep in the attic), and public and utility rooms accounted for, space must have become tight when the newly-weds moved in. During the 1730s, relations in the Blair family had been harmonious. Between 1733 and 1737 Grizell Blair lent money to her son John totalling at least £113 sterling. She signed three requests for repayment of different loans with the words 'your affectionate mother'.[36] John had borrowed money to buy: 'black cattle and horses, the cattle being partly milch [milk] and partly yeld [literally barren or dry but may also mean young], for stocking the lands of leigh [low] Borgue' – that part of the estate of Borgue he farmed directly.[37] Mother and son continued to act in concert. In March 1742 they granted a 'tack' or lease of the lands of Boreland to William M'Kitrick and William Porter for seven years.[38] The rent was 168 merks plus 22 'small bolls' of grain, half 'bear' (a type of barley common in Scotland), half corn. A boll was a standard measure of volume. John made a bold and fluent signature in which he simply wrote 'Blair', though it is possible that the 'J' of his first name is part of the initial 'B'. For her part, his mother made a neat if less precise signature in which she spelled her name 'Grissall'.

Domestic harmony changed to discord around harvest time 1745 when John and his mother had a falling out, allegedly leading to his physically assaulting Lady Borgue. It was claimed that Hugh intervened on his mother's behalf. The incident is referred to throughout the case, although John's lawyers quickly stepped in to head off any extended discussion of it by the witnesses. In the court transcripts which mention it, John is always referred to as 'a certain person'. Hugh's lawyer repeatedly tried to introduce questions about the alleged beating into the examinations in order to prove that his client was a loving son while John was disrespectful and disobedient.

Out of pique or practicality, the mother cooked up a scheme to marry Hugh to Nicholas, daughter of the surgeon Archibald Mitchell. Nicholas's parish minister, Rev. Gartshore, was reluctant to comply and referred the matter to an assembly of his peers, Kirkcudbright Presbytery. On 12 November 1746 they unanimously refused to proclaim the banns on the grounds that Hugh was 'quite incapable of giving consent or of taking marriage vows'.[39] In spite of this, the designers pressed ahead with the marriage, which was conducted at Edinburgh at the very end of 1746. Indeed, Lady Blair and Mr Mitchell must have anticipated the Presbytery's decision, because they, Hugh, and Nicholas were ensconced in lodgings in Edinburgh by 3 November.[40]

Events moved swiftly. No later than 8 January 1747, the Presbytery received a letter from John Blair's lawyer asking for an extract of their opinion and judgement.[41] John demanded the marriage's annulment and took the case to the Commissaries of Edinburgh. They agreed with the Presbytery, finding that Hugh 'has been from his youth a natural fool and void of that degree of reason and understanding which is necessary to the entering into the marriage contract, and therefore find and declare the pretended marriage between him and Nicholas Mitchell to have been from the beginning and to be in all time coming void and null'. The grounds were straightforward. As Stair noted: 'who cannot consent, cannot marry, as idiots and furious persons'.[42] The issue with Hugh was one of idiocy or an absence of reason, but the same principle applied to temporary losses of this basic human faculty attributable to madness. During insane periods a person could not give the free consent necessary for a valid marriage but during lucid intervals such consent could be given.[43] Other cases before the Consistory Court involved instances of melancholic (and sometimes suicidal) men whose marriages were upheld on the grounds that they had been *compos mentis* when they agreed to marry.[44]

All the Blair children had been 'served heir' to their share of their inheritance in February 1722. In descending age, Jean, Hugh, John, and Margaret (also known as Grizell) were termed in law 'co-heirs of provision general' to their father.[45] Margaret died in 1735 or early 1736, and John registered himself as her heir in June 1736.[46] The reason why Hugh and Jean were cognosced in 1737 was that their brother John had reached the age of 25 years and was therefore deemed in law to be old enough responsibly to take on the guardianship of a dependent relative.[47] The circumstances of the family had been changing during that decade. While their father died in the early years of George I's reign, he had never made a will or testament, known in law as a 'testament testamentar'. The testament proved (probated) before the Commissary Court nearly two decades after David's decease was a 'dative' one, registered by John to prove himself the heir to his father's moveable estate.[48] That was in 1734, the year when Hugh, the eldest of the three surviving Blair children, reached 25 years old and was thus himself 'of full age'. The late David Blair had died intestate not through negligence but because he had agreed to bestow his heritable lands on his children in the marriage contract of 1705. His widow's interests were protected by the marriage contract.

Much happened in the decade before the Commissary Court case. Jean Blair, the eldest of the siblings, died sometime in the early 1740s and Hugh, as her immediate younger brother, was heir to her share of the estate. His attempts to gain her portion of the estate were thwarted by John, despite the fact that John was charged at law with protecting his brother Hugh's best interests. Indeed, John's evident venality and certain flagrant acts of maladministration allowed his mother to have his guardianship ended in July 1745. After his younger sister Grizell's death, John immediately had himself served as her heir but did nothing following the death of Jean to secure Hugh's interest in her portion of the estate.[49] The law required him always to act in the best interests of his charge. The mother herself took over as Hugh's 'tutrix', an arrangement confirmed on 4 February 1747.[50] John was not formally served heir to Jean's portion of the estate until November 1765 (the same time as he succeeded to Hugh's quarter). Hugh must have died sometime between January 1763, when he is named in a legal document, and the latter date: probably some time in 1765 given that John would have wasted little time in formalizing the inheritance.[51] Whereas he registered his heirship to Margaret at Kirkcudbright, John chose to secure his inheritance from Jean and Hugh before Edinburgh Sheriff Court.[52] Perhaps he feared the long memories and forcefully expressed opinions of his Kirkcudbrightshire neighbours.

All the evidence suggests that Hugh Blair had suffered from mental defects since birth or early childhood. We need to explain why, in his late thirties, Hugh married, and why his brother, John, was so vigorously opposed to the union. If the decision to cognosce Hugh and Jean in 1737 was the result of issues of inheritance and family, the scheme to marry him was principally a function of changing familial circumstances. It seems clear that Grizell Blair and Archibald Mitchell, the prospective father-in-law, were the instigators. A naive person like Hugh would have been easily persuaded of the scheme, though the lawyers' submissions make it plain that Nicholas, Archibald's daughter, was initially reluctant to contemplate the match and had gradually to be won over. Beyond this, motives are difficult to unravel. According to a former schoolmaster of the parish, Hugh Blair's mother had acted logically in marrying him off. For one thing, she was old. Even if she had married at the age of 20 years – rather young by contemporary standards – she would have been in her mid-sixties by the time of the case.[53] Worse, her options were running out as she had already failed to get any of his near relatives to care for Hugh.[54]

There was evidently no question that Hugh would dwell anywhere except in the family home, at least while his mother lived. This seems to have been the preference for all social groups, though financial constraints and the absence of institutional facilities may have necessitated the emphasis on domestic care.[55] Until the nineteenth century, Scottish idiots, imbeciles and mad people can be found in a wide variety of circumstances. They might be cared for in their families of origin or boarded out on an individual basis with other families; maintained in workhouses, 'hospitals' or jails; housed temporarily in the infirmaries of the larger cities; placed in the few private madhouses which existed around Edinburgh; or incarcerated in one of the still rarer public asylums (from 1743). Other lunatics and idiots were left to their own devices: 'at large' in the words of late-Georgian reformers like Dr Andrew Duncan. Formal asylums were generally only for the mad until well into the nineteenth century. In any case, south-west Scotland had no formal provision until long after Hugh's death. Dumfries hospital or infirmary was completed in 1778 with a room set aside for four cells for lunatics. In 1791 a separate building was added with six cells.[56] Idiocy and imbecility remained a domestic rather than a public issue until the nineteenth century. Indeed, the absence of any medical testimony in the case, or of any reference to medical treatment (even for Hugh's deafness and dumbness), suggests that his condition was not perceived as one which medicine could help. While keeping Hugh at home, the Blair family also relied on a consensus in the neighbourhood about the impropriety of doing business with a man who was plainly unable to manage his own affairs, and on the licence given to his behaviour by long familiarity. One witness, Rev. Welsh, reported that 'he never knew Hugh Blair make any bargain or common transaction in life, or that he ever was employed that way'.

The principally domestic focus of care for the mentally incapable is demonstrated in other documents. Two surviving volumes of Dumfries burgh chamberlain's accounts for 1773–78 and 1779–85 contain only two mentions of insanity, each involving the transportation of a mad person back to their home parish.[57] In 1773 town officers were paid to take a 'mad woman' outside the boundaries of the burgh of Dumfries.[58]

Wanderers who showed signs of derangement might be treated in the same way as other poor people who looked as though they might become an enduring burden on a community's exiguous poor relief funds. The insane and stupid were treated like other paupers, even if (depending on the extent of disability) their care was generally more expensive.[59] This shows not a lack of discrimination, but a willingness to care for the mentally incapacitated within the limits of available charity. While the 'furious' who posed a threat to the public and to themselves might be incarcerated by order of a magistrate, there was no law against harmless idiots wandering at large, provided they had residence in a parish for poor relief purposes.[60] Speaking with the voice of a later and perhaps more sensitive age, J. Clerk Rattray (Sheriff-Depute of Midlothian) argued in April 1817 that it might be desirable to change the law to allow magistrates 'to confine such idiots as prove a nuisance to the public by their irregular, vagrant life or indecent appearance in public places'.[61] His comment reminds us that then, as in the 1740s, there was no prohibition on such people, provided they had residence or were simply passing through. Hugh was hardly on the breadline and, while causing puzzlement, did nobody any harm and posed no threat to the parish purse.

The only 'secure' accommodation for violent lunatics was a jail or 'tolbooth'. A Dumfries merchant petitioned the burgh council in 1704 about the damage to his business caused by Thomas Crosby, who was imprisoned in a prison cell above his shop. He claimed he was 'greatly molested and troubled almost continually by the said Thomas his speaking at the window and ignorant people's attention thereunto at my shop door and particularly by the said Thomas his throwing out sometimes stones and often the stoups and vessels he receives with meat'.[62] Incarceration in a prison was viewed as a temporary expedient. However, release required agreement from 'friends' (relatives) that they would themselves protect the rest of the community from any violent behaviour on the part of their mad kin. Alexander Logan was imprisoned at Dumfries by order of the Justice of the Peace on or about 13 August 1728 after three or four days of furious behaviour, 'the country [being] in hazard'. A warrant was issued for his release to relatives on 26 August since there were no charges against him, and the justification for his imprisonment was: 'the delirious state he was in . . . [and] to secure him . . . in order to preserve him from doing violence to himself or others'.[63] In the early and mid-eighteenth century the presumption (and necessity) was that the fatuous and the furious would be cared for in a family.

Hugh was a minor oddity rather than a major curiosity. He was certainly not a violent man. In many ways, he seems to have posed no problem to his family and community, let alone a threat. Nevertheless, John Blair and his wife plainly had no time for the childlike eccentricities of a man then in his late thirties. John Blair's wife was neither happy nor comfortable with Hugh in the house. For her part, she disrupted his routine and, perhaps understandably, ordered his verminous clothes to be boiled and his room to be cleaned out of accumulated twigs, birds' feathers, scraps of cloth, and unwashed garments. Grizell Blair's concern can only have been with protecting Hugh, or with spiting her younger son after their falling out. In the absence of further evidence, John's actions in 1737 can be read as both venal and altruistic. It is at least possible that John believed his actions were best for all the family. What he did in 1747 can only have been an attempt to regain control of the administration of his brother's section of their inheritance, and to frustrate the chances of Hugh fathering legitimate children. John had half the heritable estate following Grizell's death: if Hugh died without issue the other half would eventually pass to him and his only son, David.

Marriage was viewed as the normal state in this society, even if anywhere between 10 and 20 per cent of men and women remained single all their lives. We do not know how old Nicholas was or whether she had previously had problems attracting a partner. Apart from her initial reluctance, we know nothing about her reactions to the prospect of marrying Hugh or her later experience of the marriage's physical or emotional side. Archibald Mitchell had known Hugh since his infancy and his daughter Nicholas Mitchell must also have know Hugh's character as 'she had long lived in his neighbourhood'.[64] However, a fictionalized account of a cognition published in the 1820s may give us some flavour of her motivations. It is contained in John Galt's novel, *The Entail*.[65] Galt knew and wrote about the rural society of Ayrshire and Renfrewshire. Jenny Purdie, a former servant of the inquest's fictitious subject, Walkinshaw of Grippy, describes him as 'daft': 'he's just silly, and tavert [senseless], and heedless, and o' an inclination to swattle [wallow] in the dirt like a grumphie [pig]'. On concluding her evidence, the judge said jocularly he was sure this was not the sort of man she would like to marry. Her reply was swift. 'There's no saying . . . the Kittlestoneheugh's a braw [fine] estate; and mony a better born than me has been blithe to put up wi' houses and lan[d]s, though wit and worth were both want-ing'.[66] This is not simply a literary device. A court submission written on behalf of Hugh and Nicholas cites:

> marriages of such persons as are defective in their understanding, but not quite void of reason . . . though at the same time such persons pass in the country for fools or idiots. There was a gentleman of that character in Galloway, that died not many years ago [Gordon of Knockbrex is named in the margin], who was married, and had issue still alive, and they are no fools.[67]

There is strong evidence that Grizell Blair herself may have made just such a marriage. A later court case mentions the alleged mental weak-ness of David Blair during the late 1700s and early 1710s. The tutors to the children of Borgue spoke of securities for loans granted by David under dubious circumstances: 'the same was fraudfullie elicit from the said David Blair, a weak, facile person who was addicted to a habit of drunkenness, acted as a madman for several years before granting, there-after, and at the very time the same was made he was so drunk that he was insensible of what he did'.[68] In the 1825 publication, *Jamieson's Dictionary of the Scottish Language*, one of the less-than-flattering adjectives used to describe Grizell's husband is explained thus: 'A facile man is a forensic phrase in Scottish, which has no synonyme in English. It does not signify one who is weak in judgement, or deficient in mental ability, but one who possesses that degree of softness of disposition that he is liable to be easily wrought upon by others'. However, the term could also be used of someone who had more serious mental problems. Thus, in 1756 the trustees for James Fawside, a Lanarkshire clergyman's son, made the following statement. They were seeking the 'reduction' or invalidation of certain unwise (not to say deranged) transactions entered into by Fawside, 'a poor unhappy man, who from his infancy was weak and simple, in his more advanced years became quite distracted and has been twice since confined to a mad-house in Glasgow'.[69] They referred to 'open madness' in 1745 and 1750 but suggested that James was al-ways:

so weak, facile, and simple that he was . . . an easy prey to any man who would be bad enough to take the advantage of him, under the colour of sincerity and friendship, and stir up the unreasonable prejudice and jealousy which he appears to have entertained in his madness against his father and sisters; and which appears to have been the prevailing extravagance which broke out upon every occasion in his distracted fits.[70]

As a local stonemason put it: 'The people in the neighbourhood did not choose to contradict the said James Fawside, as they knew he was wrong in the head'.[71]

Another example suggests that the strict legal meaning of the term (suggestible) was in practice extended to include implications of deeper mental difficulties. Ann Blair (no known relation to Hugh) was cognosced as an imbecile by Perth Sheriff Court in March 1812.[72] Her own agent, Charles Hay of Beech Hill, spoke of her as: 'incapable of judging or acting for herself, and he conceives her always to be under the influence of the person who has the charge of her in some shape being of a facile or fatuous disposition'. As with Fawside, there was an elision between gullibility and imbecility. Asked what he thought of his parishioner, Rev. John Findlay, minister in Perth, 'conceives she is not in possession of her right mind'. Interrogated for the other siblings: 'if he means that she is possessed of no reason or that she is only to a certain degree facile . . . he does not consider her altogether devoid of reason [an idiot] . . . but that the reason she possesses is of a low degree'. Grizell Blair must have known what her prospective husband was like – he was also her cousin – and may have felt that Nicholas could make the same adjustments as she had done on behalf of herself and her kin.

Archibald Mitchell's interests are easier to infer. Marrying his daughter to Hugh Blair opened up the prospect of sharing Hugh's inheritance while at the same time enhancing his family's status by becoming linked to landowners. Mitchell's main occupation carried less status than it would later attain. Being a surgeon was decidedly less prestigious than being a physician. Conventionally, surgeons performed bleeding, amputations and other techniques involving cutting. Physicians administered medicine and advice, offering a more learned diagnosis and a more rounded set of cures. Surgeons tended to learn from practical experience gained through apprenticeship, while the élite physicians were more 'bookish', often attending a Scottish or European university's medical faculty. While medical students were gentlemen undergoing a liberal education, surgeons' apprentices enjoyed a more servile standing.[73] The result was a medical 'profession' divided by wealth and status. The respective charging scales reflect the differentiation. Depending on the distance travelled and the time of day, the basic consulting fee of a physician was one guinea (21 shillings) in late-eighteenth-century Glasgow, that of a surgeon approximately five shillings. Not surprisingly, surgeons tended to be considerably less wealthy on average than physicians.

Mitchell himself was an entrepreneurial man, in all senses of the word. The Town Council Minutes show he was admitted burgess of Kirkcudbright on 26 April 1721.

> The said day Archibald Mitchell, 'apothicary chirurgeon' in this burgh is created, adjudged, and received freeman and burgess of this burgh to all the privileges and benefits and advantages that other burgesses therein [enjoy], without any composition but for his encouragement in setting up here his shop of surgery and apothecary that may be useful and helpful to the whole inhabitants and others in time coming. Who being sworn made faith, owning and professing the Protestant reformed religion, true allegiance to his majesty King George and obedience to the magistrates and their lawful successors, and to bear scot and lot according to the exercise of trade or calling.[74]

His 'cautioner' or surety was Samuel Ewart. Mitchell made an elegant signature with a prominent flourish under his surname. There are two points to note in what is otherwise a formulaic document. First, he must have come from outside the town since it was more usual to enter burgess as someone's son, or by marrying a burgess's daughter or by apprenticeship. Second, it was normal for a small fee to be paid by incomers. The town may have been short of medical practitioners though there was at least one other surgeon present during the 1720s (John Clark).[75] Alternatively, Mitchell may have been a particularly persuasive man. His wide-ranging business interests are shown in later references to him. In a document of 1724 involving a deal with a merchant in the Isle of Man, Archibald Mitchell is described as 'chyrurgeon, apothecary and merchant in Kirkcudbright'.[76] Later, he branched out even further, renting one of the burgh's pastures. On 4 March 1745 we find in the Town Council Minutes: 'Set [leased], the common grass to Mr Archibald Mitchell, surgeon in Kirkcudbright, for £38'.[77] The following year, the grass was rented to Samuel Herries, wright, for £44 Scots with Mitchell as his cautioner.[78]

Whatever the financial advantages of the union, we should not underestimate the attractions of social mobility for the Mitchells. Hugh came from a landowning family. He was Blair *of* Borgue and therefore quite different from someone who simply lived in the parish without owning land. The latter would simply be described as *in* that place in Scottish historical documents. For example, the first witness in the case was William Taggart, tailor in Borgue. In a traditional society like that of pre-industrial Scotland, land was the principal source of wealth. It provided food, fuel and raw materials such as wood, wool and hides. Of course, this was also a commercial society with complex economic relations primarily based on money rather than barter. New sources of wealth were opening up in the shape of early industrial development in nearby Lanarkshire and Ayrshire and throughout the Central Lowlands. Overseas commerce was expanding rapidly, notably the tobacco trade through Glasgow. Dumfries and Kirkcudbright shipping had long been involved in coastal commerce and had some links to colonial North America. Smuggling was held to be rife in Galloway because of its proximity to the Isle of Man. Yet land remained the most important commodity. Additionally, it conferred social status and political rights. The predominant values of Scottish society in the early eighteenth century were landed values.

With rights went responsibilities. Local landowners were liable as 'heritors' (owners of heritable property) for providing a manse, paying the salary of the parish minister and supplying a school house for the community. Their families and dependants (including tenants) had pews in reserved areas of the parish church, confirming their prominence in the social and economic life of the community. Her family's privileged position as a major contributor to the clergy's salary may explain Lady Borgue's haughty attitude to the Presbytery's enquiries into her son's mental capacities. In 1799 David Blair of Borgue was second only to the Earl of Selkirk in his share of the rental value of the parish – even if that was only 16 per cent.[79] Heritors also had responsibilities for the administration of roads and bridges, and were expected to contribute to the relief of the poor on their estates or in their parish. Landowners or 'lairds' (as they were also known colloquially) were viewed as the natural leaders of a community, looked up to, and expected to provide example, guidance, and arbitration in the event of disputes. Special form of address ('of' rather than 'in' a place) reinforced the distinctiveness of landowners. Mrs Blair consistently gave herself an exaggerated style: a contract of 1742 describes her as 'Mrs Grizel Blair, Lady Borgue'.[80]

This was also a close-knit society. On 2 November 1705, Hugh McGuffock of Rusco signed over to David Blair authority to settle his debts by collecting rents from the estate of Borgue. On the same day a notary gathered the tenantry together in the low hall of 'the place of Borgue' formally to advise them of the assignment.[81] The tenants had been convened by their lord's authority at what was termed 'the head court of the barony of Borgue'. Baron courts were community courts, presided over by the landlord's steward to protect his interests, to organize aspects of agriculture which required a degree of joint decision making, and to maintain 'good neighbourhood' among members. All those owing suit to the court were supposed to attend a head court, the purpose being to convey information in such a way that none could claim ignorance: another aspect of a face-to-face society where, for some purposes at least, written communication was not good enough. To take another example, when John Blair registered himself as executor of his father's moveable estate, the event was done publicly at Kirkcudbright tolbooth on 15 April 1735.[82] Baron courts were retained (only to atrophy) when other heritable jurisdictions were swept away by the London government in the aftermath of the failed Jacobite rising of 1745–6. Changes there certainly were, but while other parts of Scotland were modernizing rapidly around this time, the opinion of late eighteenth-century agricultural writers was that the south-west of Scotland was enclosed but not much improved.[83]

The fact that life was rather self-contained in eighteenth-century rural Scotland does not mean that geographical mobility was absent.[84] Some of those who gave evidence in the case had worked for a year or two in the Blair household before moving elsewhere for better pay, conditions or work experience. Such people were very typical of ordinary men and women in their teens and early twenties. Most would have left their parental home to live and work as domestic or agricultural servants and apprentices in order to gain independence and the savings necessary to achieve that level of economic independence which would enable them to marry and set up their own household. While apprentices might move long distances to a town like Edinburgh or Glasgow, servants normally took positions within a day's walk of their previous place of residence.

They moved rather frequently, more than half moving annually and three-quarters changing their employer within three years. Service was the characteristic experience for young people of the eighteenth century. The modern equivalent is extended ('secondary') schooling, higher education, and/or vocational training.

In this part of eighteenth-century Scotland, 'The farm servants all receive their victuals in the farmer's family'.[85] By this was meant both live-in servants and the cottagers and labourers, often married, who worked for a farmer. Hugh was exposed to a wide range of such people 'of a low rank'. The economy of Galloway also benefited from a long distance cattle trade from the south-western counties of Scotland into the north and Midlands of England, and even as far south as London, then a major city of nearly three-quarters of a million people. Those of the landowning and professional classes had wider horizons, visiting the major cities of Edinburgh and Glasgow for their leisure opportunities and for the legal, medical and educational services they provided. England and Ireland were just a short boat journey away.

The witnesses were selected for their intimate knowledge of Hugh Blair's life and are not a random sample of Kirkcudbrightshire society. Indeed, the fact that they had generally stayed in the area for long periods may make them atypical in a era of considerable change. Yet much geographical movement, notably of hired labour, was short-distance and temporary. Even communities experiencing profound upheavals would have contained a core of stable population. Furthermore, people sometimes retained an association with the areas where they had grown up. Alexander Goldie was a lawyer cognosced as *incompos mentis* by Edinburgh Sheriff Court in March 1765. Goldie came from Dumfriesshire and had estates there despite spending most of his time living and working in Edinburgh.[86]

If society and economy were changing around this period, there were certain important institutions which retained a place in the lives of most eighteenth-century Scots. In particular, the church played a far more important role in everyday life than modern readers might expect. Attendance at church was expected. Taking communion at least once a year remained an important part of civil as well as religious identity. The famous Ayrshire poet, Robert Burns, later disparaged communions as 'holy fairs', but the significance of religion to eighteenth century people should not be under-estimated. Outward behaviour in moments requiring gravity of dress and demeanour was regarded as an indication of social acceptability and integration. Nowhere was a display of conformity more vital than in church. Conduct in the pews was highly visible and deemed

Plate 7: 'A sleepy congregation'
Regular attendance at church was both accepted and expected in eighteenth-century Scotland. However, sermons could be long and densely theological. Hugh Blair liked to sit in the same place every time he went to church.
Source: John Kay, *A series of original portraits and caricature etchings, by the late John Kay, miniature painter, Edinburgh; with biographical sketches and illustrative anecdotes*, 2 vols (Edinburgh, 1838), vol. 1, p. 28.

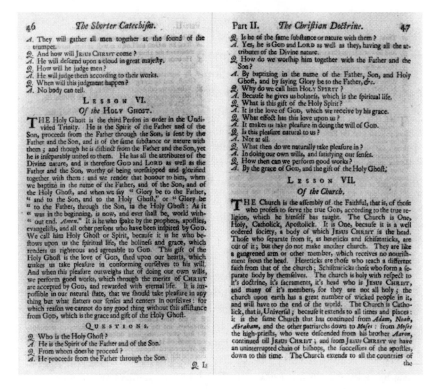

Plate 8: Pages from a catechism
These pages from a 'shorter' catechism of 1748 show the sorts of detailed questions and answers which comprised this basic resource for religious education. We know that Hugh Blair had an excellent knowledge of both this and the more complicated 'proof' version. Some of the questions which the judges in his case asked of him resemble the form and content of catechism.
Source: St Andrews University Library.

to be of the greatest significance. Calvinists in particular were required to display awe and reverence before the pulpit.[87] They were on view before the rest of the church community who could, among other things, test any gossip they might have heard about melancholic, foolish or furious talk or behaviour.

Family worship was prescribed by the church and was probably widely practised in the period under scrutiny. Depending on their own inclinations, the head of a household might catechize their servants and children or require them to learn for themselves. Catechism was a basic tool of religious education in early modern Europe, involving a long list of questions on central aspects of the faith to which there were set answers. The 'shorter' catechism (actually a substantial work), involved questions, answers and a biblical reference to substantiate the latter. The 'proof' version, which could be up to three times longer, had the same information but it also reproduced the full text of the reference.[88] That religion was not a mere formality is shown by the religious revival movement in the west of Scotland during the early 1740s, the most famous at Cambuslang, south of Glasgow. One individual who had worked in the Blair household during the 1730s – John McEwan, a land labourer in Borgue – singled out Hugh's perceived failings in religious observance and understanding:

> When the deponent was in the house of Borgue it was usual for the servants to examine one another upon the catechism. One night the deponent put several questions to Hugh Blair but he could not answer any nor distinguish question from answer. In time of family prayer he has frequently seen the defender stalking through the room with the back side of his wig foremost, making sport or diversion to the servants and sometimes standing by the chimney side or trifling with candlesticks, without regard or sense of family worship.

The Church of Scotland was the ecclesiastical establishment. It had the authority to require conformity to its moral precepts and behavioural norms not only from voluntary adherents (though their compliance was much easier to secure), but from all Scots. With growing religious divisions and changing political priorities in the eighteenth century, that authority proved difficult to maintain in the long term. It had always been easier to enforce on those who needed the many things the kirk provided. The church of the seventeenth and eighteenth century was involved in much more than spiritual ministrations. Through the parish 'Kirk Sessions' it administered poor relief to both parish residents and needy passers by. A Kirk Session comprised the parish minister and a number of lay 'elders'.[89] The 'precentor' or clerk who aided the minister generally also acted as a junior schoolmaster, helping children to learn the catechism, to read the Bible and to sing psalms.[90] Importantly, the church made into issues of public concern aspects of what we now regard as deeply private life. While they exaggerate, the authors of a recent general survey of Dumfries and Galloway offer the following useful description:

> The Presbyterian church in power was an immensely powerful organisation, the only education authority and social welfare agency, a court of morality interfering, censoring and controlling the most trivial aspects of human behaviour, and extending its multiple intolerances not just to religious opponents, Catholics, Episcopalians, and Quakers, but to nonconforming persons of any variety – outcasts, gipsies, troublemakers.[91]

One example was the observation of the Sabbath. Work was forbidden on the Lord's day (as was drinking in time of divine service), and this explains why a farmer was able to persuade Hugh not to muck out the stables on a Sunday, by 'signing that the minister would take him by the gorge [neck] and hang him' if he persisted. It was quite normal for elders of the Kirk Session to go around their areas of the parish to check on how people spent their Sundays.

Sexual behaviour is another area in which the Kirk Session took a close interest. The church taught that pre-nuptial fornication was wrong and, where possible, punished by fines and public humiliation those found to have engaged in it. On the page before the Presbytery's judgement on Hugh Blair's banns is a case from the Kirk Session of Anwoth about a couple, married on 21 November 1745, who produced a child on 8 June 1746 with 'nails such as ripe [full term] children ordinarily have, and could suck'. The session had quizzed them repeatedly 'in order to bring them to an ingenuous' confession but without success. It ordered them to be rebuked publicly in their parish church.[92] Adultery was proscribed also. The entry immediately prior to the minutes of Lady Borgue's petition is a reference from the session of Borgue about exactly this. Having an illegitimate child was both a secular and ecclesiastical offence because it transcended moral norms and involved the possibility of expenditure on poor relief. The Kirk Session was the basic unit of church government in each of Scotland's 900 or so parishes. Difficult cases involving recidivism, contempt of an individual minister, or aggravating circumstances were referred to the next level of Presbyterian church organization, the Presbytery. This body comprised the ministers and leading or 'ruling' elders from a group of parishes. It met less frequently and dealt with bigger issues.

Lady Borgue and Archibald Mitchell, surgeon in Kirkcudbright, had applied to the minister of Kirkcudbright, Rev. Gartshore, for proclamation of the banns between Hugh and Nicholas. The clergyman was reluctant to agree, sceptical as he was of Hugh's ability to comprehend what he would be doing in marrying the surgeon's daughter. The parents agreed to await the judgement of the Presbytery of Kirkcudbright. The minutes of the meeting read as follows.

> Upon this the several brethren present being asked by the moderator to declare their minds gave their judgement unanimously the greatest number from their personal knowledge and two only from the character they had received of the said gentleman, that he was incapable of rational consent to marriage or of coming under the religious tie and sacred bond of a marriage oath. But as these two brethren were not otherwise acquainted with Hugh Blair than by common character it was moved that he should be sent for to appear personally before the Presbytery. A committee was appointed to wait upon Lady Borgue and her son to desire that he should attend the Presbytery and that the lady, if she pleased, might come along with him. The committee being returned made the following report, that the lady did not think it proper that either she or her son should come before the reverend Presbytery. And they report further that when at her desire one of the two members had asked Hugh Blair her son whom he would have for a wife, thought he answered in this way: Nickie Mitchell. Yet that member naming another young gentlewoman he consented to the one as to the other.[93]

The Presbytery therefore refused permission for the union to be celebrated under the aegis of the Church of Scotland. In the extract from the Presbytery's judgement, it is plain that Hugh was well known within the county. Only a minority of the ministers of Kirkcudbrightshire had to rely on his 'character', a second-hand opinion derived from others. On the surface, he might seem to have been the victim of hearsay and innuendo. Yet, in societies where face-to-face interactions were the norm, it was quite acceptable to rely on what others of respected opinion thought of someone. In criminal cases, a person could be found guilty wholly on the basis of their reputation as a malefactor. By the same token, those of previously good character might be given the benefit of any doubt or, if found guilty, might receive a lesser punishment. In this sense, Hugh was treated no differently to anyone else who found himself an object of discussion before a civil, criminal or ecclesiastical tribunal. And the church tribunal ensured that all its members had had the opportunity personally to evaluate Hugh's mental capacities. The Church of Scotland retained the ability to pronounce on the sexual and moral behaviour of its parishioners and to deny its offices to those who transgressed its prescriptions or who failed to live up to the standards of religious knowledge it required. Hugh Blair was refused proclamation of the banns for his marriage on the grounds of stupidity. But the same thing happened to countless others who had committed fornication, or whose religious faith was not firmly Protestant.[94]

Despite the church's refusal to allow one of its officials to perform a marriage for Hugh and Nicholas Mitchell, the couple were married. Furthermore, their union was a legal one. Until 1855 in Scotland there were a number of ways to marry. Technically, acts of the Scottish Parliament in 1641 and 1649 (subsequently repeated) obliged people to marry before a Church of Scotland minister.[95] However, the church recognized that it was consent which made a marriage, and that a young man and woman above the ages of 14 and 12 respectively could make a valid marriage provided they were not within the prohibited degrees of kinship. If questioned, proof of willing consent given by the parties themselves or by independent witnesses was enough to substantiate a claim to be married. A couple could form a marriage in another way. They might promise to marry in the future (*per verba de futuro*) and then follow this by having sex, the latter act indicating the required consent. A man and woman could live together as husband and wife: in this case the canon of proof was 'by habit and repute'.[96] Sharing food and a bed, being seen together, producing children, and being called man and wife in the community were what constituted evidence of a union in this case.

Thus, legally binding marriage required free consent, an outward display of that willing agreement, and the absence of impediments.[97] The essence of a binding marriage was the exchange of willing and informed consent between a man and woman who had no impediment to their union on the grounds of consanguinity or pre-contract. Marriage could be achieved by the exchange of vows in church before a Church of Scotland clergyman, following the proclamation of banns. Importantly, marriages did not have to be conducted in the Church of Scotland to be valid. They could be celebrated by a minister of another denomination, usually an Episcopalian in the early eighteenth century. Ceremonies without the approval of a recognized church were deemed to be 'irregular' or 'clandestine', but they nevertheless constituted a binding marriage. An Act of the Scottish Parliament in 1649 recognized the motives behind clandestine marriage: 'to eschew the censures of this kirk, or to falsify their promise of marriage formerly made to others, or to decline the concurrence and consent of their parents'.[98] Such marriages were common in certain parts of Scotland in the early eighteenth century, notably in the Edinburgh area, which is where the union was performed.[99] Hugh Blair and Nicholas Mitchell were 'irregularly' or 'clandestinely' married in that the Church of Scotland frowned on the path they had taken to become man and wife. By whom the couple were married is unknown since that section of a document which states the information has crumbled with age. But they were certainly married.

One conventional image of the past is that, for those of property, marriage was too important to be left to the people getting married. Over the late seventeenth and eighteenth centuries, it is true that a mixture of demographic chance and intermarriage between branches of the Blair/McGuffock families created substantial landholdings. Hugh's grandfather's two marriages had both been highly advantageous. Thus, we have the notion of the 'arranged' marriage where a partner was selected by the parents or wider kin group on the basis of material advantage rather than by a man and woman for reasons of personal emotional compatibility. It is indeed hard to exaggerate the importance of a proper marriage among members of the moneyed classes. The correct partner would ensure the financial and social future of offspring, and add to the family of origin's store of contacts and prestige. There was certainly an active (and sometimes highly venal) marriage market in early Georgian Edinburgh, though in the narrower world of rural society personal contacts would have been more significant.

However, the idea that partners were selected for, and imposed upon, nubile young people is difficult to apply to Scottish society as a whole in the eighteenth century. On the one hand, the ease with which marriage could be contracted made it difficult to control free choice. On the other, the absolute requirement for willing and informed consent made it very difficult (if not impossible) to force someone into a union. For the bulk of the population, the notion of arranged marriages is wholly inaccurate.

For the propertied classes it has a kernel of truth but is nevertheless misleading. When seeking their spouse, those marrying for the first time were guided by the assumptions of their class, the indirect influence of parents and kin, and their own complex ideas of what constituted personal attractiveness. When Hugh was teased about his marriage prospects or questioned by the Commissaries, the women who were mentioned were (as far as we can tell) all landowners' or ministers' daughters and thus most appropriate for his station – other things being equal. In the end, Hugh Blair and Nicholas Mitchell were steered towards union by their respective parents. As Professor Christopher Smout has written, 'marriages were not so much arranged as artfully contrived'.[100]

The formal marriage was the most easily achieved part of the relationship. But if the church made it easy to form a marriage, it made it difficult to dissolve one. The reason why Hugh Blair's life is so well documented is because of his brother's attempts to have his marriage annulled. We must be careful about using the word 'divorce' here, at least in a modern sense. For there were in reality two forms of formally sanctioned marital break-up in eighteenth century Europe, neither exactly comparable with the late twentieth century – even if the canon or ecclesiastical law used the word *divortium* or divorce for both. The first was called separation *a mensa et thoro* – known in the vernacular as bed and board in Scotland. It did not allow the possibility of remarriage and was indeed intended, by the church at least, ultimately to lead to a reconciliation. The second, closer to our understanding, was divorce *a vinculo* with the possibility of remarriage. Divorce for adultery by either party was introduced in Scotland (and in Holland) at the time of the Reformation.[101] This was because marriage became more a civil contract rather than an ecclesiastical sacrament. While divorce may have been easier (and cheaper) than in England, there were still only 347 petitions before Edinburgh Commissary Court 1708–1800, of which just a quarter came before 1770.[102]

The Witnesses

So much for the legal and social background to the case. We have explained in detail the laws of guardianship, property and marriage because they bear directly on the way Hugh Blair's life is presented to us in historical sources. For further information about his life and his mind we have to look beyond the motives of family members and religious or legal institutions to the opinions of those who lived and worked with Hugh. For it was largely on the basis of their views that Hugh's marriage was annulled.

Who were the witnesses who gave evidence both for and against Hugh? Twenty-one were men and eight were women. The imbalance may be because men were more likely than women to interact with Hugh. However, legal filters also enter into the equation. Courts much preferred male to female testimony on grounds widely accepted by contemporary (male) writers that women were more easily influenced, more emotional and therefore less reliable.[103] Lady Borgue and Helen Lamont could not speak in the case because they had a material interest in its outcome, as did Hugh's brother John. Seven of the women who did give evidence were single and one was a widow, reflecting the subordinate legal status of married women. Witness ages ranged from the early twenties to the mid-fifties. Age reporting was approximate in this period. In the absence of the need to know and report an accurate age and of the record-keeping required to verify it, a number of the witnesses gave some imprecise indication such as '20 and upwards'. Mr William Jamieson gave his age as 40 but he must have been 43 years old at the time of the case.[104] Except for some of the clergy and those living in Edinburgh, all the witnesses lived within five miles of Borgue kirk as the crow flies.

The witnesses came from a wide range of professional, farming and artisanal backgrounds. Most people in eighteenth-century Scotland lived on the land or in small villages; most got their living directly or indirectly from the land and its products. Apart from the west-central Lowlands and patches of the south-west where small-scale owner occupation was common, land was owned by a small number of lairds. It was generally worked by tenants along with their sub-tenants (sometimes called 'cottars') and servants. The backbone of rural communities were the tenant farmers, men like John Porter who had lived in the area for 30 years and had been a Blair tenant for 16 years. The term 'labourer' is more ambiguous. It could be used to indicate a person who worked with his hands for wages but a 'land labourer' could be another term for a tenant. A 'portioner' like John Tudhope was an owner-occupier of land: the word meant heir to a part or portion of a heritable estate (usually shared with siblings).[105] Portioners were minor lairds.

The notion that pre-industrial families were self-sufficient – for example, spinning their own yarn to make into cloth and then clothes – is quite inappropriate for eighteenth-century Britain. The division of labour was already advanced in rural Britain (if less so than in more urbanized regions) and all aspects of life were highly commercialized. Tailors might work in their own homes or shops, or spend days or weeks working at the house of a family which could provide sufficient demand for their services. Weavers and shoemakers too made commodities for local and regional markets. These artisan-traders may have varied considerably in wealth and status within the community. Some worked on their own, possibly with the help of family and a servant or apprentice; others may have employed several workers and operated on a larger scale. Even an allegedly 'under-developed' economy like that of early-eighteenth-century Scotland had a considerable variety of economic experience.

If most of the witnesses lived in Kirkcudbrightshire and had known Hugh's family for many years, the final deponents were newer acquaintances who met him, his wife and his mother during the court case of 1747. They hailed originally from a place called Binns near Linlithgow, a few miles to the west of Edinburgh. However, they rented or owned a flat or apartment on or in a 'close', or narrow lane, off Edinburgh's High Street. The location was probably to the east of what is now North Bridge, for it is reported that on one Sunday Grizell Blair went to Canongate church while Hugh attended the Tron.[106] We do not know if widow Balfour was a relation of the Tudhope family but we can say that it was the norm for people in urban and rural areas alike to rent rather than own their homes. 'The Binns' itself, now a National Trust for Scotland property, is a substantial country house which dates from the seventeenth century, since when it has been the seat of the Dalyell family.

For most of the witnesses we must rely on general observations. Without hours of possibly fruitless labour on local sources it would be difficult to build up a detailed picture of the lives and works of individual artisans and farmers on the fringes of the Blair orbit. In contrast, the clergy are much better documented. Potted biographies of them appear in the *Fasti ecclesiae Scoticanae*.[107] To take just one example, Robert Walker's career was meteoric. Educated at Edinburgh university, he was licensed to preach by the Presbytery of Kirkcudbright in 1737 at the tender age of 21 years. From the south-west he went to Straiton in Midlothian, from where he was formally called to be assistant minister of South Leith (Edinburgh's

Plate 9: The Revd. Robert Walker (b. 1716)
Robert Walker was a witness in the case because he knew the Blair family
between 1733 and 1737. Gloves and wigs were a normal part of a gentleman's
attire.
Source: John Kay, *A series of original portraits and caricature etchings, by the late John Kay,
miniature painter, Edinburgh; with biographical sketches and illustrative anecdotes*, 2 vols
(Edinburgh, 1838), vol. 1, p. 347.

port) on 15 May 1746 and admitted to the charge on 20 November of
that year. His removal to the prestigious charge of St Giles, Edinburgh, in
October 1754 marked the pinnacle of his career.[108]

Kinship links between the clergy are particularly pronounced. For instance, Robert Monteith, minister of Longformacus, was the son of James Monteith, who had been minister of Borgue from 1693 until his death on 24 March 1744. It was that event which caused Hugh to say 'O! Die'. The clergy are over-represented among the witnesses because of their position in the community and their perceived integrity. Five men of God and two ministers' daughters gave evidence (including Margaret or Peggy Veitch, one of those about whom Hugh was teased or questioned). Interestingly, the parish minister of Borgue did not give evidence in the case. This was James Brown, correctly identified by Hugh in his verbal reponses to the Commissaries of Edinburgh. He was formally installed as assistant minister to the ageing Rev. Monteith in September 1741. Brown was a native of the parish, born just two or three years before Hugh Blair. They almost certainly went to school together and would therefore have sat in the single class of different ages and abilities that made up most early-modern schools. Hugh sat directly beneath Brown in church and the minister cannot have been ignorant of his marriage or the court case. Yet, Brown's was an invidious position, trapped between the competing material interests and opinions of the opposing parties, some of whom were not only his parishioners but also his paymasters.

It is unclear whether Brown was a graduate but he had been to university. Certification at the end of a university career was less important in those days than was forming the personal contacts and patronage ties through which most worthwhile jobs were obtained. Rev. Robert Walker had a glittering career without being a graduate. Certainly, those with a university education formed nearly a third of male witnesses in the case of Hugh Blair. For modern readers, putting 'Mr' before a person's name is useful only in showing that the person referred to is male and perhaps has no other title such as 'Dr', 'Professor', or 'Sir'. In early-modern Scotland, the addition 'Mr' to a person's name normally indicated that he was a *magister* or Master of Arts: usually a graduate in theology. It was not until the later eighteenth century in the cities that the modern, honorific use of the addition became more common. Recent graduates who were unable to find a parish might earn a living as a parish schoolmaster by teaching Latin grammar, the core of post-elementary education everywhere in early-modern Europe.[109] Thus, Mr Thomas McCourtie, schoolmaster at Twinholm (modern Twynholm), was in his early twenties and had to wait another decade before being called to the parish of Dolphinton.[110] Mr John Gordon, who had once been a schoolmaster at

Borgue, seems never to have secured a post and was, at the time of the court case, in his forties and a 'residenter' at Balmangan (south of Borgue): a term generally used of genteel folk with private means. He was also an uncle by marriage to Hugh Blair.[111] Roy's military map of the 1750s shows a tower or castle at Balmangan. Those who never made it were sometimes known as 'stickit' (stuck) ministers.

Chapter 3

Understanding Mental Incapacity

We shall now investigate how these people from all walks of local society understood what it meant to be mentally capable. In doing so, we explicate what constituted incapacity, but we shall also be able to explore the conventions of normal functioning which underlay judgements. Those understandings are fundamentally non-medical ones. Whatever the extent of lay knowledge about medicine, none of the witnesses in Hugh Blair's case was a professional medical practitioner. Of course, folk and professional medicine do not exist in separate compartments, but can be seen as part of a spectrum from amateur neighbourly advice to the most highly qualified physician. Medicine was part of the consumer revolution of the eighteenth century, with quacks or mountebanks selling patent medicines to eager customers. Self-help was also common and the eighteenth century saw the proliferation of medical manuals for ordinary people.[1] Of these, the best known is that authored by the Edinburgh physician William Buchan. His *Domestic medicine; or, the family physician . . .* was first published in 1769 and went through many editions before the end of the Georgian age. It was said to be as widely owned as the Bible in late eighteenth-century Scotland.

For all this, the language of the depositions contains no distinctively medical terminology or jargon of the kind which could be found in Buchan or other near-contemporary texts such as Robert Whytt's *Observations on the nature, causes, and cures of the disorders which have been commonly called nervous, hypochondriac, or hysteric* (1765). The predominance of lay people in court cases is not unique to this investigation, and it is true of both civil and criminal courts which discussed issues of mental capacity and personal responsibility. As we read them in the court transcripts, the definitions of mental capacity were those of lay people and were based on what was termed by contemporary thinkers 'common sense'.[2] Judge, jury (in cases where there was one) and witnesses sought secure ground by reference to a general or common standard of what constituted normal mental functioning. Such definitions were predicated on the notion that sanity and/or mental capacity was to be taken for granted and that its obverse, insanity, could be readily identified by any competent lay person. Witnesses offered specific instances of odd behaviour and, usually, a judgement of the mental capacity of the person in question. Those who sought to lend greater authority to their testimonies did so by an appeal to widely shared public opinion rather than to some objective scientific standard.

All the witnesses called against Hugh concluded with some variation on: '[he or she] looked upon the defender as an idiot and mere natural fool. The neighbourhood commonly looked upon him as such and usually called him the fool laird of Borgue'.[3] The criterion used by witnesses was whether Hugh was like them and other ordinary people. John McEwan, a 39–year-old land labourer in Borgue, said he regarded 'the defender as wanting the exercise of reason, void of common sense and understanding like himself or other men'.

Opposite and p. 56
Plates 10-13: The daft Highland laird, John Dhu or Dow, alias MacDonald, and Jamie Duff, an idiot
– Jamie Duff alias Bailie Duff
– Dr Glen and the daft Highland laird
– Thomas Fraser (a natural)
These four images show Edinburgh 'characters' etched by John Kay. While Hugh Blair was called 'daft', an 'idiot', and a 'natural', there is no testimony to suggest that he looked anything like these representations – or that he was physically unusual in any way.
Source: John Kay, *A series of original portraits and caricature etchings, by the late John Kay, miniature painter, Edinburgh; with biographical sketches and illustrative anecdotes*, 2 vols (Edinburgh, 1838), vol. 1, p. 4; vol. 2, p. 17; vol. 1, p. 26; vol. 1, p. 184.

Plate 10: 'The daft Highland Laird, John Dhu or Dow, alias MacDonald, and Jamie Duff, an idiot'

Plate 11: 'Jamie Duff alias Bailie Duff'

Plate 12: 'Dr Glen and the daft Highland laird'

Plate 13: 'Thomas Fraser (a natural)'

What Does it Mean to be a 'Natural' Fool?

The noun most often used to describe Hugh's capacities was indeed either idiot or fool. Certain as they may have been about their judgements, witnesses rarely gave an explicit statement of what they meant by this level of mental impairment. Lawyers for Hugh Blair submitted that he was not a complete idiot in law because he knew who his mother was, he could dress himself and he could count, he understood the basics of religion ('has impressions of the deity'); and he could behave properly in church. A former teacher said 'he believed Hugh Blair had sense and reason and a notion of religion and worshipping of God'. By those standards, only the most profoundly stupid would ever have been classed as an idiot. Whatever Hugh's basic competence in some areas, John Blair's counsel focused on the *extent* of his intellectual capacity, and this is how most of the lay witnesses were asked to approach Hugh's mental and social abilities. In some instances witnesses were reluctant to state categorically that Hugh was an idiot, though they were clear that his mental capacities were at best weak and at worst insufficient to allow him to take decisions for himself.

Most witnesses seem to have agreed with the 1737 judgement that whatever defect Hugh had was congenital or 'natural'. The latter word could mean total, but was also applied to origins. The famous author Daniel Defoe wrote in the early eighteenth century of 'persons born without the use of their reason, such as we call fools, or more properly, *naturals*'.[4] The distinction is summed up in the legal arguments offered in the case of Sir Peter Halket of Pitfirren Bart., heard before the Court of Session in 1761. His curator and heir apparent contended that as a congenital idiot Sir Peter could not succeed to an entailed estate. While he failed, the line the curator followed summed up legal thinking on the origins and nature of idiocy.

> It is necessary to distinguish between that total deprivation of judgement, which accompanies those unhappy objects from birth, which answers to the legal description of a natural idiot, and the same degree of incapacity, arising from external or supervenient causes, whereby those who were formerly endowed with reason, are by the afflicting hand of Providence deprived thereof.[5]

Natural idiots could not recover the use of their reason but others might, just as anyone could from 'any other disorder incident to human nature'. In a submission on his behalf, Hugh's lawyer argued that it was years of neglect which had turned a congenital defect in hearing and speech into a serious social disability.

> And tho' this natural defect and infirmity, both in hearing and speech, might in a great measure have been removed and rendered less conspicuous, had proper care been taken during my younger years, it was my misfortune, as is but too often the fate of such like unhappy children, to be neglected by my parents and exposed to the ridicule of servants and others about the family.[6]

There is, of course, no proof of this claim, however much the modern reader might sympathize with it. The reason why John Blair's lawyers stressed that Hugh had been kept at school into his twenties was to prove that he had had ample opportunity for socialization and education to overcome any remediable weakness of mind.

Education and Literacy

While there is some ambiguity about dates, Hugh Blair remained at the parish school of Borgue until well into his twenties. In some ways, this was not unusual. Young men (rarely women) in their late teens and early twenties can be found in Europe's schools alongside children of five or six years old. Young people might enter and leave schooling for long periods as their family's financial circumstances dictated. Except in the largest and most advanced schools, pupils were taught in a single class. By the same token, men (never women) could enter university as young as twelve, the entrance requirement being simply a proficiency in Latin. Nevertheless, universities also contained a high proportion of fully adult students, some in their thirties. The practice of flexible and life-long learning was rather well developed in this period. Thus, being at school in one's twenties was not itself noteworthy, even if most boys would have left school by the age of 13 or 14 at the latest and most girls even earlier. Deponents did not comment on the fact that Hugh had apparently been held back at school. Nor was he 'illiterate' in any conventional sense of the word, being able to read and write fluently. Able to write, he was like all but two of the 21 male deponents who gave evidence in his case and who signed their statements, however poorly. Among the women who spoke, four could sign their statements and four told the clerk recording their words that they could not. Hugh's superficial attainment of religious knowledge and basic literacy may explain why the family did not employ a personal tutor for Hugh as others of their social class sometimes did. Or perhaps they thought he could not benefit further.

What those in and out of school found odd was the way Hugh Blair related to the products of literacy. He could certainly write, or rather copy. He had a command of literacy, but no ability to use reading and writing independently in order to compose. When the Commissary Court

Plate 14: Sir George Harvey, 'The Village School' (mid–nineteenth century)
Rural schools of the eighteenth and early nineteenth century generally had children of all ages taught in one classroom. Prolonged education was not normal and most children had finished formal schooling by their early teenage years at the latest. Note that all but two of the pupils are boys.
Source: National Gallery of Scotland, NG 2090.

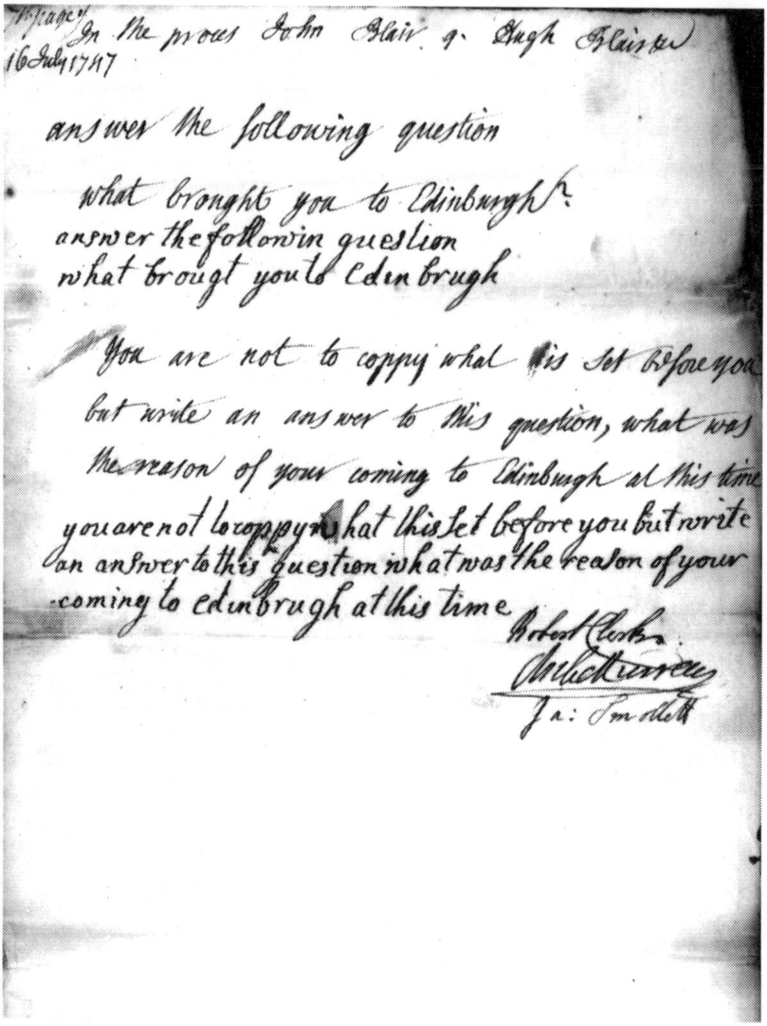

Plate 15: Hugh Blair's holograph replies to the court, 16 July 1747

As well as hearing testimony from others about Hugh Blair's mental abilities, the judges or Commissaries of Edinburgh also posed verbal questions to him. Because of his unsatisfactory replies and his apparent hearing and speaking difficulties, they also submitted written questions. This image shows what they wrote down, and Hugh's holograph replies. Nothing signed by Hugh Blair survives. These writings are the only known material trace of him. (For a transcription, see p. 91).

Source: National Archives of Scotland, CC8/6/15, Blair v Blair (1747–8).

judges wrote down questions for him to answer in writing, he simply copied out the questions again. What this case tells us is that those who thought themselves sane and mentally capable made a clear distinction between composition and copying as skills within the broad definition of writing. Hugh Blair had learned to write and that gave him some status, but his skill was useless to protect him against the charge that he was mentally incapable. Worse, his copying gave the court valuable evidence of his mental incapacity. Neat and accurate as his handwriting was, Hugh learned the hard way that writing gives people power over you.

His lawyer argued that the test of answering a question in writing was strange to his client, who 'was never accustomed to converse in writing, or to make answers in that manner, but had always been in use to copy the writings set before him, and could not readily apprehend any other intent in doing the same'.[7] The problem here was that a man of 40 years of age, especially one who was considered by some to be deaf and dumb, *must* have had experience of this form of communication. The lawyer himself stated that Hugh could not hear unless people shouted at him and that he had trouble talking intelligibly. The court could only conclude that Hugh's failure to answer was the result of a lack of wit. The other problem with this line of argument is that, even outside the court, Hugh's copying had no purpose other than performing the act itself. A clerk might copy out a document of record, but Hugh wrote without apparent purpose.

If people wanted to transmit their own thoughts other than through speech they had to learn to compose – an advanced skill which required considerable training and practice, and which effectively marked 'full' literacy for most people. The other, more common, level of writing was in fact copying: writing without necessarily understanding. This is what Hugh Blair did. Copying might create the potential to move on to other types of more creative writing, but Hugh was unable to do this. He suffered not from the inability to learn but from the inability to think as other people did.

Then as now, there were appropriate and inappropriate ways of relating to the written and printed word. Rachel Courtey told how, during her service with Hugh's family, 'she has seen him looking on the Bible or other book turning over the leaves from place to place without settling as people ordinarily do when they read'. At school in the 1720s, recalled another witness, 'when he was examined on the question book he never could be made to distinguish between question and answer' and simply repeated the whole of the catechism, questions and answers, until stopped. Hugh was still at school in his twenties doing basic reading, memorizing, and copying. Even at that age, a former school friend remembered: 'That he the deponent did never see the defender write anything as of himself or out of his own head but has seen him copying after what was laid before him' – though he did this well. Hugh had a command of the written and printed word, but no ability to use reading and writing independently. Before the judges in his case he showed he could read parts of the Bible, but did not know what book he was being shown. Hugh was not just slow. He reacted differently to the products of literacy than did mentally able people.

The Appeal

Hugh Blair appealed to the Court of Session against a judgement from the Commissaries annulling his marriage. Among the papers is a 15-page printed 'advocation' explaining why he was not an idiot. It is an exhaustive justification of actions and answers designed to refute the case brought by his brother John. Rendered in the first person singular, the document was, in fact, wholly written by his lawyer.[8] Of course, Hugh might have copied it out for the printer – as he was very capable of doing. However, the voluminous manuscript case papers make it obvious that Hugh could not *compose* anything freehand, let alone a document as complex and erudite as this. His lawyer made a great deal of his ability to write, pleading also that the circumstances in which the Commissaries' questions were put to him prejudiced his replies. He admitted that to some questions Hugh:

> gave absurd and improper answers, occasioned no doubt from his not perceiving the import of the questions, or their not apprehending his answers. Whereas had they admitted his mother or father-in-law to be with him at the time, who might have made him understand the questions, he might have answered the same properly, as he did several of them even with the disadvantages he laboured under.[9]

Unfortunately for the defence, Hugh only managed to answer correctly seven from the 41 questions put to him. The judges concluded that he did not really understand what was being asked of him and that his intelligible responses were accidental. Hugh's lawyer conceded that his client was 'a man of weak understanding', but claimed that he was no idiot.

The Case of Cecilia S.

We can compare what was asked of Hugh Blair with another (rare) example where the interaction between judges and the subject of a cognition is recorded in full. This comes from the case papers about Cecilia Stevenson, a young woman of 25 years who was cognosced before Edinburgh Sheriff Court in 1783. She was an epileptic. The lengthy exchange began when the final deponent in the case made an impromptu interjection.

> Miss Stevenson being asked by the witness if she knew him and would name him she did name him and likewise said that he lived at Leith. But upon being asked his business she made no answer and being asked said this day was Wednesday and that she saw the witness two days before this. And being asked whether this was summer or winter she answered she believed it was winter; and whether or not it was raining she answered it was 'unko rainy'; and being shown an ink-holder, she said it was ink and that there was two pens in it which was the case.
>
> Being shown a shilling she knew it, half a guinea the same, and sixpence the same. And the judge having shown her a watch, she said it was a watch; and being shown the outer case she said it was the silver which held it. And being shown the seal she said she did not know what use it was for nor what it was. And being shown a spy glass she said it was glass but she did not know the use of it. And being shown a silk handkerchief she knew what it was and being desired by the judge to look at the dial plate of his watch and asked what o'clock it was she said it was one and nine o'clock, the hour hand then being at one and the minute hand at nine; and being desired to say how many minutes it wanted of one she said may be twenty.
>
> And being asked if ever she went to a kirk she said many times. And being asked if this was a kirk she answered it was a court and the judge having asked her the meaning of his having on a gown she answered maybe it was not a gown: it might be a cloak. And being asked if he was a minister she answered perhaps he was. And being again shown half a guinea she said perhaps it was half a crown and maybe half a guinea. And being asked how many shillings she could get for half a guinea she said she could

not tell, and being asked how many shillings she could get for a whole guinea she answered maybe six. And being asked how many sixpences or shillings she could get for half a crown she answered she did not know nor for a whole crown. [paragraphing added][10]

The clerk recorded answers and added glosses where a future reader of his transcript might not be able to assess their accuracy. Some errors he did not trouble to write down since they were too obvious. For example, it was not Wednesday but Tuesday, 26 August and thus it was plainly not winter. Nor, in all likelihood, was it raining and Cecilia had seen the last deponent Robert Neilson, painter in Leith, before the current court session and earlier the previous day, not two days before. Cecilia started fairly well and did her best to field the puzzling questions in a non-committal way which might have passed in normal social intercourse. Her problem with guineas and half-guineas may have been because she was unfamiliar with higher-value coins. Nevertheless, both the gaps in her knowledge and understanding, and her descent into confusion are tragically plain. We do not know what tone the judge used when asking her questions, or how much time she was given to reply, or to compose herself between enquiries. Being in court was obviously a stressful experience for all concerned, even witnesses whose sanity was not in doubt. Whatever the pressures, the result in Cecilia's case is unsurprising. She was found to be 'fatuous, silly and unable to manage her own affairs'.

A Preference for the Company of Animals?

While the questions asked by judges were more or less standardized, each case involving mental incapacity has its own special aspects. If we return to the investigation of Hugh Blair's capacities we can explore some of these. Sparing nobody's feelings in the search for a legal victory, the lawyers for John Blair wrote of his brother Hugh in 1748: 'except with respect to his figure, he differed very little from the brute creation'.[11] They even sought to cast aspersions on Nicholas Mitchell for sleeping with 'one who had nothing *human* about him but the external figure'.[12] Apparent confusion in distinguishing man from beast, and in preferring the society of animals to that of people, struck observers as odd. People who chose to associate themselves with the beasts seemed to be eschewing human company. Those whose relationship with animals was too close might risk being put on a level with them. The description of Hugh Blair of Borgue and the household animals is fascinating in this regard. A local tailor called William Taggart who had frequent cause to be around the Blair mansion told the following tale of Hugh's behaviour:

> That for ordinary when he was taking his pottage the cats and dogs were about him in the kitchen or in the middle hall. That both dogs and cats were very familiar with him and would be now and then taking a lick of his pottage when he was supping them. That he has frequently seen the cats get upon his shoulders, put in their fore feet into his spoon when he was putting the supp to his head and lick their feet notwithstanding whereof he still continued supping and the cats continued to put in their feet in the supp until he had done.

At one level Hugh's behaviour was questionable on the grounds of simple hygiene. This witness and others told how he allowed dogs to lick his spoon and cats to dip their paws in it without cleaning the utensil prior to putting it into his own mouth. Despite the fact he used a tool rather than his tongue or forelimbs to feed, there is also a sense in which Hugh was acting like a brute beast by doing this. Furthermore, he was 30 years of age at the time when the incident described took place. Children might play with 'pets' on their own level, adults did not. Hugh's lawyer tried to argue that his behaviour showed 'an excessive fondness of these creatures, as some ladies are of their lap-dogs'.[13] Witnesses and judges thought his familiarity much more unusual.

Too much should not be read into this section of the evidence. It is sometimes claimed that the mad and idiotic of the eighteenth century were perceived as beasts. According to Professor Anne Digby, 'the mad, having lost their rationality, slipped off the lowest rung of humanity and thus took on an animal character'.[14] In reality, it was the idiotic who were most often likened to beasts. In Hugh Blair's case, the tone of the depositions is curious rather than appalled. His lawyer offered the following argument, which would have won over all those who gave evidence in cases involving mental incapacity.

> However the human understanding may be darkened and obscured in different persons, to a greater or lesser degree, 'tis believed none ever was found so absolutely deprived as not to have some rays of light and human

65

understanding in some particulars common with brutes who act by impulse, what in rational creatures proceeds from the rays and dictates of judgement and understanding.[15]

The lawyer went on to clarify that Hugh, like all people of 'weak understanding' had 'rays of understanding, wherewith their minds are enlightened', and was therefore quite distinct from the animal kingdom.

Dining Habits

Those who observed Hugh Blair's feeding tended to stress his apparent failure to say grace and give thanks before and after eating, rather than the other oddities of his dining habits. Moral sense and an awareness of religious precepts were components of mental capacity. Hugh's apparent failure to say grace was one suggestion that he might have lacked an awareness of the deity. Mr John Gordon, the former schoolmaster at Borgue, gave evidence for Hugh Blair and his mother. He believed Hugh 'had sense and reason and a notion of religion and worshipping of God' and was not 'incapable of receiving any impressions of a divine being'. Enlightenment thinkers debated whether people had an innate sense of God or whether all knowledge was learned. Whichever, it was generally agreed that an awareness of one's creator and of the nature of the Trinity were fundamentals of humanity. This explains why the Commissaries asked such questions of Hugh. Gordon affirmed he 'believes him capable of religion and that he has impressions of the deity'. William Taggart compared Hugh Blair with others of his family: 'the rest of the children behaved very decently at table and were there when a blessing was asked and did not rise from it till thanks were given. That he has frequently seen the defender take up his coge [bowl] and eat by himself but never observed him either to ask a blessing or give thanks.'[16]

Witnesses were more likely to remark on *where* a person ate since familial dining was the norm. Those who were peripheral to, or absent from, the table were regarded as socially marginal. One contemporary definition of a family was the people who lived in a house under the dependence of a head, and who ate at a common table. That definition might include not only kin but also servants. Exclusion from the table therefore symbolized distancing from those closest to the person and from

Plate 16: Alexander Carse, 'Grace Before Meat'
'The deponent never observed the defender say grace before or after meat [meals] though possibly he might have done it as he the deponent does not know his heart.' Testimony of John McEwan, land labourer in Borgue. Following the correct religious observances was an important part of normal life in eighteenth-century Scotland. Regular dining together was also a crucial symbol of family unity. The domestic interior portrayed here is more modest than the Blairs'.
Source: Scottish National Portrait Gallery, B8214: from a private collection.

the fundamental unit of society. Solitary consumers like Hugh Blair broke social rather than dietary norms. Those who sought to portray him as mentally normal emphasized participation in the rites of eating. For example, his mother's woman-servant 'has frequently seen the defender carve meat at the table and serve it about'. Rituals surrounding meat were particularly significant in this society.[17] Eating patterns were more important as social than biological symbols or, for that matter, as indicators of animality. Eating with animals was inappropriate behaviour, but only on a par with a man in his thirties playing with five-year-old boys outside the church during a service, as Hugh did.

Dressing Habits

Whatever word deponents chose to apply to Hugh, they offered rich and varied descriptions of the sorts of words and deeds which had caused them to form their opinion of him. In a society where face-to-face interactions were the norm, dress was a crucial preliminary indicator of a person's status and could have a lasting effect on how they were judged. Thus, Hugh 'was always very nasty and mean in his clothes, that he ordinarily wore the pursuer's [his brother John] old casten [cast-off] clothes'. One deponent, John Porter, dated the change in his appearance to soon after the death of his father David Blair. His lawyer tried to claim that Hugh was forced to wear his brother's cast-offs and to live in a verminous garret.[18] Perhaps that had once been the case though Hugh seems to have adapted to the way he was treated and to have adopted as his own way what may initially have been an imposition.

It appears that after he left the house of Borgue, Hugh's mother looked after him better than she had for much of his life. She realized that now he was in the public eye more than he had been in the circumscribed world of Galloway society. Maintaining his appearance was important to the figure he would cut. Being properly dressed as a gentleman also made it less likely that people would initially take him for an eccentric or fool. Hugh seems to have adjusted to such new routines as changing his shirt when he came back to his lodgings, shaving regularly, and keeping clean. For all this, the depositions make it clear that Hugh's lifestyle at Borgue Old House was ultimately one he chose. He refused to allow servants to make his bed and was evidently discomfited by his sister-in-law's attempts to clean his clothes and bedclothes. He apparently got satisfaction from mending and using cast-off (or 'appropriated') clothes. Being badly dressed for one's social station was a cause for remark. So was inappropriate dress. Hugh was also an avid attender of funerals in Kirkcudbrightshire.[19] According to a local tailor: 'he never put on mournings at these occasions but when he was desired by his mother and brother, which was when he was at the burial of his relations'. Not knowing how to dress for solemn occasions was worthy of comment.

None of the witnesses commented on the most important part of appearance, the face. This silence is important because it suggests that Hugh looked much the same as any other man. The same is implied by the lawyers' comments on his 'external figure' we quoted above. Contemporaries regarded the set of a person's face as a powerful indictor of lunacy or stupidity.[20] The human face, uniquely expressive among all creatures, was a signifier of reason but also a betrayer of its failure. Apart from touch, all the organs of sense are concentrated there and speech originates from the face. Non-verbal communications between individuals depend to a degree on the movement of the hands and the posture of the body, but much more on the great diversity of facial expressions. Sir Charles Bell wrote in his 1806 *Anatomy and Philosophy of Expression*: 'In the lower creatures, there is no expression . . . while in man there seems to be a special apparatus, for the purpose of enabling him to communicate with his fellow-creatures, by that natural language, which is read in the changes of his countenance'.[21] According to a local schoolmaster, Hugh could be seen 'stalking and wandering along the streets of Kirkcudbright, staring and gazing about him like a fool and in such a way that nobody who saw him would take him for anything else'. It was his actions rather than his facial appearance which indicated foolishness. Hugh played with his hands and focused his attention in ways which suggested he lacked the intellect of most men.

The appearance of the face is defined by more features than the eyes, the attitude of the head, and the set of the mouth. Hats and wigs are artificial additions designed to protect and ornament. Gentlemen of the age wore wigs over their own hair, which had thus to be cropped quite closely. They were generally clean-shaven. Hair could be decorative but, unlike hats and wigs, had to be dealt with as an organic growth of the body.[22] Like clothes, such visible symbols 'are not read as naturalistic attributes of an individual in eighteenth-century society but understood as components in a language'.[23] Wearing hair in a certain way may have had meaning for the wearer, but what we are concerned about here is the reaction of others to the meaning they read into a hairstyle.[24] What was done or, more likely here, not done to hair conveyed important social meanings which were taken as indicators of mental states. In the case of the apparently deranged, the point about their hair was that it was not styled at all but left in a state of nature. Contemporaries condemned the carelessness, moral decadence, or insanity such a failure might imply. Long hair meant also that a man could not wear a wig and thus did not sport that important symbol of social status – a leisured, measured lifestyle – and of masculinity. One of Hugh Blair's many oddities was that he was always washing his wig and therefore often went around with his head uncovered, in contravention of social custom. Wigs had come into fashion by the 1680s in Scotland and they remained fashionable into the early nineteenth century, whereas their wearing was given up in England and France at the end of the eighteenth century.[25] Proper dress and attention to personal appearance were important to the way people presented themselves in everyday life. Dressing was one of several culturally specific conventions concerned with self display. Wearing a hat and a wig, keeping facial and head hair at a conventional length, and cutting one's fingernails were powerful symbols of civility – and mental capacity.

Sociability was a central aspect of eighteenth-century life. The Blair household had visitors and its occupants were expected to return the visits. There were set forms to be followed for arrival and subsequent behaviour. When callers arrived at the door of the house they waited to be admitted; unannounced calls were only to be made in daylight; hosts always offered food and drink, giving undivided attention to the caller; guests participated in conversation. Hugh broke all of the conventions of

Plate 17: Resco (Rusco) Castle, 1807
Rusco Castle, owned by one of his cousins, lies north–north–west of Gatehouse of Fleet and represents the furthest known limit of Hugh Blair's wanderings.
Source: The Stewartry Museum, Kirkcudbright.

both guest and host at one time or another. His nocturnal wanderings and unannounced visits were made easier by an apparently liberal tradition of hospitality among the gentry in this part of Scotland. Those who gave evidence that he had visited them spoke of offering food and a bed, which explains why Hugh was able to 'wander from the house, sometimes for a fortnight together'. His standing in the community meant his visits required special consideration. All of Hugh's wanderings were within ten miles of his home, the furthest point being Rusco Castle (a tower house of *c.*1500 with seventeenth-century additions), where he picked up a coat belonging to the laird. His peregrinations were aided by the fact that his kin (specifically, cousins at the time of the case) owned most of the land in the area, including the adjacent estates of Dunrod, Senwick and Rusco (which belonged to his cousin William). A near equal, Robert McMillan, took Hugh in: 'being a gentleman's son . . . [and] out of regard to the family of Borgue was kind to him and gave him meat and drink'. McMillan had known Hugh for 25 years, lending the weight of personal familiarity to social convention. Another family which received a call was that of the parish minister. In this case accepted ideas of hospitality were given additional force by the clergyman's profession and by the need to fulfil what for others may have been more the rhetoric of Christian charity.

It is important to note that Hugh's visits were not privileged in any other way, either because he was a stranger or because he was a fool. Regarding him with neither fear nor reverence, his hosts were at best accommodating, sometimes bemused, occasionally anxious. Nocturnal arrivals were undoubtedly seen as an unwelcome intrusion. Hugh did go through some of the motions of visiting – arriving, greeting, sitting, smiling – but without entering into the verbal interactions which were the most important part. Callers to the house of Borgue, or at least those from the landowning class, tended to ignore Hugh – tactfully so, since he might be found emptying chamber pots during their visit. Even had he made himself available, those who 'knew of him never reckoned him capable of any conversation . . . [and therefore generally] had no conversation with him'.

Gifts and Services

Hugh's hosts cannot have expected much in return except an intangible addition to their stock of good will and social credit. For his part, Hugh gave unusual gifts. Societies which value gift exchange are not necessarily those where commerce is poorly developed. Kirkcudbrightshire was undergoing a significant transformation at this period to a specialist cattle-raising region; Hugh bought his ale at a tavern as did everyone else; the family servants were paid cash wages as well as their keep. Nevertheless, a 'crucial series of transactions which expressed central social values could not be articulated in terms of money or the associated absolute rights of possession'.[26] It was not the fact that Hugh gave people things he had made, but their evidently useless quality which struck the recipients as odd. He might even destroy perfectly serviceable items to make useless ones. In a legal submission we learn that he took the wainscoting off the walls to be cut into spindles.[27] He also cut up his mother's prized swan-skin blanket to mend his clothes.

While lodging in Edinburgh during the Commissary Court process, Hugh was invited in to the room of Barbara Balfour, a fellow lodger. He picked up a religious book belonging to the lady. 'Making another bow to the witness (as if he had been asking her permission) he took up pen, ink, and paper which were lying on the same table with the book and wrote out the Lord's Prayer and gave it to the deponent.' Barbara Balfour, widow of John Robertson, had heard of the Consistory Court case but must have done so by word of mouth rather than reading about it in the press. The 'Edinburgh' section (the other two parts are news from London and advertisements) of the two newspapers of the day, *The Edinburgh Evening Courant* and the *Caledonian Mercury*, contains news of commercial, military, and political affairs along with brief obituaries and short accounts of house fires, freak accidents, heat waves, arrests, riots, celebrations, atrocious murders (including one committed by a madman), sensational suicides and assaults – but no mention of the Blair case.[28]

Work and Leisure

Hugh was fascinated by the machinery associated with spinning and weaving (like looms) and he enjoyed carving wood, but seems always to have fashioned spindles for which nobody could see any use. Mr Robert Monteith, minister at Longformacus, had seen him bringing stone from a quarry to build walls which did not enclose anything and thus served no

purpose. As described by Monteith, Hugh's action seems odd. It is from
a local weaver that we discover that Hugh was building his dykes at the
time when the estate was being enclosed. Since the 1680s and 1690s
large areas of south-west Scotland had had walls built to divide property
and make the breeding and management of cattle easier. A weaver, Andrew
Taggart, did not question the purpose of the wall. Instead he confined
himself to a consideration of whether it was 'ill or well built'.[29] It is
possible that Hugh really was competent at building dry-stone dykes but,
without guidance, his erections had no function. One of the Blair tenants
thought Hugh a good worker in the fields: 'in time of harvest the said
Hugh helps to stack the corn when the deponent who was stacking could
not over take it and that any stacks he put up appeared to the deponent at
a distance to be as well set as his own'.

In the end, it did not really matter whether Hugh was good with his
hands. His labours outside the home generally seemed to have no purpose, to be based on imitation rather than understanding, and to have
been compulsive rather than discriminating. Almost every witness picked
out some apparently trivial or pointless act:

[he] frequently brought in ash wands to use as flails on the corn sheaves
but they were quite unfit for that purpose. Sometimes he used scrap cloth
and wood to make windmills such as bairns ordinarily divert themselves
with or are stuck up in corn fields to frighten away the birds . . . sometimes [he] tried to mend wheelbarrows with these scrap materials.

Those who opined that Hugh could fix the latch of the kitchen door 'as
sufficient as any tradesman would have done', build stacks of cut corn,
erect dry-stone walls as well as anyone, or carry stones to fill a hole in the
road, ignored the fact that this was inappropriate behaviour for a landowner's eldest son. There were many other examples of activities unsuited to a landowner. On a visit to Kirkcudbright town, a witness saw
him sitting upon a stair foot beside an 'apple wife' who was selling her
fruit, and remarked that this was 'a very odd place for a gentleman to sit'.
There were other indicators that Hugh did not know how to behave
correctly for a man in his social position. Poor people might gather dried
dung for their fires but those of Blair's standing bought peat, wood, or
coal for heating. Had they required such fuel, they would not have gone
looking for it themselves.

Plate 18: Walter Geikie, 'The Fruit Seller' (1824)
'At this time he also saw him sitting upon a stair foot besides an apple wife who was selling her fruit: a very odd place for a gentleman to sit.' Testimony of Mr Thomas McCourtie, schoolmaster, concerning the behaviour of Hugh Blair on his visits to Kirkcudbright.
Source: National Gallery of Scotland, NG 2335.

This is not to say that Hugh Blair was unresponsive to social convention any more than that he lacked emotional responses. Knowing and caring about one's close family was a central indicator of socialization and an important aspect of life in eighteenth-century society. Ignorance of, or indifference to, the well-being of one's closest relatives left a person socially detached as well as personally disoriented. Deponents acknowledged Hugh's affection towards his mother and his attempt to protect her against the alleged attack by his brother John. On balance, witnesses also found Hugh suitably loving to his wife. However, the silences in the documents about any other close ties within his family or friendships with outsiders suggest that his social circle was far more circumscribed than for most people.[30] Hugh seemed unaware that his sister was dying and showed nothing more than the briefest exposition of emotion at her death or that of others who were important to family or parish life. Appropriate displays of affection towards close family helped create the most important bonds in this society. Conversely, a failure so to react was socially isolating and might suggest a defect in a person's thought processes.

Social Conventions

Nor was Hugh devoid of all social awareness. When meeting people at church or at home, he certainly followed most of the normal social conventions. He would bow and lift his hat, and also bared his head when (apparently) asking God's blessing. To a casual observer, Hugh Blair was sociable and socialized. Bowing was one gesture of respect which regulated relations between individuals.[31] So too was toasting their health, a ritual referred to by John Carsan who 'has seen him, at table, drink and bow to strangers'.

This society had a rich and powerful vocabulary of gesture. Recent research in history and anthropology shows that many gestures were specific to a time, place, or social group.[32] In the eighteenth century, Samuel Johnson observed that etiquette books required updating every couple of generations. Witnesses mention the use of gestures characteristic of the age, such as bowing, which were not practised a century later, as well as hand shaking and hat doffing, which had longer usage. Yet, even something as simple as a bow may have many components: does one stand

75

close to or away from the person greeted; how low does one bow; are the eyes averted or raised; in which position are the feet to be placed; what happens to the hands? It was not just the movement or posture which mattered but when it was used and with whom. Hugh responded correctly to greeting gestures and seemingly performed the mix of ritual and gesture that surrounded drinking. But he also indulged in an unstructured use of bodily movement – gesticulation – as when he was seen 'playing with his hands, like a fool'. At times he did not move at all, or made the wrong gesture, as when he answered questions with 'a foolish smiling stare'. There are indications that he greeted servants as he would his social peers, strangers as he would a close acquaintance.

Those who knew Hugh better doubted that he understood why people went through these actions, noting that he only did them by way of response to others and never initiated the sequence of greetings. He followed certain social forms, such as doffing his hat, but did so by imitating other people in a way which suggested he did not appreciate the significance his acts had. What witnesses described was a man who could follow the forms of everyday life without properly understanding their meaning. When acquaintances asked after his health, he always said he was 'very well', even when he had a 'bloody flux' (dysentery), and gave the same reply about his sister's health even when she was plainly dying.

Hugh copied actions just as he wrote out passages of words or counted through a memorized sequence without knowing an individual number. He did the latter for the Commissary judges who questioned him and showed a similar difficulty over numeracy, coupled with a fixation on a number, in conversation with a minister's daughter. When 'asked who made him he answered "five" and when she asked how many fingers he had he answered "five", when she asked how many toes he had he answered "five"'. His preoccupation with the number five becomes more puzzling when we discover that he normally counted in multiples of four. A former servant gave the Commissaries an example: 'One night when some sheep skins were hanging over a rope in the kitchen he pointed to them and said "one, two, three, four skins" but there were more than four skins hanging there and it was his ordinary way of counting to say over and over again "one, two, three, four".'

An important occasion for hospitality and conviviality was provided by funerals. English visitors remarked on the significance which eighteenth-century Scots placed on funeral rituals. Among them was Edward Topham, who visited Edinburgh during the 1770s. An astute observer, Topham noticed that at marriage 'there is no occasion for any particular ceremony'. In contrast:

> I know no place where you hold more frequent funerals than in this city, and they are conducted with a silence and solemnity . . . instead of applying to an undertaker for a group of grim figures, and dismal faces, they send a card, as the French do, to all the persons of their acquaintance, desiring attendance at the funeral . . . They all dress themselves at these meetings in a suit of black . . . the procession is always on foot. The coffin is carried by four people, the minister walks before it, and all the friends and relations follow. They proceed with a slow, solemn pace to the kirk: and as the relationship extends itself a great way in this country, a whole street is sometimes nearly filled with this sable procession.[33]

Funerals were a means of remembering the dead and celebrating their lives, but they were principally for the living. Attendance reinforced the bonds of friendship, neighbourhood, and kinship. The religious service and associated secular gathering appealed to notions of community both as a residential grouping of people and as an association of religious believers. Events before and after a burial emphasized continuity rather than a decisive break or gap in the social fabric. Helping to carry the corpse (as Hugh did) indicated solidarity with the kin of the deceased and created a bond amongst the living. Funerals could be an occasion for eating, drinking and the giving of charity. Significantly, one had normally to be invited to a funeral and one had to dress in an appropriately sober fashion. We have seen that wearing mourning was a hit-or-miss matter for Hugh and witnesses were either puzzled or looked askance at his promiscuous attendance at interments.

The Butt of Jokes

Some of Hugh's behaviour was regarded not only as odd, but also as amusing or even ridiculous. Truly genial laughter may not have as its focus criticism or discomfiture of a third party. However, men and women had to be careful not to become objects of ridicule, since a degree of personal dignity was expected of adults. The distinction between intended humour and unintended foolishness, between laughing *with* rather than being laughed *at*, was a fine one. Hugh Blair was the butt of servants who 'broke ludicrous jests upon him . . . the servants both men and women and the boys about the house did for their diversion and to make sport of him cause him hobble and dance which he did in a very ridiculous manner and so as to occasion abundance of laughter'. Laughter here might be: 'society's weapon to criticize departures from the norm, from the expected, to punish and to correct idiosyncrasies'.[34] However, Hugh himself apparently had no fear of ridicule. Laughing at him cannot have been seen as a sanction because he did not alter what he did on this or other occasions. This suggests that making fun of Hugh served purely selfish individual or group goals for the servants. They found it difficult to interact with him, and making Hugh an object of fun was a way of easing their sense of awkwardness, albeit at his expense. Any incongruity was deliberately created with a view to releasing the tensions employees found with a social superior who shared their tasks, but not their perception of him. Laughter here was a reinforcement of the lack of respect the servants had for Hugh Blair. We are reminded of the seventeenth-century philosopher Thomas Hobbes's acerbic remark that, in a certain type of person, laughter:

> is caused either by some sudden act of their own that pleaseth them; or by the apprehension of some deformed thing in another, by comparison whereof they suddenly applaud themselves. And it is incident most to them, that are conscious of the fewest abilities in themselves; who are forced to keep themselves in their own favour, by observing the imperfections of other men.[35]

Servants and children laughed at Hugh, the former admitting it openly. Laughing at him bound them together, but also separated them from their social superiors. In contrast, Hugh's social 'set' tended to ignore him rather than laugh at him. For them it would have been indecorous to laugh or to make fun quite so crudely.

Hugh Blair was disrespectfully treated by servants and others partly because his mother allowed them to. He was given menial tasks partly because his mother had told the servants to find something useful for him to do: 'that his mother desired the deponent to take the defender to any of the out work that was not oppressive', such as feeding horses or binding sheaves. Hugh Gordon, farmer in Borgue, saw Hugh Blair being led around Kirkcudbright by a young lad, as did his mother who said: 'fool thing that boy will gar [make] him do what he likes and the youngest boy about the town will do the same with him'.[36] A number of deponents said explicitly that Hugh's mother 'neglected' him and that neither she nor the servants nor (while he was at school) his fellow schoolboys treated him with any respect.

Mental Capacity and Incapacity

For those so minded, making fun of Hugh was easy. He had no sense of social inhibition but he did possess a naive innocence. He was eminently biddable on almost any matter except kissing girls. He would hobble, allow himself to be led around, even expose his genitals. Those who thought him an idiot emphasized these aspects of his behaviour, along-side his propensity for emulation, as an indicator of his lack of wit. He seemed unable to initiate actions by himself. Of course, that was not entirely true. He might help his mother on and off with her clothes, perform manual labour around the house, pay for drinks he had ordered in a public house. Yet, the point was not whether Hugh could do any-thing off his own bat but whether he did enough to be deemed mentally capable. The weight of opinion among witnesses and judges was that he did not.

Issues of volition and intention were central to eighteenth-century judgements of mental capacity. Understanding the reason for performing an act was important, but the deed itself could be a useful indicator of intellectual ability. Friends and neighbours had plenty of opportunity to observe what Hugh did. However embarrassing he may have been to acknowledge, he was not shut away from society. He went on his own to taverns, was politely entertained in homes even when arriving unan-nounced, and was invited to at least some funerals. All these suggest that he was regarded by some as worthy of inclusion in social events. He cannot have been seen by everyone as the worthless, ragged, brutish idiot portrayed by his brother's lawyers. Indeed, Hugh was often out and about.

Much of the above bears on what Hugh did rather than what he said. This emphasis also applied to most eighteenth-century cases where men-tal capacity was at issue. The problems Hugh had with speaking and hearing forced the focus on his actions. Importantly, those around him not only recognized his communication difficulties but also believed that he was stupid. Legal texts allowed that the deaf and dumb might need some help in managing their affairs, but lawyers did *not* assume that those with problems hearing and speaking necessarily had mental incapacity. In law, 'Curators are given, not only to minors, but, in general, to every one who, either through defect of judgement, or unfitness of disposition, is incapable of rightly managing his own affairs'.[37] Thus, 'curators may also be granted to lunatics, and even to persons dumb and deaf, though they are of sound judgement, where it appears they cannot exert it in the management of business'.[38]

Having a speech or hearing defect meant that the law deemed a curator necessary to guide one's affairs. But inability to hear and/or speak was not by itself a sufficient criterion of lunacy or, more likely, idiocy. A later case illustrates the distinctions made. John Adam, portioner of Kilfapet in Stirlingshire, gave evidence about Catherine Leny. Aged about 40 years in 1798, 'she is deaf and can speak none altho she can make a noise but no person can understand her except by signs', and has been so since birth.

> He thinks she is not capable to negotiate any money transaction by receiving . . . cash due to her or lending it out upon security but she is capable of acting as a servant in the country and can make herself to be understood a little by making signs to persons who are acquainted with her and she can understand by signs what others want her to do.[39]

A curator was appointed because Catherine had a physical rather than a mental defect.

The discrimination shown in legal provisions is also evident in the perceptions of educated people. Describing Hugh Blair variously as 'a weak creature' and 'a natural fool or stupido', Mr Andrew Boyd, minister at Twinholm (Twynholm), drew a comparison. He told the inquest: 'though the defender's sister Jean was both deaf and dumb yet she by signs showed a great deal of sagacity and intelligence but the deponent could never observe anything like that in the defender who though deafish hears when loud spoke to and can speak though not quite so distinct as other people'. Jean had a congenital physical problem communicating with others through sound. Hugh had a less acute physical condition since he could speak and hear. His lawyer put the following words in his mouth:

afflicted by the Hand of Providence from my infancy upwards, with a difficulty of speech and slowness of hearing, and thus rendered improper for the management of my estate and fortune, am neither so deaf as not to comprehend what is audibly spoke by voices with which I am acquainted; nor so dumb, but that by articulate pronunciation I can make myself understood.[40]

But the way he used his voice was peculiar. More significantly, what he said suggested he was defective in the processes of his thought. He had the ability to use language but did so in an idiosyncratic way which meant he could not communicate effectively. Brother and sister both had impairments of hearing and speaking but Hugh's communication failures went far beyond these. Contemporaries perceived a clear difference between being simply deaf and dumb, and having those disabilities plus mental incapacity. The distinction is reinforced by incidental information in the depositions. For example, Jean followed the conventional forms of behaviour at table whereas Hugh did not.

It may, of course, have been thought more decorous to cognosce someone as having a speech or hearing defect rather than being an idiot or an imbecile. Hugh's brother John, who applied for the curatorship in 1737, claimed in the subsequent court case to nullify Hugh's marriage that Hugh had been an idiot since his infancy. Witnesses gave evidence that this was true long before, and at the same time as, the 1737 cognition. In papers from the subsequent appeal before the Court of Session John explained that a brieve to investigate if Hugh was deaf and dumb 'was thought more decent' than one of idiotry:

as no more was intended but to obtain a tutory for managing his affairs, it was sufficient for that purpose to find him deaf and dumb, and the finding him so is no evidence whatever that he was not an idiot, especially that it now appears, and is confessed on all hands, that he is neither deaf nor dumb, nor ever was. On the contrary, it clearly appears that he is, and always was, a natural idiot.[41]

In a submission on his behalf, albeit written in the first person singular, Hugh's lawyer confirmed this. He acknowledged that sister Jean had indeed been 'from her cradle quite deaf and dumb'.[42]

There is just one occasion on which deponents specified what they meant by a use of language which signified a lack of reason. Three clergy-

Plate 19: A riding master
In common with many of those of his social class, Hugh Blair liked to ride on horseback. This was the fastest means of personal transport available in eighteenth-century Scotland.
Source: John Kay, *A series of original portraits and caricature etchings, by the late John Kay, miniature painter, Edinburgh; with biographical sketches and illustrative anecdotes*, 2 vols (Edinburgh, 1838), vol. 1, p. 69.

men gave evidence in Hugh Blair's case, including Mr William Jamieson, minister at Rerrick. Condemning Hugh as 'an idiot and mere natural fool', Jamieson had always thought him not 'capable of connecting ideas regularly or of perceiving any moral obligation, or entering into any paction or covenant whatsoever. That he the defender did never connect any entire proposition with its verb and person'. Hugh Blair spoke English, but not in a grammatical way because he could not make logical connections between different words and phrases. His reported speech never involved more than a few words, usually repeated twice. Examples include: 'Hugh Blair ride' when he wanted to go on horseback' 'Hugh Blair, bonny coat, bonny coat' when he was given an old liveryman's jacket, and 'Hugh Blair no die, Hugh Blair no die' when neighbours teased him about mortality. A simple question was 'whar i calf' meaning 'what is a calf?'

While Hugh is known to have spoken more than four separate words at a time, deponents could not remember them exactly because they did not make sense, and could not be fitted into their existing perceptual sets. When they could make out what he was saying, his words served to reinforce the opinion that Hugh Blair was a man of weak intellect. Another minister, Robert Monteith, had seen Hugh 'chalk upon the walls words without any manner of connection'. A third minister tried to communicate with Hugh by imitating his sounds and simplified grammar. Mr Robert Walker, a minister at South Leith near Edinburgh when the case was raised, had known the family well between 1733 and 1737. Sometimes 'he asked Hugh where he was to which he made no answer but if the deponent had asked him "whar you" or "you whar" he would have answered "dyke"'. Walker explained that 'for his own curiosity frequently [he] put that question to him and he always made the same answer. He did not look upon him as capable of regularly connecting ideas or of perceiving any moral obligation but looked upon him as void of judgement and a mere natural fool.' Having tried to communicate with Hugh at his own level, Walker concluded (like everyone else) that his problems lay with his intellect rather than his speech and hearing.

Examples of the Depositions of Witnesses

William Taggart, tailor in Borgue, 37, married [witness for John Blair; spoke sometime between 18 and 22 September 1747]. Knows the pursuer John Blair and the defender Hugh Blair, being sworn, purged [of malice, partial counsel, good deed, and the promise thereof], examined, and interrogated.

He has known the defender Hugh Blair of Borgue these 24 years past and was at school with him and was frequently going and coming about the house of Borgue and for some 12 years last past has been frequently employed as a tailor about the house of Borgue. Ever since the defender was 12 or 14 years of age the defender's mother Grizell Blair used and treated the defender as a fool taking almost little or no notice of him or of what he did till about two years ago when she had some sort of difference with the pursuer John Blair. Hugh Blair sometimes sat at table and ate with his mother and the rest of the children and sometimes not for he was frequently out of the way at meal time and ate often by himself in the kitchen among the servants and sometimes in the common hall. Sometimes he sat when he was eating but more commonly stalked about with his coge [a wooden bowl] below his oxter or in his arm. He was not called upon at meal times to eat with his mother and the rest of the children but if he came he either sat down or not as he thought proper. For ordinary the rest of the children were called upon at meal time. When the defender did not sit at table he would go in to the kitchen and take up his own coge. When he dined at table with the family he would sometimes go off before giving thanks and sometimes after a giving of thanks would sit still and eat. The rest of the children behaved very decently at table and were there when a blessing was asked and did not rise from it till thanks was given. He has frequently seen him take up his coge to eat by himself but never observed him either ask a blessing or give thanks. For ordinary when he was taking his pottage the cats and dogs were about him in the kitchen or in the middle hall. Both the dogs and cats were very familiar with him and would be now and then taking a lick of his pottage when he was supping them. He has frequently seen the cats get upon his shoulders put in their fore feet into his spoon when he was putting the sup to his head and lick their feet, notwithstanding whereof he still continued supping and the cats continued to put in their feet in the sups until he had done with his pottage. This the deponent has seen when the defender was near 30 years of age.

The defender was always very nasty and mean in his clothes. He ordinarily wore the pursuer's old cast-off clothes until the pursuer was married. He lay in a garret room where there was a bed meaner than any in which the common servants lay. He kept the key himself and did not allow any of the servants to make his bed. So often as the deponent has seen this bed it was very ill made up and nasty. The servants always treated him as a fool, paid him no manner of respect, not so much as they did one another, despised him and broke ludicrous jests upon him and frequently put him upon drudgery work such as bringing in water or peats or raking the dirt from before the doors or mucking the stables or washing the kail and several other drudgery things. When the defender did these pieces of drudgery work he was sometimes desired to do so by the servants by word of mouth and at other times by signs. Sometimes he did these drudgery things of his own accord and he did them both in foul weather and in fair weather and in day time and under night.

The deponent has seen him employed when company came about the house who saw him but seemed to take no notice of him. That is to say did not speak or talk to him nor did he seem to take any notice of the strangers but went on with his drudgery work. He has sometimes seen the defender when strangers came about the house taken notice of by these strangers. That is to say he has seen the strangers hold out their hands and shake hands with him. When these strangers took no notice of him he took as little of them. He has heard strangers ask him how he was and he answered 'very well'. When he was at school and about 15 years old he was seized with a vomiting and upon being asked by the scholars what ailed him he answered 'fever, fever'. About 12 years ago when the defender was very ill of a bloody flux but not confined to his bed one day being at a burial he heard some of those there ask Hugh Blair how he was to which he answered 'very well'.

About ten years ago when John Ewart, wright, and the deponent were fitting up a new bed and were missing one of the newly made cornices they asked the defender if he knew anything about it, alleging that he had taken it away. To which he answered 'spintle, spintle' and in a little time brought it back. He frequently diverted himself by cutting and shaping small sticks which he called spintles [spindles] and which he offered as compliments to some of the neighbours. He has frequently seen these spindles which were very ill-made and of no use to anybody. About a dozen years ago the deponent observing the defender carrying up to his room something below his coat tails in a hidden way which was a flagon of water and upon the deponent's asking him what he was going to do with it he answered 'bed, bed, lice, lice, flea, flea'. Hugh Blair stuck up part of the curtains of the grey room upon his own bed in the garret with whin sticks without taking off the bark. The deponent looks upon the defender to be at this time a man of about 40 years of age.

When he was at school and about 19 or 20 he has seen the meanest of the school boys and the youngest of them lead him about and command him to go where ever they had a mind and do whatever they bid him. They ordinarily made their diversion of him and the boys used him the

85

same way within these three years. He did never see Hugh Blair write anything as of himself or out of his own head but has seen him copying after what was laid before him. He has seen him copy things that laid before him very distinctly. About ten years ago the defender brought to the deponent a bit of paper with the word 'calf' printed upon it and by way of question said to the deponent 'whar i calf'. The deponent answered 'nolt' [calf] upon which the defender cried out 'calf nolt, calf nolt' and seemed to be pleased.

During the time he was under his mother's care which was within these ten or twelve years his clothes were mostly so ill-smelling, nasty, and overrun with vermin that the servants and tradesmen about the house shunned sitting near him. After the pursuer's wife came to the house of Borgue the defender's linen were by her order all boiled and steeped in boiling water. His body clothes and bed clothes were often boiled or steeped in boiling water. When the pursuer's liveryman left the service the defender got hold of the livery coat, that was of coarse blue cloth faced up with blue plush with white linen and white metal buttons, and carried it to his room calling it 'bonny coat, bonny coat'. He seemed very fond to wear it, pointing to his own body and saying 'Hugh Blair, bonny coat, bonny coat'. While he was under his mother's care it was his custom to mend his own clothes notwithstanding of the tailor's being in the house who he would not allow to mend them. That he would have done this with clouts or shapings of any sort of cloth and of any sort of colour, however unlike to his clothes. When the deponent and his brother were in the house working the defender would sometimes steal away shaped work or new cloth from them of which he made a sort of bonnet. He gave away these bonnets to the boys of the neighbourhood, particularly one to one of the servant lads of the house. He never saw the defender wear any of these bonnets himself. While he was under his mother's care about 12 years ago he went about to gentlemen, ministers and other houses in the neighbourhood and particularly one morning he came in with a coat under his arm and slipped it down upon a chair. The deponent asked him where he got the coat to which he answered 'Rusco coat, Rusco coat'. The deponent has seen this very coat upon the Laird of Rusco's body whose house is about six miles from Borgue.

The defender had a particular place at the head of a pew belonging to Borgue where he usually sat. If the seat had been never so full of company or of whatever quality they were he always endeavoured to go to the head of the seat and never rested till he got to that particular place. He sat decently in church. He has often seen the defender drying his wig on the branch of a tree and has been often told by the defender and his mother and others that he was in use of washing his wig. He once saw Hugh Blair shave himself.

He has frequently for his own diversion desired the defender to dance before him which the defender as often as desired did and which was several times done in his presence. He did this in a very foolish and ridiculous manner and it was for that reason that the deponent asked him to dance, meaning thereby to divert himself and the company. He has several times bid Hugh Blair discover his nakedness or privities which he did without any ceremony or seeming to know that there was any indecency therein and this he has done when others were present and he has bid him do so when women were present who always ran off and did not stay to see him discover his nakedness. The last instances of this kind were about two or three years ago.

When the defender was at school and when he was examined on the question book he never could be made to distinguish between question and answer. The last time the deponent heard him examined on the question book was at age 17 or 18. While at school he has heard the defender frequently repeat the Lord's Prayer without missing out one single word. When the master of the school came to his turn of examining the defender he ordinarily put the catechism into the master's hand and the defender himself began with the question and went on with the answer without being questioned till such time as he was stopped. The master never asked him any particular question in the question book. In the ordinary examination with the other scholars the method which the master observed was to ask the question and the scholar to answer. He has frequently known that the defender when asked how his brother, mother, or sister were answer they were very well and at the same time the deponent knew that some of them were not well or sick and living in the same house as Hugh Blair.

He went to all the burials about whether rich or poor and that whether he was invited or not. This he did before and after he was a man or arrived at the years of majority. He has done this in the last three years. He never put on mournings at these occasions but when he was desired by his mother and brother which was when he was at the burial of his relations.

Several times at the school and since and even within these two or three years when the deponent or others said to him that he would die or 'Hugh Blair die' the defender said 'Hugh Blair no die, Hugh Blair no die' but that when the deponent or others said to him that such a one whom the defender knew would die the defender said that these persons whom the deponent or other persons named 'would die but Hugh Blair no die'.

Often after it was well known to the family of Borgue and all the neighbours round that Mrs Grizell Maxwell was married to Mr Andrew Hunter writer in Edinburgh he has heard the defender being asked who was his wife answer 'Grizell Maxwell'. Several times within these three or four years the deponent and others have asked the defender if Peggy Veitch was his wife, to which he answered 'yes' and the very next question the deponent and others have asked him if Betty Monteith was his wife, to which he answered 'yes'. Before Miss Nelly Lamont was married to the pursuer the deponent asked Hugh Blair if she was his wife, to which he answered 'yes'. He has known Hugh Blair since he was a schoolboy and he has always looked upon him as one void of understanding, common sense, and reason such as he the deponent and other ordinary people have and that the neighbourhood have the same notion of him. He was commonly called the daft lad or dumb lad of Borgue. [paragraphing added]

[signed]

Mr John Gordon, residenter at Balmangan, 40 and upwards, married [former schoolmaster at Borgue and a witness for Hugh Blair; spoke on 1 January 1748 and again a week later (see below)].

Before he was cited as a witness he was in company with William Taggart, tailor in Carletown, who was then working in the deponent's house. In conversation, the said William told him that he had been cited as a witness for the pursuer, upon which the deponent said 'What can you say in that matter? For you remember that when Hugh Blair and you were at school together I used to make you and he, as well as the rest of the scholars, kneel and say your prayers and answer the questions in the proof catechism.' To which Taggart answered that he did not remember anything of Hugh Blair praying. The deponent at the same time said to Taggart that if he swore that Hugh Blair was a fool and knew him as well as the deponent did, he would have more freedom in his conscience than he the deponent had.

Robert McMillan, brother to McMillan of Barwhinnock, after he had been summoned as a witness for the pursuer in this cause, came to the deponent's house (before he himself had been summoned) and told him that he was cited. Upon which the deponent asked him what he could say in that matter. He answered that he thought he could have freedom to swear that Hugh Blair was an idiot. The deponent then said that as he took an idiot to be one void of reason and incapable of receiving any impressions of a divine being, he believed that McMillan would get none to concur with him in his opinion if they knew Hugh Blair as well as the deponent did.

Since the deponent came to town, he has visited the Misses McGuffock, of the family of Rusco. The conversation having turned upon the present process, the deponent did justify the conduct of Lady Borgue in marrying her son Hugh, as the lady had in vain applied to his nearest friends on both sides to take the proper care of him, which they having declined and the lady herself being an old woman, the deponent thought she had acted a reasonable part with regard to her son. In the same company, Miss McGuffock having asked the deponent's sentiments about Hugh Blair, the deponent gave his opinion that Hugh had sense and reason, and a notion of religion and worshipping of God, that he could say a grace and was regular in his secret devotions, and asserted that he could repeat more of the proof catechism than he the deponent could. This he knew to be the case when Hugh attended the deponent's school. [All the depositions for the defender were conducted on 1 January. Exactly a week later, after noting some objections to John Gordon's testimony, his evidence continued.]

The deponent first knew Hugh Blair in 1723 when he came to be schoolmaster at Borgue. Hugh Blair was then about 14 years old, and had already been attending the school there. On arriving at the school the deponent found Hugh both wrote and read pretty well, and that particularly he read the Old and New Testaments as well as his indistinct manner of speech would allow. He likewise answered the questions in the proof catechism but sometimes instead of answering the questions in the shorter catechism he has heard him repeat over the questions instead of the answers. The deponent endeavoured to bring him from this, but he still continued sometimes in his old way.

Some years after this, when Hugh had left school, the deponent has seen him quarrying stones, and carrying them in a hurle-barrow [wheelbarrow] to the dykes, which were then being built at Borgue. He knew also the defender mend a piece of a deep mirey way, leading from the house of Senwick to the church of Borgue. He saw Hugh carrying some till in a hurle-barrow to the same and, as far as the deponent observed, the defender was not desired by any person to mend the said way; neither did anybody assist him in it. He worked several days on this piece of road. He believes him capable of religion and that he has impressions of the deity and believes also that he is capable of understanding the marriage contract. Asked if ever he knew or was present at the defender's making any bargains, even if the simplest sort, depones that he never was present at any such bargains. [paragraphing added]

[signed]

16 July 1747 (at 3pm) interrogatories put to Hugh Blair by the commissaries of Edinburgh with the said Hugh Blair's answers.

When came you to town? Nickie Mitchell.

When came you to Edinburgh? Yes.

Where did you live before you came to Edinburgh? Edinburgh.

Do you hear me when I speak to you? Speak.

Did you ride or walk from the country? Ride.

Is this a fair day or rainy? Fair.

Is this a fair day or a foul? Foul.

Have you got your dinner? Hugh Blair.

Is your mother alive? Yes.

Came you from the west or from the east country? From the east.

Who made you? God. Being asked the same question a second time. Christ. And being asked the same question the third time. Holy Ghost.

What age are you? Hugh Blair.

Have you any brothers or sisters? Yes.

How many brothers or sisters have you? Yes.

What is the name of your parish minister? Brown.

How many fingers have you? At first he made no answer but his fingers afterwards being pointed to he counted the fingers of each hand twice without stopping.

Being desired to hold up his right hand he held up the left.

Is your finger or leg longest? Longest.

Is it forenoon or afternoon? Afternoon.

Is it forenoon or afternoon? Forenoon.

The said Hugh Blair being shown the Bible he read the first two verses of Genesis and being shown the title of the Old Testament and likewise of the New Testament both which titles he likewise read and being several times asked what book it was he hummed but made no articulate answer.

What brought you to town? Kirkcudbright.

What brought you to Edinburgh? Yes.

Being shown a guinea of gold and asked twice what it was he answered a shilling. And being shown a shilling and asked what it was he answered a shilling. And being shown a half penny and asked what it was he answered a half penny.

Being shown a pen knife and asked what it was he answered a knife. And being shown a pair of spectacles and asked what they were he answered glass.

Being shown a watch and asked what it was he answered: do not tell.

What is your name? Hugh Blair.

Whose son are you? Yes.

Can you write? Yes.

And having set before him in writing as follows: answer the following question. What brought you to Edinburgh? In place of giving an answer in writing when desired he transcribed verbatim the writing so set before him.

And he having thereafter set down in writing before him thus: you are not to copy what is set before you but write an answer to this question. What was the reason of your coming to Edinburgh at this time? And in place of giving a written answer he copied this over in the same way which writing is upon a paper hereto appended. [The original piece of paper on which the writings occur is reproduced on p.60 as Plate 15.]

Are you married? Nickie Mitchell.

Is Nicholas Mitchell your wife? Yes.

Is Peggy Veitch your wife? No.

Do you live with Nickie Mitchell? No.

Do you live with May Gordon? Yes.

Do you live with Peggy Veitch? No.

Do you live with Mary Brown? Mistress Mitchell. Being asked a second time. Marion.

Was you ever in bed with Peggy Veitch? Nicholas Mitchell.

Whom do you love best? Nickie Mitchell.

One of the Commissaries having asked Hugh Blair if he would marry him he answered yes.

Is your wife alive? Wife.

Have you any bairns? Bairns. And upon the question being put a second time. Yes.

The Significance of the Case in the Eighteenth Century

Hugh Blair was an individual. So was each person who commented on him. Yet the way people reacted to his behaviour brought out the more general criteria of mental capacity shared by those around him. Awareness of the body, its presentation and its care was central to normal life. Close family had to be recognized and respected. Behaviour in public places like churches and at ceremonies such as funerals was dictated by certain well-known conventions. A person should know and show their place in society. Realistic self-assessment would create the correct balance between pride and humility. Proper functioning by an individual in civil society required basic literacy and numeracy, and an appreciation of the value of material items as well as their cost and nature. In all social contexts, behaviour had to be appropriate.[43] In contrast, Hugh showed a limited range of social interests, resistance to change, and stereotypical behaviour.

Witnesses and observers frequently offered additional information about gestures, actions, and facial expressions which added nuance to the impression of an apparently incapable person. Indeed, they are central to the definition of mental incapacity for we cannot abstract one or two types of behaviour as unacceptable when it is really all of them together which are indicative of madness or stupidity. Hugh was not judged idiotic simply because he washed his wig frequently, or gratuitously copied passages from religious texts. The definition of capacity was based on an accumulation of signs rather than a particular action. Those who knew an allegedly incapable person assessed the whole context of that person's behaviour, interpreting it in a flexible and contingent way. Some acts reinforced the opinion that a person was stupid, others detracted from it. Yet, in the final analysis an opinion was reached. In the case of Hugh Blair it was that he was idiotic, lacking sufficient reason to enter into an irrevocable contract such as marriage. Underlying psychology was dealt with by summary nouns or adjectives – idiot or idiotic – or by inference, rather than by an extensive or explicit discussion of underlying thought processes. As John McEwan put it: 'The deponent never observed the defender say grace before or after meat though possibly he might have done it as he the deponent does not know his heart'. However, the abiding impression most people had of Hugh's mind was that it was deficient in its reasoning when compared with the average person.

For the lawyers, Blair v Blair had one enduring legacy. It was used by subsequent legal authorities to illustrate the principle that an indissoluble tie like marriage could not be made by a person defective in their reason (though showing some little sense), while a revocable one like a last will and testament could.[44] Until we read the appeal submissions, the marriage of Hugh Blair and Nicholas Mitchell seems important more as a legal fact than as a personal experience. The case's emotional content is largely hidden from view. Yet Hugh was described as doting on his mother, and (by some) as loving and attentive to his wife. In a document, admittedly framed by Grizell Blair and Archibald Mitchell, it is stated that Nicholas agreed to the marriage reluctantly ('in compliance with my father's advice'), but has had no cause to regret it because Hugh: 'ever since the marriage, has behaved himself with great tenderness and affection to me, and even to outward appearance is a quite different person from what he seemed to be, when kept as a scullion about the house of Borgue'.[45]

That their union was more than a material arrangement or a weapon in familial struggles became apparent only during the appeal. For in June 1748 the Court of Session was told that Nicholas Mitchell was with child, and soon to give birth. She had twice previously been pregnant but had suffered miscarriages on both occasions.[46] On one, 'Nicholas Mitchell parted with child, after she was pretty far gone, occasioned by a fall, as can be proved by the midwife, and others that attended her on that occasion'.[47] The old parochial register of births and baptisms reveals that on 27 June 1748 David Blair, the son of Hugh Blair and Nicholas Mitchell, was christened at Kirkcudbright. Coming just a week after the Court of Session's confirmation that their union was invalid, the child would have been officially illegitimate – a bastard. Thus, the entry reads: 'David son of Hugh Blair, portioner of Borgue, and Mrs Nicholas Mitchell, 29 June 1748'. All other male babies baptized at this date are styled 'lawfull son' or 'son lawfull'.[48] In medieval English law, the ability to beget children was regarded as an indicator of mental capacity.[49] Hugh's lawyers referred to this, but only in passing.[50] Baby David was baptized by the same Rev. Gartshore whose refusal two years earlier to sanction Hugh's marriage had set in motion the events described above.

Whatever umbrage Lady Borgue had taken against her son John was carried to some lengths. On 1 July 1748 she was still involved in a Court of Session case against him for payment of the £113 she had lent him during their happier days of the 1730s.[51] She had summoned him on 11 June 1747, perhaps out of anger or in the hope that the threat of multiple law suits might weaken his resolve and deplete his resources. The summons is annotated on 26 June 1747: 'Seen and returned with this defence that the bills charged on are more than paid and compensated by the pursuer's intromission with the defender's effects and rents, but besides she cannot demand payment of the bills here because they are produced in another process depending before my Lord Drumore'. John had much on his plate in 1747 and 1748, including sequestration for debt, multiple court cases, and lawyers' bills.

The modern reader may struggle to sympathize with him. Yet John had learned some hard lessons in his life about greed and the limits of familial loyalty. Between 1740 and January 1742 John Blair pursued an action against Alexander Blair of Dunrod, one of his cousins.[52] The issue was two allegedly usurious loans made to the late David Blair around the time that Hugh and John were born. It seems that David had made a number of questionable dispositions or bonds and that, on attaining majority, John had to pursue actions against several individuals for the reduction of these. Alexander Blair claimed that David, 'being pinched in his circumstances and having occasion for money to pay off his creditors', asked his two brothers (James of Senwick and Hugh of Dunrod) for 600 merks; this not proving enough, David's brothers paid out a further 600 merks to creditors. He issued a second bond which gave the tack of the lands of Risk Croft to the creditors. John claimed successfully that the two bonds were 'usurious' because they charged 6 per cent, not the 5.5 per cent legal maximum interest set by Act of Parliament. Commonly for a landowner who had to resort to the law, John Blair himself had to borrow money: in this case 600 merks from a cousin in December 1741.[53]

This was not the first time that John experienced a clash of material interest with his kin. From his teenage years onwards, he had bitter experience of the limits of family love. The papers for the Court of Session process of the early 1740s include a copy of an earlier 'decreet of reduction' from that court (1725).[54] This document was in favour of John, Hugh, Jean, and Margaret Blair; the defender was William McGuffock, eldest living son to William McGuffock of Rusco. The litigation was pursued by the tutors dative to the Blair children: their maternal grandfather John Blair of Dunskey, and their uncles Hugh Blair of Dunrod and James Blair of Senwick. McGuffock had obtained a disposition (18 January 1711) from David Blair of the lands of Borgue. On behalf of the children, the tutors claimed successfully that the marriage contract specifically stated that the lands and barony of Borgue should pass to the children. Thus, it was illegal for David Blair to do anything to the contrary.

For the purposes of our story, we should allow that John, sometimes aided by his mother and tutors, had been fighting his cousins over money for as long as he could remember. Sadly, John himself lapsed into some form of mental incapacity around the age of fifty. In the early 1750s he was said to have been 'in a state of mind like that of the rest of mankind', but was described in a document of January 1763 as 'having lately become furious'.[55] His son David was appointed factor to his father and uncle by the Court of Session sometime in 1761 or 1762. Grizell had continued to follow a different course from her son John. The reason for the documentation just cited is a dispute over an augmentation of the glebe and a repair to the manse of Borgue following the death of Rev. Brown in 1751 and the ordination of Rev. David Forbes as parish minister in 1752. Lady Borgue had joined with a number of other heritors in opposing the Presbytery whereas John had agreed to the augmentation and repair. Relations between landowners and Presbytery were poor around this time. According to Andrew Hunter, the heritors' lawyer: 'matters were conducted full of invective and bitterness on the part of the heritors, and on the part of the presbytery with indecent warmth and precipitancy'.[56]

Grizell Blair's own pockets were not bottomless: she haemorrhaged money on lawyers and accommodation during 1747 and 1748. Soon after losing the court case over Hugh's marriage, Lady Borgue was sued before the Sheriff Court by a Kirkcudbright merchant for unpaid bills amounting to £31–19–10 (£31.99) sterling.[57] This was more than her normal annual income from her annuity, due under the terms of her marriage contract. On 8 August 1748, another merchant sued her for £2–4–8 (£2.23) sterling. The larger debt was from the previous year but this one is based on an IOU dated 20 July 1748. It looks very much as if Lady Borgue's credit-worthiness had been called into question. Worse was to come. On 18 November 1748 she was further sued for £348 Scots (approximately £29 sterling) by William Gordon, Writer to the Signet, for legal fees. She is described as 'tutrix dative to Hugh Blair, now of Borgue'.

In effect, the story ends in the summer of 1748. Hugh would have been in his mid-fifties when he died, probably in 1765. We have only indirect evidence and therefore imprecise dates for the demise of any of the principal players in this drama. Perhaps they chose not to spend money on durable headstones; they may have been buried out of the shire even if their roots were there, or their monuments may not have survived. Whatever the reason, we find none of them or their offspring listed in a careful study of Kirkcudbrightshire gravestones prior to 1855 (when civil registration of births, marriages, and deaths was finally introduced into Scotland).[58] John Blair himself did not survive long after taking control of the entire heritable estate of the family of Borgue. His son, David, succeeded him in February 1769.[59] David's mother, Helen Lamont, registered a legal document or 'sasine' concerning her right to her annuity in that same month.[60] Grizell Blair died in late 1760 or early 1761, probably in her late seventies or early eighties. Of the other principals, the only thing currently known is that baby David gained a sister, Grizell, baptized on 3 November 1752. Curiously, she is described as 'Grissel, lawfull daughter of Mr Hugh Blair and Mrs Nicholas Mitchell'. There is no record of another marriage and, unless Rev. Gartshore had had a change of heart, the only explanation is that Hugh and Nicholas had become recognized as husband and wife 'by habit and repute'. However difficult it may have been, Hugh and Nicholas had remained together.

Chapter 4

Autism and its Relevance to the Case of Hugh Blair

In the short history of psychiatry, autism has come to mean much more than social detachment. Leo Kanner, the author of the first textbook on child psychiatry, is credited with identifying autism as a diagnostic syndrome. Autism was the name he gave to the disorder which he first described in 1943, using case material from his clinic at Johns Hopkins University, Baltimore.[1] The children were beautiful but aloof. They were unable to relate to others. They had no language, or else, very peculiar language. Either way, they did not communicate. The behaviour of these children showed many puzzling features: they performed the same actions repeatedly; they insisted on events having a fixed order and things having a fixed place; they showed an obsessive desire for sameness; finally, they had islets of ability which hinted perhaps at some hidden intelligence.

Kanner's descriptions chime in with the witnesses' accounts of Hugh Blair. Hugh Blair had poor speech and even poorer communication. He did not properly take part in the social life of the family or community. Many of his activities were baffling to others. He performed repetitive tasks unsuitable for his station in life, such as carrying stones. He insisted on having the same place at church and, according to a former servant to the family, 'was very careful to set everything right that was in any way out of order in the house'. While generally thought of as feeble-minded, his memory was praised by his former schoolmaster as better than his own. Uncannily, Hugh's ability to recite the Presbyterian catechism was also shared by one of the children that Kanner saw.

97

The clinical picture evoked by Kanner's description induced many clinicians to identify autism among their own existing cases. There is no reason why it could not also inspire others to identify similar cases in the past. While Kanner's textbook on child psychiatry has become obsolete, his seminal article 'Autistic disturbances of affective contact', remains a milestone in twentieth-century psychiatry. Its impact is still seen in the diagnostic criteria for autism in the handbooks that clinicians use today.

A Prehistory of Autism

Why is it that no one before Kanner described autism in children? Did it exist? Or is autism a new phenomenon? There are in fact earlier descriptions of children with mental handicaps, which are strongly reminiscent of autism. Most of these never reached the scientific journals, and nobody related the cases to each other. The condition had no name and was not recognized as a clinical entity.

The case of AIDS and mad cow disease show that new disorders can arise suddenly, be it from a genetic mutation, a newly spreading virus, or some other factor, possibly induced by the conditions of modern industrialized societies. It would be very important to know whether or not autism existed long ago. Case studies can answer this question. However, they can not tell us whether a disorder has become more common, or simply more recognized, in modern societies.

John Haslam, apothecary at Bethlem, the famous London asylum, reported in his *Observations on Madness and Melancholy* the case of a five-year-old boy admitted in 1799.[2] This boy did not speak until aged four, never joined other boys in play, but played obsessively with toy soldiers. He was able to whistle several tunes 'very correctly'. 'Although he was acquainted with the names of many things and also with expressions which characterize passion, he applied them in an insulated way'. These symptoms might be described by modern psychiatrists as impaired relations with peers, narrow and obsessively pursued interests, good rote memory and impaired expression of emotions. All these symptoms are consistent with autism.

An argument for considering at least some of the 'holy fools' of Russia as suffering from autism was first proposed by the historian Horace Dewey, who also had a deep knowledge of autism based on personal experience in his family.[3] One of several documented cases dates from the sixteenth century: a boy who sought to avoid human contact and was captured by peasants and put in the care of the local priest. This boy grew up to be the Blessed Simon of Jurev. His case is reminiscent of the wild boy of Aveyron, who was found in the late 1790s in the woods of the Auvergne. He has also been considered a possible case of autism; his disorder having perhaps led to his abandonment in the first place.[4] We know the details of this case through a scientifically motivated study by E. M. Itard, who was a physician at the National Institution for Deaf-Mutes in Paris.[5] Itard attempted to educate the boy, whom he named Victor. He made much progress, but after five years he gave up the task. Victor never learned the ways of society and never learned to speak fluently. From Itard's account, as well as others, we can infer that Victor showed some characteristically autistic features, especially his inability to relate to others and his inability to communicate even by sign. Various experts examined the boy and came to the conclusion that he was very similar to other children of 'incomplete and damaged constitutions' and that he was mentally defective from birth.

Even earlier cases might be suspected. A character out of the thirteenth-century legends of St Francis, the unworldly Brother Juniper, strikes a chord with autism in a particularly benign guise. The stories tell of strange behaviour – foolish but wise, and always at odds with common sense. Brother Juniper may have been modelled on a real person who suffered from autism with its concomitant problems of communication and flexibility. If so, he had a niche; he was tolerated and even admired for his humility. It is tempting to speculate that even if cases of autism have not been documented earlier, the condition did exist. This is one reason why the case of Hugh Blair is of scientific importance. If the diagnosis of autism can be made on the basis of the historical facts that we have available, then this would unequivocally establish the existence of the disorder at the beginning of the eighteenth century, considerably earlier than John Haslam's case and the case of the wild boy of Aveyron.

The Pioneers

At almost the same time as Kanner wrote his famous paper, Hans Asperger, a young paediatrician in Vienna, was engaged in writing a thesis on what he called 'autistic psychopathy in childhood'.[6] Asperger described strange children who gazed about them as if 'they had just fallen to earth', who did not take part in peer group activities, and who had extremely limited 'relations to the outside world'. Although showing sometimes high intelligence, some had nasty habits and all were liable to be teased and bullied. Again we are reminded of Hugh Blair. He was frequently said to 'gaze about him', he was clearly unable to fit in with his position in society, he evoked disgust in others and he was cruelly teased by servants and children. Asperger's paper was published in 1944, but was understandably ignored, given the historical context of the Second World War and its aftermath. This neglect has recently been rectified. The label 'Asperger syndrome' has come into use to describe a particular variety of autism, in tribute to Hans Asperger's pioneering insights. This variety encompasses individuals of high levels of ability, that is, they reach good scores on intelligence tests and are generally better socially adapted than individuals who suffer from other varieties of autism. However, their better adaptation may be due to assiduous effort and may not necessarily be the result of a minor form of the disorder.

The coincidence of the choice of the word 'autistic' by both Kanner and Asperger can be explained by the influence of adult psychiatry. The label had been used by the influential Swiss psychiatrist Eugen Bleuler at the beginning of the twentieth century to describe the negative symptoms of schizophrenia. Patients suffering from these symptoms appeared to be in a state where they were entirely uninterested in the outside world, but exclusively preoccupied with themselves (*autos* in Greek means 'self'). The label autistic therefore seemed an apt choice to describe the essentially egocentric world of these strangely aloof children, who seemed supremely indifferent or unaware of what other people felt or thought about them, and appeared to be utterly absorbed in their own world. The differences between these children and the patients described by Bleuler were, however, greater than the similarities: the age of onset of the disorder was different, and so was its course. Despite borrowing from Bleuler's insights, each author was adamant that autism was not a form of schizophrenia. Schizophrenia was defined as a disease which started after a normal childhood, and showed progressive deterioration throughout its course. In the case of autism, the disorder existed from birth and, following an often very difficult childhood, the adaptation of the child often improved markedly.

100

The coincidence of the choice of label is one thing, the coincidence of interest in these children in different countries is another. Various forms of 'congenital idiocy' had been known for a long time. Some of these forms were successfully linked to medical conditions and became treatable. For instance, hypothyroidism, which was endemic in Alpine countries, was found to be due to iodine deficiency and could be treated by dietary supplements. The most severe conditions of brain abnormality and consequent mental handicap often went hand in hand with physical signs, for instance malformations of the face and body, or sensory and motor impairments. Knowledge steadily accumulated concerning mental deficiency with physical signs, such as Down's syndrome and other chromosomal disorders. The existence of mental impairment in otherwise physically normal and healthy children presented a more complex problem.

In the early part of the twentieth century better health care had brought about an increasing awareness of other disturbed children who did not seem to carry physical stigmata. Some of these were severely deprived children, a not uncommon phenomenon in Europe after the First World War. More puzzling were those who came from good homes and were well cared for, but who behaved strangely and failed to learn like other children. They conveyed the impression of intelligence despite evident failure at school and maladaptation to everyday life. Brain disorder did not seem to apply to misfits and unhappily excluded children. Had they withdrawn from a hostile world, retreating to a mental fortress of their own making? Could a key be found to release them? This was a romantic notion, but a highly influential one. It induced people to try to 'rescue' these children by various types of psychotherapy. These efforts were to be cruelly disappointed.

Changing Ideas on the Causes of Autism

No sooner was autism described than causes and cures were suggested. The dominant image that the first descriptions of autism conveyed was of an aloof and withdrawn child, cut off from emotional contact with others. It seemed that it should be possible to break through and establish contact. The idea was that with appropriate therapy the child would be led out of isolation to emerge with intact mental powers. From a modern perspective, the failure to consider brain disorder is a strange oversight. It is now generally assumed that our brain evolved to make social and emotional contact possible in the first place. From there it is but a small step to imagine that brain abnormality could cause such contact to be broken. Even in the 1950s and 1960s, professionals spotted frankly neurological signs in autistic children that pointed to an organic rather than psychogenic basis of their disorder. Signs were detected in movement patterns, such as tiptoe walking, and more strikingly in various types of epilepsy. Some theorists tried to interpret neurological signs as effects, rather than causes, of the mental disorder. This idea found little empirical support, and by 1978 a neurological model of autism was possible.[7]

When Kanner and Asperger first described autism, in 1943–4, most of the world was in acute turmoil. Asperger's paper, published in German, was largely ignored. Kanner, in the United States, was influenced by psychoanalytic thinking – the dominant trend in psychiatry at the time. Nevertheless, each of the pioneers initially proposed that the condition they had identified had a biological basis. Kanner suggested the possibility of a disruption in what he considered an innate, and hence physiologically based, capacity for affective contact. However, later, when under the influence of psychodynamic notions, his interest turned to the relationship between mother and child, suggesting that the root cause of autistic aloneness was a mother who was incapable of showing emotional warmth. Indeed Kanner propagated the powerful and pernicious term 'refrigerator mother'. This theory was speculative and not based on evidence. Nevertheless, the idea took hold in popular imagination. Furthermore the prevailing belief was that a socio-emotional disorder was more likely to be caused by a breakdown in interpersonal relationships than by a neurological fault.

Asperger's view, which remained untested until recently, was that autism was an inherited personality variant. He wrote about seeing similar but milder features of autism in the parents. At the time when psychogenic theories put the blame on mothers, and also in the backlash which followed, such work was 'politically incorrect'. It seemed more pressing to demonstrate that autism could occur in families of all sorts. However, after initial reluctance, researchers turned their attention to the features of autism in family members.

The strong genetic contribution to autism – as opposed to environmental contributions – has been demonstrated in twin studies.[8] The rare cases of children with autism who also were twins showed that only identical twins who share all their genes, but not fraternal twins, shared the diagnosis of autism. As one would expect from a genetic disorder, autism does run in families. The risk for a sibling to be affected is 3 per cent, 50 to 100 times higher than in the general population. Recently, data have been published suggesting a site on chromosome 7 as a critical locus for autism-related genes.[9] Between three and ten genes are thought to be involved. However, there is still a long way to go before these genes can be identified. Some non-genetic factors, including viral infection, auto-immune disorder or other biological adversity, have also been considered as potential causes of autism. Both genetic and non-genetic causes are likely to be probabilistic and not deterministic, that is, they have to be viewed as risk factors. As risk factors they may combine with other factors to produce the full-blown disorder or a milder form. In the case of Hugh Blair we cannot examine evidence that could clarify the biological causes of his disorder. Nevertheless, a biological basis can be assumed.

Some facts and figures

Autism was quickly established as a recognizable disorder. It was not a quirky constellation of features confined to rare cases in university clinics. Many clinicians and researchers worldwide responded to the challenge to explore the natural history and the causes of the disorder. Foremost was the need to define the disorder and to establish its prevalence. The signs and symptoms of the disorder had to be systematically investigated by comparison with other types of mental incapacity. An explosion of studies followed as more and more cases were diagnosed, and as clinicians were moved by the plight of the children and their families. From early on, studies of the effect of different treatments were conducted. Biological and genetic studies into the origin of the disorder followed later. The investigation of the causes, the nature and the treatment of autism is still in progress in many different countries with ever-intensifying efforts. Only a small number of selected studies can be touched on here.

The first prevalence studies were based on Kanner's criteria, which emphasized aloofness and indifference to others, absence of speech or peculiar idiosyncratic speech, and insistence on sameness as well as elaborate repetitive routines. Children with these precise characteristics were

103

relatively rare: 5 in 10,000, with a ratio of 3.7 boys to 1 girl.[10] With the benefit of hindsight it is now possible to say that Kanner's criteria were too narrow, and hence this prevalence estimate of autism is too low. It became increasingly clear that the variation in the clinical picture of autism is very great, both between individuals, and within one and the same individual over time. The concept of an autism phenotype based on well-defined cognitive rather than purely behavioural criteria, was pioneered by the psychiatrist and leading autism researcher Michael Rutter at London's Institute of Psychiatry. This laid the foundations for explanations of both the clinical and neurobiological aspects of autism.[11]

In the 1970s, a landmark study by the London-based epidemiologist Lorna Wing found that a proportion of mentally retarded children had some form of manifestation of the three core features of autism, which could vary in their manifestation to include quite subtle forms.[12] The social impairments could take the form, not only of indifference, but also of passivity or enthusiastic but inappropriately egocentric interactions. The communication impairments could be seen even in children who had acquired fluent speech, but were still unable to take part in proper two-way conversation, not only in children with obvious speech and language problems. The repetitive routines could be very simple, or they could be highly abstract, involving preoccupations with words or facts, not just manipulation of objects. These findings led to the notion of an autistic spectrum, characterized by a triad of impairments in social interaction, communication and imagination associated with repetitive activities and interests. This triad was estimated as affecting 16 in 10,000 children, based on a geographically defined sample of 35,000 children. Subsequently Lorna Wing elaborated the notion of an autism spectrum.[13] The term 'pervasive developmental disorder', as used in the current editions of psychiatric handbooks, covers a similar range of manifestations of autism including Asperger syndrome.[14]

The identification of a wider group of individuals with consistently co-occurring autistic features overcame one particular problem, namely the arbitrariness inherent in diagnostic criteria that had been initially derived from a small clinical base of school-age children. It also made sense of the fact that multiple cases of autism in the same family, presumably due to the same genetic cause, tended to show different manifestations in form and severity of symptoms. Kanner's criteria were not proved wrong, but they were considerably loosened. The prevalence of the whole range of autistic disorder, including children without mental retardation, remains to be established. On the basis of some initial studies, it is likely to lie somewhere between 0.2 and 0.7 per cent – remarkably high. Has autism increased over time or has only the diagnosis of autism increased? The answer is unknown at present, but increasing numbers are to be expected with a loosening of the criteria and an increasing awareness of the disorder.

A curious association of autism with upper social class was at first suspected, but was later revealed to be an artefact: professional and more affluent parents were more likely to describe and document their children's problems in detail and managed to attract the specialists' interest in their children. They formed the first parent's organizations, which in time were joined by similar parents. When few professionals had yet heard of autism, access to centres of knowledge favoured well-educated and well-connected families. In the case of Hugh Blair too, we see an individual from an important and well-connected family. Only a relatively well-to-do family could afford to mobilize the legal system to assess the mental capacity of their eldest son. A similar bias is likely to operate today in countries where health and education services are neither free nor comprehensive.

The Many Shades of Autism

The claim that it is possible to recognize autism in different cultures and over several centuries is a strong and possibly reckless one, given that there are vast individual differences between people with autism, even if they are of the same historical and cultural background. At one extreme are the withdrawn individuals who never speak and who are entirely engaged in apparently pointless repetitive activity. At the other extreme are the socially inept individuals who talk at length about their abstruse interests although unable to converse with others in the normal way. In between are those who have limited use of language and strange habits.

The two extreme cases can be disregarded in the comparison with Hugh Blair. He was neither mute nor fluent; he was not totally disinterested in others, nor did he crave constant company. He was not foolish in everything he did, but neither was he wise. Hugh resembled those cases who have a craving for social interaction as long as pace and content is adapted to their ability to respond. Yet, like many people with autism today who are far from aloof, Hugh did not take part in the flow of everyday communication.

The reasons for the variable picture of autism and the unpredictability of individual outcomes are as obscure as are the reasons for individual differences in the normal population. Some of the variability in the clinical picture of autism may be due to degrees of severity in the underlying pathology. Some of it may be due to additional impairments in intellect, hearing or vision. However, some of it may be due to factors largely external to the individual. It is here that historical cases may be informative. Take, for example, lack of public awareness of the disorder, and lack of provision for special education. A host of other factors should be considered as well. For instance, a difficult temperament can stand in the way of teaching by alienating people who might otherwise be eager to help. In this respect Hugh Blair was fortunate. He was by all accounts exceptionally good-natured. Hugh's poor hearing and speech, on the other hand, were much commented upon and might have aggravated his condition.

Autism in Adulthood

Hugh Blair was a middle-aged man at the time of the court case, and the information we have is mainly about his life as an adult. Yet, historically, autism has been studied as a disorder of childhood. All of the early psychological experiments were conducted with children. The reason is not difficult to fathom. After all, autism was still a novel diagnosis in the 1960s, not the household word that it has since become. Hardly anyone reported experience with individuals at later ages. Young parents, understandably, hoped that their children might grow out of autism. Older parents wondered what would have happened if their children had received early treatment and special education. Few people appreciated that autism is a lifelong disorder.[15]

In 1989 a popular Hollywood film, *Rainman*, showed for the first time an adult with autism. It departed from the still haunting stereotype of the beautiful withdrawn child to show a different side of autism with neurological implications. The adult Raymond (or Rainman as his younger brother nicknamed him), portrayed by Dustin Hoffman, was based on a composite of several real cases, one of whom had been diagnosed by Kanner and was middle-aged at the time. Typical autistic behaviour, mannerisms and special interests were represented quite faithfully in the film, so much so that the film has been used as a teaching aid and a means of raising public awareness.

The adult with autism was shown as awkward and gauche, with easily recognizable neurological signs. For instance, he had a peculiar stiff gait and a wooden expression, altogether a rigid and obsessive demeanour. Despite the lack of what we might call lost child appeal, he was an engaging character. That is, he was essentially innocent of the ways of the world. He was supremely egocentric (and hence autistic in the original sense of the word), yet he was uncorrupted by the base motives which seem to govern so many transactions between ordinary people trying to get advantages for themselves. At the same time he was shown as exhibiting acute powers of perception, albeit in ultimately useless skills, such as remembering a page of a telephone book. The combination of rare skills, whose potential the owner does not realize, and guilelessness, was set in sharp contrast to the worldly and venal ways of Raymond's brother. The story of the film rests on the idea that a handicapped person with autism can have a strong moral impact even on a near-villain. Unhappily, in the case of the Blair brothers, where John, the younger brother, has some claim to villainy, the outcome was far bleaker: John usurped Hugh's hereditary rights.

The case of Freddie

Contemporary biographical and autobiographical accounts are often based on autistic people of exceptional ability. A detailed account of a case near the lower extreme of the spectrum is that of Freddie the Weaver.[16] Freddie was born in the UK in 1946 and adopted by a society beauty who devoted her life to him. Mark Frankland, her journalist stepson, gives a fascinating account of the different theoretical and practical approaches to severe forms of autism in England from the 1950s onwards. There are extraordinary parallels between Freddie and Hugh, such as their shared interest in weaving. However, Hugh seems to have been less incapacitated than Freddie, and also better adapted to his own environment. Freddie never learned to speak and only communicated by grunts. He was temperamentally difficult to manage. Yet, despite turbulent ups and

Plate 21: Photograph of Freddie weaving, dated 1970s. Hugh Blair too was reported to have an interest and skill in weaving. By kind permission of *Yorkshire Post* and with thanks to Mark Frankland.

downs, he too had episodes of a quasi-normal life. For instance, at age 29, after a succession of different placements and attempts at both orthodox and unorthodox treatments, Freddie returned to a village community (governed by the Camphill Trust) which cared for handicapped people. There he had a reasonably contented life. He lived in a home run as a family unit where he helped with the daily chores. He learned to weave well until one day he suddenly stopped. He also worked a printing press, chopped logs for firewood, broke stones for a new car park and worked in the candle shop. Then the seemingly suitable placement had to be changed again, partly because of administrative changes, partly because of Freddie's intermittent violent behaviour.

Opposite
Plate 20: Still from the Hollywood film *Rainman* (released 1989). Dustin Hoffman acted very convincingly the part of an adult with autism and Tom Cruise played his scheming brother.
Photo: Kobal Collection.

Finally, after a spell of hospitalization, Freddie ended up in a small home in rural Devon. This home is run by capable carers with a strong ideological commitment to the dignity and independence of people with mental disorders. It is close to the ideal model of care in the community. Freddie has some privacy and can again do chores he likes to do: he puts the milk bottles out, draws the curtains, brings in the shopping, makes tea, and goes to church. Despite a mostly humdrum existence, Freddie was adored by his mother and loved by many of his caregivers. Frankland reports that a doctor who had known Freddie at his most difficult, wrote in his hospital notes, that he had 'an attractive personality when you got to know him'.

The cases of Sumner and Ted

A touching account by the American writer Charles Hart describes his experience with an autistic brother, Sumner, and later on an autistic son, Ted.[17] Sumner was born in 1920. Coping mainly by themselves, the

Plate 22: Photograph of Sumner aged 55, with his mother. He is attempting to smile for the camera.
By kind permission of Charles Hart and family.

Plate 23: Photograph of Ted aged 25 standing at a swimming pool with smile for the camera. Note the difference to his uncle's attempted smile. The younger man's habilitation due to tailored educational programmes gave him much more confidence and poise.
By kind permission of Charles Hart and family.

family carried a heavy burden of responsibility. For example, ten-year-old Charles had to take over in an emergency and lead his 30–year-old brother safely to bed, in the same step-by-step routine that his mother had followed, year in, year out. He patiently taught Sumner to read and write, where others had previously failed. Sumner remained with his widowed mother in her old age, assisting her with the housework. 'He would carry the groceries for her and help with the peeling, cutting, and cleaning that her cooking required. But he couldn't ask a question, tell a joke, or respond except by repeating a few words of her last phrase' (p. 37). Sumner could initiate a few words, characteristically repeating them, for example, 'I'm being good, I'm being good' (p. 144). He could read and write after a fashion, but not so that it was a useable skill. In all these respects he closely resembled Hugh Blair.

In the cultural context of the time the senior Hart family felt obliged to hide the truth about their handicapped son from others. 'My home life seemed to revolve around Sumner's problems. We chose not to become involved in the community – we were simply too embarrassed by Sumner and sought to avoid even the friendly questions of others who were puzzled by his behavior' (p. 32). 'My embarrassment about Sumner and his inexplicable behaviour had burdened me for as long as I could remember. Like my parents, I tried to hide him or at least conceal his disability. I thought that just as others avoided him, they would also avoid me if they understood our relationship' (p. 39). Did John Blair ever experience similar feelings? Perhaps not, as there was no way of hiding the truth in the Borgue household. Every servant, every neighbour, knew what went on in minute detail, as the depositions make plain. On the other hand, the extent of the burden that fell on John's shoulders must have been considerable: caring for his foolish older brother and looking after his interests for the whole of his life. The documents indicate that John failed in his obligation. This is not perhaps too surprising given the harsh code of conduct this implied. All but the most saintly would try to avoid such obligation.

Eventually Sumner was placed in a home. 'For sixty years our mother had provided gentle but unyielding authority over his schedule. She had been his clock, telling him when to rise, dress, perform bodily functions, etc' (p. 146). Would Hugh's mother have played a similar role? The fact that Hugh lived with her in lodgings after they had to leave the house at Borgue, suggests that she did. It seems likely that she organized Hugh's daily life with the help of servants and Nickie Mitchell, the wife she had chosen for him. It is interesting to note that Hugh survived his mother by three years. Somebody else must have taken over responsibility for his care.

The description of Ted Hart, who was born in 1971, shows him to be more able than his uncle Sumner. Even though his father had intimate knowledge of autism he did not spot the condition in his son particularly early. At first, Ted's indifference to other children seemed to indicate that he was merely too bright to find them interesting. Soon, however the parents realized that their son did not develop in the way that his peers did. Ted was able to learn to speak and to read and write fluently. In fact, he could read anything upside down and mirror reversed as rapidly as in an upright orientation. Ted developed other astonishing talents, in particular an uncanny memory for dates and trivial facts. Calendar skills and prodigious feats of memory are not uncommon among autistic savants. Although we have no direct report that Hugh had any special skills (the defence lawyer would no doubt have used such information had it been available), Hugh's ability to read and write was unusually good in a man who hardly spoke.

Despite his impressive abilities, Ted showed evidence of a communication failure that is typical of autism. Such a failure is demonstrated in the following anecdote (pp. 109–111). Ted was taught how to use a telephone by two of his communication therapists. Nancy would phone Susan, who was working with Ted in an adjoining room connected through a one-way mirror. Susan let the phone ring, asking Ted to pick it up. Nancy then said: 'Can I speak to Susan please'. Ted would hand the receiver to Susan and say 'It's for you'. Ted learned the procedure successfully. This was demonstrated to his father who watched via the screen. Then Nancy had the idea of sending Charles to the next room to be with Ted. She phoned again, and when Ted lifted the receiver, she said: 'Can I speak to your father please'. At this point, Ted gave the receiver again to Susan with a cheerful 'It's for you'. Ted had learned a routine without in the least understanding that the message given over the phone had an intended meaning. This is reminiscent of another telephone anecdote which appears in accounts by a number of families whose autistic children sometimes pick up the phone. When the caller asks 'Is X in?', they are apt to reply 'yes' and put the phone down. This example highlights just how profound the failure of communication can be even without defects in hearing or speaking.

Ted's life with autism is different from and better than that of his uncle. Some of this difference can be attributed to intrinsic factors but beneficial cultural changes enter the picture as well. Better understanding of autism has led to appropriate provisions for education and behaviour modification from early childhood. Social services now provide more generous means for relieving the family's burden of care. Ted experienced a series of enlightened educational placements. He can now live independently with some supervision. This contrast in community support between two generations of the Hart family shows what can be done as a result of increased understanding. We can only speculate on how Hugh Blair might have benefited from modern educational resources. Ultimately, community resources might have lightened the burden of care which tore the Blair family apart.

Family members tend to suffer as a result of autism too – often in a way that is barely acknowledged. Charles Hart made this clear when he said, 'Living with Ted created growing stress for our family. Nick [his younger brother] seemed chronically angry and frustrated as he saw his favourite property defaced or destroyed' (p. 109). Imagine the reaction of the Blairs when Hugh purloined bits and pieces from the household and destroyed good clothing to mend his own ragged garments. Hugh's family must have been every bit as frustrated as similar families now.

Many other cases of autism in the public domain could be quoted for comparison with Hugh Blair. In particular, it is worth exploring literary accounts of autism in autobiographical form. The authors of these accounts are exceptional in that they show great writing talent, which Hugh certainly did not have. Nevertheless, the autobiographical writings are strangely revealing. They show an inner world of sensations, perceptions and emotions unique to each author.[18] All the accounts give vivid examples of interests that are odd from the usual social perspectives. For example, the enthralling experience of feeling sand running through your fingers, or looking at rainwater. Hugh, too, seems to have been fascinated by rainwater. Thus it is possible that these accounts can throw some light on Hugh's strange interests and what they must have meant to him.

Problems and Prospects in the Diagnosis of Autism

There was a time when a diagnosis of autism could only be trusted when made by a foremost expert with first-hand experience. Nowadays, training in child psychiatry and psychology not only includes, but highlights, autism as a prominent disorder. The criteria for autism are behavioural criteria. They are internationally agreed and can be looked up in one of two handbooks that are periodically updated. One is published by the World Health Organization (the most recent edition, ICD-10, 1993) and the other by the American Psychiatric Association (the most recent edition, DSM-IV, 1994). The criteria in the latter stipulate that there must be a qualitative impairment in three areas:

> social interaction, for example, impairment in the use of gestures, failure to develop relationships, lack of emotional reciprocity;
> communication, for example, lack of spoken language, poor ability to initiate and sustain conversations, repetitive use of language;
> repetitive and stereotyped patterns of behaviour, for example, preoccupation with one or more restricted interests, compulsive adherence to specific routines, preoccupation with parts of objects.

In many ways this list still retains the essence of Kanner's earliest descriptions, but uses wider criteria, without emphasis on aloofness. The first two criteria seem plausibly related. Impairments in social interaction and communication might arise from a fault in the same underlying mental and neural process. The question is how can such a fault best be conceptualized? The third criterion is strikingly different from the first two. How can one explain the repetitive behaviour and restricted interests, and do they necessarily constitute an impairment? Later in this chapter, we shall consider how these intriguing questions are being tackled by current theories.

The final diagnostic criterion listed by the manuals requires that the abnormalities must have been present before the age of three years. Although autism exists from birth, this does not mean it can be recognized at birth. Autism is seldom diagnosed in the first year of life. One reason is that there is tremendous individual variation in the speed and manner with which babies develop. A developmental delay in language and communication in the first 18 months, while not necessarily significant, would be taken very seriously if it persisted. From around 18 months of age many differentiated language and communication patterns emerge and, above all, the pleasure in make-believe play. Now differences between normal and abnormal development start to become apparent. There are various early signs focused on communication, which can alert the paediatrician or general practioner. These form a screening test which has been used experimentally for the early detection of suspected autism.[19]

The findings so far suggest three particular signs. One is when a child seems uninterested in where another person looks. Another is when a child does not point to things or show them to others, and a third, when a child shows impoverished understanding of make-believe. Since we do not have evidence about Hugh's childhood, it is impossible to form an opinion about his abilities in early life.

Autism is sometimes diagnosed quite late in life. Even though signs were present from early childhood, they might have been overlooked. Well-meaning doctors and teachers sometimes feel that an otherwise able child will grow out of social communication problems. Ignorance of the condition in the past means that there are many adults who were never diagnosed correctly. When they eventually find a specialist, their persistent difficulties fall into place. Those who live with the affected person are able to be more accepting of a handicap that has a name. The diagnostic tools available today are based on extensive clinical interviews. Much of the information will be retrospective about the early development of language and non-verbal forms of communication. Direct observation of behaviour and neuropsychological testing are used as complementary tools of assessment. A biological marker of autism is still not available. Genetic tests and brain scans, while suggestive, cannot as yet be used to determine a specific abnormality that identifies autism. Once clear markers are available, the diagnosis of autism will proceed at a different pace.

Contributions from Experimental Psychology

The first experimental studies investigating the autistic mind were carried out in the 1960s in parallel with the first clinical and epidemiological studies. The findings played a vital part in overturning the romantic notions about autism that had insinuated themselves into public consciousness. Strict laboratory procedure, rather than anecdotal clinical observations, set a new standard. At first psychological experiments targeted children with severe degrees of autism. Testing these children was a great challenge to the experimenters' ingenuity. Tasks were designed so that the children could do them with a minimum of social interaction, preferably without the need for verbal instructions.

The extent of learning disability that emerged in these children was devastating to those who had mistaken their islets of ability as signs of hidden intelligence. Outstanding talent was rare. There were, however, measurable differences between learning-disabled children with autism and those without. The differences seemed to be specific to responsiveness in social interactions, particularly in their use of language and nonverbal gestures. There were also differences in the pattern of abilities across different subtests of standard intelligence scales. Typically, the pattern for autism was jagged, with ups and downs on different subtests, rather than uniformly low. The best skills were associated with abstract constructions or rote memory, the worst skills with answering common sense questions or making up picture stories.

A minority of autistic children – about 20 per cent – were found to have average or above average IQ. However, this statement does not imply that their intelligence is like that of the average person. Despite their high performance level, the profile of their test scores showed the same peaks and troughs as that of children whose performance was much poorer. Once these high functioning children were identified, they soon became favoured experimental subjects. Their cooperation tended to be high and any impairments on particular tasks were unlikely to be due to poor motivation or poor understanding.

The question about intellectual capacity in autism is still not resolved. Why do so many individuals obtain scores on IQ tests in the range of mental retardation? Why are those with good IQ test scores still so handicapped? Even highly intelligent individuals with autism seem to lack 'common sense', that is, the ability to solve everyday problems which an average person would be expected to solve with ease. The basic capacity to process information cannot be considered the stumbling block. Instead, experiments indicated that it is some specific type of information which cannot be processed. This in turn creates a bottleneck which impairs intellectual development and results in a lack of everyday knowledge and skills. We shall have to bear this point in mind when interpreting Hugh Blair's presumed lack of common sense. He was judged to be a fool. But was this because of poor general intellectual ability, or because of his inability to deal with the demands of everyday social life?

The possibilities for experimental research into the psychology of autism are far from exhausted. So far, the studies can be seen to fall into distinct phases. In the 1960s and 1970s two scientists working in London, Neil O'Connor and Beate Hermelin, carried out trailblazing work exploring basic processes in perception, memory and language.[20] From the beginning they asked questions about the mind of the autistic child that were crucial to understanding both origin and possible treatment of autism. Did children with autism really avoid looking at people? Did they in fact show complete indifference to social interactions? Contrary to popular belief, the answer turned out to be negative. They did not avoid people; rather, they could not make sense of people. There were stark impairments in many cognitive skills. Yet there were also islets of ability, for instance, in memorizing facts and reading aloud. In many cases, rote memory for unconnected information turned out to be superior to memory for meaningfully connected information, quite the reverse from normal. Again and again, results indicate that autistic children cannot make sense of things in the ordinary way. They truly look at the world differently. They have different minds.

The Recognition of Autism as a Brain Disorder

Many studies worldwide have been inspired by these early experimental investigations. Their goal remains the understanding of the core impairments in autism, the possible mechanical faults in the mental machinery and, eventually, the neural processes that sustain them. The same questions are still motivating the research efforts of laboratories around the world. Increasingly, scientists are attempting to look at the anatomical and physiological basis of autism.[21]

There were several reasons for the decisive shift of focus towards cognitive and neurophysiological processes. One was a mounting volume of evidence: in particular, observations of individuals with autism over a longer time span. Enduring features could be distinguished from transient problems. Despite remarkable progress in social understanding in individual cases, the lack of true reciprocal communication appeared to be intransigent. On the other hand, emotional social aloofness often disappeared with the passage of time. Many of the previously withdrawn children became intensely interested in other people as adults. This did not necessarily mean that they became socially skilled. Often, increased social interest led them into trouble with others who felt pestered. They were sad or puzzled by not being able to make friends. Hugh Blair was by all accounts a gregarious individual but amongst the many witnesses who spoke in his defence, there was not a single personal friend.

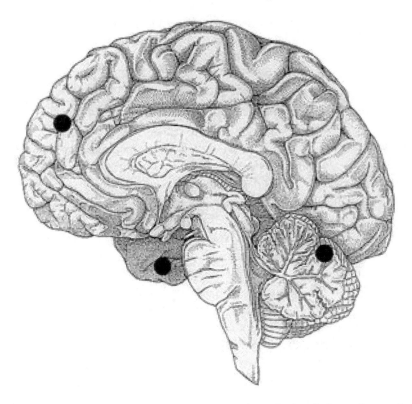

Plate 24: Medial view of the brain as if split between the hemispheres. Research suggests that anatomical abnormalities can be found in a number of brain structures of people with autism. The regions marked by black spots have been found to differ in volume compared to normal brains in a recent study using structural brain scans. The black spot at the back (right side of the picture) refers to the cerebellum; the black spot in the middle refers to the basal temporal lobes around the amygdala complex. In the front (left side of the picture) the black spot refers to an area in the medial frontal lobes, the paracingulate sulcus.

What became clear was that the social impairment of people with autism was far more subtle than had been envisaged at first. Their lack of social insight had little to do with emotional indifference or lack of social interest. Instead their difficulties were reminiscent of difficulties found in neurological patients who had sustained damage to selected regions of the brain, notably in the right hemisphere and in the frontal and temporal lobes.[22] A recent study using statistical methods to analyse brain scans

119

found abnormalities in the regions indicated by black spots in Plate 24. These findings are in keeping with earlier post-mortem studies but await replication.[23]

Mental Mechanisms and Developmental Disorders

Analogies between developmental disorders and brain injury sustained in adulthood need to be drawn with caution. Disorders with a late onset follow a period of normal development. There is no such period in the case of an abnormality which exists from birth. The consequences will necessarily be different. A child who is born with a slow developing or malfunctioning brain mechanism will find it hard to learn about certain aspects of the world, but will learn nevertheless. This would also happen to a child born blind, for example. Such a child develops compensating ways of learning about the world. Compared with an adult who becomes blind in later life, the congenitally blind child may actually have a more secure grasp of space through the habitual use of other senses. The skills of many autistic children compared to adults who suffered brain damage through accidents might be attributed to such compensation. More often than not individuals with autism show a steady increase in learning and social adaptation throughout life. This suggests that they have found a way to bypass the original problem. Hugh Blair himself showed many skills and improved adaptation in later life.

To explain the enigma of autism it is necessary to be guided by a theory. A cognitive theory is a particularly useful guide, because it makes links to behaviour as well as to brain function. Below we shall look briefly at a small number of cognitive theories. Their selection is undoubtedly biased by being associated with Uta Frith's own work. However, these theories have proved fruitful in generating new evidence.

On a technical note, the selected theories have one basic assumption in common, namely that developmental disorders can be caused by subtle faults in mental mechanisms. Vulnerable mechanisms are those involved in speech, language and social communication. The mechanisms in question are geared to process potentially complex information – much as enzymes are geared to digest food. These mechanisms have a role throughout life in processing the information they are meant to process. However, in development, they have a particularly important role: They act as start-up devices to allow ultra-fast learning in particular domains. For example, normal language acquisition shows a fast learning curve. It starts early and rises steeply. If the start-up mechanism fails, language learning will not be totally abolished, but it will be slow and effortful, and the result may be a developmental language disorder.

Not all developmental disorders can be explained as the result of a fault in a start-up mechanism that is geared towards a particular type of information. Children with Down's syndrome, for instance, have limited ability to process any type of information. This is what is meant by general as opposed to specific learning disability. In contrast to children with autism, these children are usually well able to engage in ordinary social interaction, as well as can be expected from their general ability level. Why are autistic children so different in this respect? One way to answer this question is to look for a start-up mechanism that facilitates ordinary social interaction. The idea of such a mechanism may be even stranger than the idea of a start-up mechanism for language. Nevertheless, this idea has transformed our understanding of the social impairment in autism.

Concepts Used in Understanding Autism Today

'Mentalizing'

Let us assume that the normal brain is equipped with a start-up mechanism tailor-made for social learning: a 'smart' device that enables human beings to keep track of mental states. Such a device would allow young children to latch on very fast to what people think, believe and feel. This would eventually allow them to build a theory of why people do what they do, in other words, a 'theory of mind'. Let us further assume that in autism this mechanism is not working properly. If the start-up mechanism fails in early development, there can be no kick-start for this type of social learning. Children with autism learn very slowly, if at all, that other people have thoughts and feelings of their own. This is often referred to as a lack of 'theory of mind', or lack of 'mentalizing'. Neither of these labels are very helpful, and it is best to understand the ideas by what they try to explain. As we will see, the ideas are complex, but the tests are simple. The theory has been discussed in scores of papers and books so that a brief summary here will suffice.[24]

The hypothesis of a 'mentalizing' deficit in autism was developed in the 1980s at the MRC Cognitive Development Unit in London. Amongst the researchers working there were John Morton, Uta Frith, Alan Leslie and Simon Baron-Cohen. The theory did not come out of the blue, but was built on imaginative and painstaking research conducted by primate researchers on the one hand and developmental psychologists on the other. This theory was intriguing because it appeared to go to the core of what matters in everyday social interactions and identified a critical point where the interactions of autistic children differ. Briefly, Alan Leslie proposed that normal children possess an innate mechanism that allows them to think about and distinguish things in the real world and things in the mind.[25] He pointed out that the pretend play so beloved by young children should in fact be highly confusing and lead to incorrect learning. However, children do not confuse their ideas about the physical world with their ideas about the world inside their own and other people's heads. If young children with autism do not understand nor indulge in pretend play, perhaps their brains lack that crucial mechanism to distinguish things in the world and things in the mind? In this case, autistic children should be baffled by the notion that you can know something I don't know or that one can have a mistaken or a false belief. This prediction turned out to be correct. It was first tested by Simon Baron-Cohen with the 'Sally–Ann task'.[26]

In this experiment the following scenario is enacted with two dolls: Sally has a box and Anne has a basket. Sally puts a marble into her box. Then she goes out for a walk. While she is outside, naughty Anne takes the marble from the box and puts it into her own basket. Now Sally comes back from her walk and wants to play with her marble. Where will she look for the marble first? Where does she think the marble is? The answer that seems obvious to a four-year-old child is: Sally will look inside her box. This is where Sally must think the marble is. It is really in Anne's basket, but Sally doesn't know this. She was not there when Anne transferred the marble. She has a false belief. Children with autism, but not children with Down's syndrome, had difficulty with this task. They said that Sally would look in Anne's basket.

The important part about this simple first experiment is that it shows that there is a difference between belief and reality, and that in human behaviour the belief trumps reality. Normally developing children need several years to learn to understand the relationship between belief and

Plate 25: Scenario for the Sally–Ann test. The procedure is described in the text (pp. 122) and tests children's understanding of a false belief. The child is asked where Sally will look for her marble after it has been moved without her knowledge. The correct answer is where Sally wrongly thinks her marble is, not where it really is.

behaviour fully and explicitly. They take their cue from people's expressions. They automatically follow another person's gaze. It is as if they realize that they will learn something of interest by sharing in other people's attention. Even at a tender age they begin to learn to manipulate beliefs, for example in typical hide and seek games. By contrast, children with autism have great difficulties in learning the tricks of hide and seek. It is as if they were unaware of what goes on in other people's minds – as if they were 'mind-blind'. Therefore, they do not intuitively comprehend beliefs as different from facts and as more important than facts in predicting people's actions.

You can make someone else believe that a fact is not true, but not if you are 'mind-blind'. Children with autism find it hard to understand that people deceive each other, and that sometimes a 'white lie' is the best option. They find it hard to remember that people who were not present when something important happened need to be told about it. It makes little sense to them that people engage in elaborate pretend games for the sheer fun of it and enjoy teasing each other. It is not the case that autistic children will never learn about the importance of mental states. Many do, although their slowly acquired mind-reading skills remain fragile. Lacking the start-up mechanism, their learning will necessarily be slow.

There are many cues to reading other people's minds which can be picked up for fast-track learning. For instance, children are irresistibly drawn to follow another person's gaze. Both speech and eye gaze are powerful cues for indicating that communication is imminent. Consider calling a child by name. This has little effect on young children with autism and is one of the main reasons that they are frequently thought to be deaf. Learning about the world is easy for children who have the mentalizing mechanism in place. They naturally orient to speech and track precisely what the speaker is attending to. Without this innate tendency, socialization, language acquisition and all that depends on it, will be a formidable task.

Research extending the mind-blindness hypothesis into the realms of language and social attention, in particular work by Francesca Happé in London, and by Simon Baron-Cohen in Cambridge, has been extremely fruitful. It has laid the basis for tests that are suitable for diagnosis and, importantly, that can be used in conjunction with brain scanning techniques. Brain imaging work on mentalizing ability is still in its infancy, but the results indicate that there is indeed a purpose-built neural system that is active specifically during mentalizing.[27] Two of the three black spots indicating anatomical differences in Plate 24 relate to some of the key components of this system.

The court papers in the Hugh Blair case contain many examples that would fit with the idea that Hugh was unaware of other people's thoughts and feelings while being quite sociable at the same time. For instance, he was given to visiting neighbours at inappropriate times. He was apt to 'borrow' their clothes. He gave gifts that were unwanted. Quite likely the neighbours gave hints that he was unwelcome on some of these occasions. Not everyone was polite. Hugh had some cruel experiences with servants and children but was unable to tell that they mocked him.

Sensations, feelings and emotional experience in autism are still relatively unexplored. Importantly, research by Marian Sigman and her colleagues at University of California at Los Angeles (UCLA) has shown that autistic individuals have the capacity to form affectionate attachments. On the other hand, this research also showed that they have some form of emotional impairment that makes social relationships difficult to maintain.[28] Mind-blindness goes some way towards explaining this emotional impairment. The awareness of feelings, one's own and others', is intricately bound up with the ability to mentalize. It is this awareness which also allows us to share the stream of inner experience with intimate friends. Given a malfunctioning mentalizing mechanism, relationships would necessarily be limited. Certain kinds of emotions would be unfathomable. What others think and feel about us can make us feel embarrassed, proud, or resentful – feelings that we would not experience if we did not monitor other people's mental states. Furthermore, understanding false beliefs is of the essence because humans act on their beliefs, and misunderstanding has disastrous effects on social relations. This is how jealousy is created, how paranoia thrives, but also how trust and confidence are built. This is not only the stuff of high drama but also the lifeblood of everyday social interactions. A difficulty in mentalizing would clearly limit the depth and quality of long-term relationships.

There may be other limitations too. If the propensity to monitor one's own inner states in context is weak, then feelings and sensations might be experienced differently. They might be experienced as 'too much' or 'too little', as 'black' or 'white', while normally the quality of sensations is moderated by their context. In line with this idea, autobiographical accounts of individuals with autism tell of strangely different experiences of temperature, touch, sound, light and pain. In Hugh's case too there are indications of indifference to cold and discomfort, as was evident for instance in his grim sleeping arrangements.

There is no doubt that people with autism have strong feelings and can show genuine affection and emotion. Though still a matter of debate, there are hints that the basic emotions are not impaired. In a study by James Blair at University College London (UCL) in which physiological responses were recorded while children watched emotionally laden stimuli, children with autism showed generally reduced arousal. Yet, their responses to the different emotions were just as differentiated as those of comparison children.[29]

As Hugh got older, he may well have become more aware of the feelings that others showed towards him. He intervened when his brother John was violent to their mother. The film *Rainman* illustrated what those who are in daily contact with autism have long realized, that it is possible to form emotional relationships with an autistic individual. Moreover, such relationships are not entirely one-sided. A return of affection is also possible, despite lack of social insight. Sumner Hart became a comforting companion for his aged mother. In the case of Hugh Blair his relationship with his mother and wife may have been quite affectionate, as attested by some of the witnesses. Admittedly, they were speaking for the defence, and hence would have been likely to stress Hugh's normality.

Executive functions

Much space in the preceding section has been devoted to the idea that a deficit in mentalizing may underlie the social and emotional impairments in autism. Yet it is important to stress that this theory does not explain everything. Autism has some characteristic features which have little to do with social insight. These include odd, and often obsessively pursued, interests; insistence on sameness; and occasional special talents. Some of these features are very evident in the descriptions of Hugh Blair's behaviour, for instance his prodigious memory. Two cognitive theories currently address these still poorly understood aspects of autism.

The first theory builds on parallels with patients who have suffered frontal lobe brain injury. Indeed a range of tests that are difficult for such patients are also difficult for individuals with autism.[30] The hallmark of the difficulties that are apparent in these tests and in everyday life is a lack of foresight and flexibility. They concern executive control of actions and therefore have far-reaching consequences. Admittedly, a great many aspects of our daily life are routine, but executive style decisions have to be made to guide novel actions. The distinction between routine actions and executive decisions has proved important in explaining lack of planning and flexibility as seen in patients with damage to the frontal lobes of the brain.[31] Tests for children have been developed, for instance the Day–Night test, where prepotent responses have to be reversed (see Plate 26).[32] If the executive functions are affected, then routine actions persist, along with actions elicited by exter-

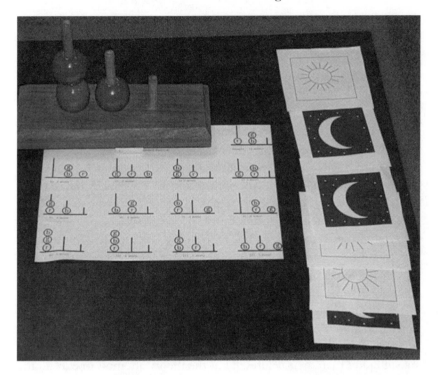

Plate 26: Examples of materials used to assess executive functions. The Tower of London test (shown on the left, by kind permission of Professor Tim Shallice) requires planning, since the coloured balls have to be moved one at a time, in a minimum number of moves, from a given starting state to a given end state (as shown on the card). On the right are shown a series of sun and moon pictures where children are asked to say 'Day' for the moon and 'Night' for the sun. Children understand this instruction, but the tendency to revert to the normal use of the label, when going through a long series, is very strong.

nal stimuli. This describes quite well a range of behaviours observed in people with autism: they keep to the same routine obsessively, they become abnormally attached to a particular object, they are unable to initiate novel activities and certain stimuli invariably tend to trigger certain actions. Examples in Hugh Blair's case include his habit of carrying stones from pile to pile, his attachment to a blue livery coat, and his repetitious answers to questions.

Central coherence

The second theory builds on the observation that there is a particular style of information processing which is prevalent in autism and is labelled weak central coherence. Some of its essence can be likened to the popular stereotype of 'trainspotting'. Of course this stereotype has nothing to do with real life train enthusiasts. The mythical 'trainspotter' is a person obsessed with collecting assorted facts in a narrow field, where these facts are odd features such as numbers, colours, shape details and statistics of train paraphernalia. In fact few people with autism are obsessively interested in trains, but they tend to be interested in odd things. Just as the stereotypical 'trainspotter' is interested in the numbers of railway engines and in the livery of carriages, so some people with autism are interested in the numbers found on lampposts or in the colour of the door of juvenile courts. By analogy, weak central coherence is a style that is characterized by preferential attention to unusual parts rather than the more usual wholes – that is, the juvenile court rather than the colour of its door.

As argued by Francesca Happé, the theory of weak central coherence as a feature of autism attempts to explain the successes of people with autism rather than their failures. Thus the theory attempts to explain the characteristic pattern of intelligence test performance with good construction skills for jigsaw puzzle type material. One key observation in the development of the theory was that children with autism were particularly good at remembering unconnected things without much influence from overall context and were apparently less likely to succumb to visual illusions which are caused by context effects, such as the Titchener illusion shown in Plate 27.[33] A related ability is copying without comprehending the meaning of the text. Another key observation is that a child with autism may pay attention to a shiny piece of metal or a pebble which other children would dismiss as uninteresting, and notice a tiny adjustment to the position of an ornament. An advantage of this style of processing is the ability to find details in hidden figures, and to construct mosaic patterns from designs which others do not immediately see in terms of their constituent pieces.[34] These phenomena suggest a preference for processing information piecemeal.

The opposite style, strong central coherence, would, by contrast, imply a preference for processing information as a whole in context. Both styles have their advantages and disadvantages. Individuals with strong

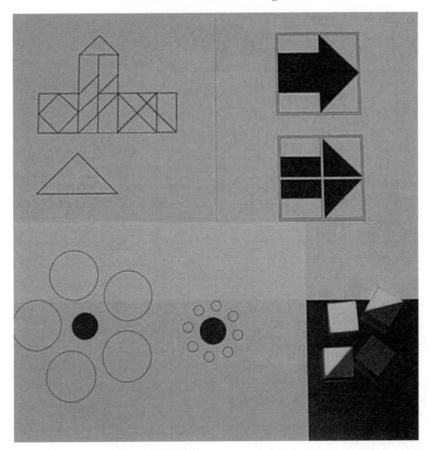

Plate 27: Examples of tasks used to test weak central coherence. Finding hidden figures is an islet of ability in autism. In the example (upper left) the task is to find the triangle in the criss-cross design above it. The Titchener illusion, shown on the lower left, normally evokes the illusion that the dark circle surrounded by big circles is smaller than the one surrounded by small circles. In fact they are the same size. People with autism are less susceptible to illusions of this type. On the right are shown examples of materials for a block design task where a design has to be constructed with little blocks. This is normally facilitated when the design is shown in segmented form (lower example) which presumably helps the identification of the embedded parts within the whole. People with autism excel at copying the unsegmented designs and derive little benefit from segmentation.

129

coherence would be good at grasping the gist of a long and rambling story, but risk losing the details of what is said. On the other hand, individuals with weak coherence would be good at remembering the story verbatim, but may miss the point of the story. This may help to explain why a child with autism may fail to understand the purpose of a message, while being able to repeat it correctly. Echoing speech parrot fashion is a common and early diagnostic sign of autism. Hugh Blair's ability to recite the catechism without understanding is an illustration of this type of rote memory. His tendency to choose unsuitable materials for mending clothes, ending up with gaudy patches, is an example of single-minded attention to detail while losing sight of the appearance of the garment as a whole. People with autism frequently fail to throw rubbish away, just as Hugh Blair accumulated feathers and sticks. They often follow exceedingly narrow interests with obsessive regularity. Hugh Blair's attendance at every parish burial is a good example of this.

The mentalizing, executive function and central coherence theories of autism all concern high level cognitive functions. Taken together they can explain quite well why autistic people have difficulty leading a normal life, even if they have high ability. In the future it may be possible to integrate these theories or replace them with a new theory capable of explaining both poor social communication and the characteristic non-social assets and deficits of autism.

The Historical Dimension

How valid are modern theories of autism for other historical contexts? Scientific explanations of autism are becoming increasingly robust and aspire to universality. The case of Hugh Blair may indicate to what extent this aspiration is justified. Similarities and differences across cultural divides can help us to distil the essence of the disorder. This is not to say that culture will not dramatically influence the course of a disorder and determine the cost of the handicap. One can imagine a society where a child with autism would not be nurtured and would have only a slim chance of survival. By contrast, other societies, such as in medieval Russia, have assiduously protected those autistic people they revered as sages.

While twentieth century accounts of autism are plentiful, some are also biased and have a particular axe to grind. In any event, they are inextricably confounded by present-day social values. A chance to make inferences from a historical account is rare. Itard's book about the wild boy of Aveyron provided one such well-documented case. The trial of Hugh Blair provides another of these exceptional opportunities.

Chapter 5

Reading the Court Case as a Clinical Case

In the judgement of Hugh Blair's contemporaries he was 'void of under-standing', 'void of common sense', and 'void of reason such as ordinary people have'. He was called the 'daft lad of Borgue'. Can we improve on this general evaluation using scientific procedures?

The Method

In the previous chapter, we related current theories of autism to informa-tion about Hugh's condition. In this chapter we do the opposite. We relate the given information about Hugh Blair's mental capacity to present-day clinical knowledge about autism. This will result in the kind of re-port used in contemporary practice where evidence from various sources is collated with a view to a diagnosis. Autism is our hypothesis to explain Hugh Blair's mental incapacity, but it is not a foregone conclusion. Here the hypothesis will be put to the test by examining all the available evi-dence, not merely pieces of evidence selected to fit such a diagnosis. Other diagnoses will be considered as well. Hugh's hearing and speech problems and his apparently weak intelligence are consistent with the diagnosis of autism, but they also raise possible alternative causes of his condition.

The Data

The various events and actions described have been analysed in the preceding chapters from a historical point of view. Now we evaluate their clinical meaning. The data for this chapter are the statements which sprang from the spontaneous reports of the witnesses and from their answers to specific questions. The statements which form the bulk of the data are listed at the end of this chapter. Many of the observations and opinions were repeated by different witnesses, but they are only listed once in their most concise form. They encompass a great many aspects of Hugh Blair's daily life, work and leisure. Most statements are about behaviour that the deponents considered unusual, but some examples of perfectly normal and even admirable behaviour were given as well.

How reliable is the evidence as the basis for a clinical assessment? In chapter 1 we have already considered the trustworthiness of the court papers that represent our data. It is understood that standard psychological tests and interviews were not available. Nevertheless, the nature of the evidence in this case is exceptionally detailed and consistent. The sources of the information are varied and to some extent independent. The informants included a variety of people of different social rank and professions. To document this variety, the witnesses and their relationship to the Blair family are listed at the end of this chapter. For the clinical evaluation of the case their statements are treated equally with no preference for any particular source.

All the deponents gave actual examples of behaviour. This is still the preferred technique for eliciting information in a diagnostic interview. While opinions were important, the court also attempted to get to the facts behind the opinions. Since half the witnesses appeared on behalf of the 'pursuer' and half on behalf of the 'defender', one might expect some blatantly contradictory statements. This was not the case. There is every reason to assume that the deponents played by the same rules of truthfulness in front of the court as people generally do today. There were, after all, dozens of people of varied backgrounds who had known Hugh Blair personally at different times of his life, in different capacities over various lengths of time. All appealed to the weight of opinion of the hundreds of local people who had some acquaintance with Hugh.

We do not have to rely only on witnesses' statements. Data exist from

133

an interrogation of Hugh by the Commissaries, dated 16 July 1747. The transcript is presented in chapter 3. It shows that this interrogation quite well approximates a psychological assessment of the ability to use language and to understand basic concepts.

There is little we can do about missing data and we are left with some uncertainties which only a series of tests in a modern laboratory could clarify. For instance, to what extent was Hugh's hearing impaired? How intelligible was his speech? The historical evidence discussed in chapter 2 suggests that any deafness was not the primary problem. The interrogation plainly showed that written communication failed just as much as spoken communication. It is therefore possible that Hugh was only thought to be deaf because his comprehension was so very poor. Although witnesses claimed that Hugh Blair was foolish from birth, there was no detailed enquiry about his childhood. The recent behaviour of Hugh as an adult was far more significant to the court. The relevance of knowing about his childhood and youth was merely to establish the long-standing nature of his behaviour and thus to assess his chances of improvement. Further, we have no direct knowledge of the feelings of the immediate family, excluded as they were by material interest from giving evidence in court.

Evidence contained in the deposition is derived from more or less standardized interviews. The interrogation itself was semi-standardized. Together the accounts are compelling. They add up to a picture that is as consistent and as factual as that provided by any modern published case study. For this reason the evidence about Hugh Blair's characteristics can be presented in the manner of a clinical case report.

Notes for a Case Report on Hugh Blair

Date of birth: 1708 or 1709
Date of assessment: 16 July 1747

Appearance and behaviour

Hugh Blair was likely to have been of physically normal appearance, even handsome. Not one deponent mentions the physical stigmata which often accompany mental disability. This is indicated in even the most deprecatory statement by the pursuer's advocate – 'except with respect to his figure, he differed very little from the brute creation'. We can assume that for his appearance in court, Hugh's mother and the wife she had chosen for him made sure he was well turned out. From the recent statements of the servants at the new lodgings, it can be inferred that Hugh shaved himself like any gentleman, and wore a ruffled shirt which he changed to a plain one when at home.

Yet while he lived at Borgue, up to his late thirties, things must have been different. Most of the time he must have looked a sight, wearing singularly odd clothing. Sometimes he wore a cast-off livery coat that he adored ('bonny coat'); at other times he wore old clothes mended with a patchwork of non-matching colours and materials. His attire was described as mean, dirty and infested. He was shunned as ill-smelling. Taken together, the statements suggest that when living at his family home Hugh did not dress appropriately for his station, except when attending church. He often disregarded the custom of wearing a wig, or put the wig on back to front, rendering him a laughing stock.

Clothes act as signals and symbols in social life. Hugh was probably not aware of their significance. His lack of awareness was a greater handicap in a society where social status went hand in hand with a number of obligations, and where dress codes were followed strictly. It is unlikely that Hugh deliberately disobeyed the dress code; none of the depositions implicates contrariness or rebelliousness. Furthermore, he did dress up for church, so important a requirement of social conduct that Hugh was probably forced into it. We can surmise that he managed to build it into his own routines. That he wore clothes discarded by others and badly patched up by himself must have been tolerated by his family for many years.

Some indirect information gives us a glimpse of Hugh's demeanour. From the accounts of his lack of resentment at having pranks played on him by others, nothing contradicts the assumption that he was a gentle and even-tempered man. One or two witnesses reported that he could fly into a passion (when a servant pretended to kiss him, and when another servant denied him a horse), but he was also said not to bear a grudge 'for more than half an hour'.

In view of the autism hypothesis it would be valuable to have an indication of whether Hugh showed odd motor movements. Indeed he was reported to gaze at his hands and play with them 'like a fool'. This scant remark is tantalizing as stereotypical hand flapping is a characteristic sign of autism.

Preliminary conclusions   A lack of mention of gross physical stigmata suggests that Hugh had none. When younger, Hugh often wore ragged clothes, and was shunned by others because of his lack of hygiene. However, this all changed after he was married. Dressed up in clean clothes he might have looked handsome. His lack of concern about maintaining the right appearance with wigs and hats suggests a lack of insight into his station in life and an unawareness of other people's views about his status. These observations and inferences are consistent with autism.

Home life

In the eyes of the servants, Hugh's behaviour did not fit at all into the pattern expected from their masters. Hugh made no effort to take part in normal family life. Unlike other members of the family, he often ate by himself and ignored calls to meals. When, on occasion, he joined the others, he felt free to leave the table before it was proper, without taking notice of the final grace said at table. He seemed to prefer to eat alone in the kitchen, amongst pets that he allowed to lick his spoon and bowl. The servants mentioned this behaviour with disgust. Altogether, Hugh's disregard for manners was consistent with his apparent ignorance of the appropriate appearance and behaviour of a gentleman.

Hugh's sleeping arrangements were also unusual. When living at Borgue, Hugh slept in a cold garret room next to the servants' quarters. His bed was mean, ill-made, and infested. It was nailed up with wooden planks, had some straw and blankets, but no chaff or feathers. He slept at times without sheets. Since the witnesses explicitly mention all of this, we can assume that it was unusual for a young man of his station. The servants claimed that he did not let them make his bed, and that he locked his room. Possible family negligence has to be considered. On the other hand they saw to it that from time to time Hugh's bedding was boiled. We can imagine that, like other people with autism who crave sameness, he would have resisted any major upheaval. Perhaps the upheaval created by cleaning out his garret precipitated the crisis which split the family. Perhaps this was when his brother John and his sister-in-law Helen knew they could no longer tolerate Hugh in the house.

After he left Borgue, when already in his late thirties, less information is available about Hugh's home life. Some odd behaviour was still noted, such as helping servants out with menial jobs. However, the accounts suggest that Hugh's daily life, especially hygiene and dress, had become less eccentric.

Preliminary conclusions   Hugh's indifference to social conventions at home is typical of autism. The indifference cannot be construed as rebellious-ness, but rather as an inability to appreciate the social relationships within the household. The picture painted so graphically by Hugh's eating and sleeping habits indicates a disregard not only for convention but also for comfort. Such disregard has been remarked upon in present-day cases of autism.

Occupations

Hugh's mother had asked the servants to find occupations for him 'as long as they were not oppressive'. His work was not considered particu-larly useful, and may even have meant added responsibility for the serv-ants who had to mind him. In any case, as we learn from the historical analysis, such work would have been considered highly inappropriate for a gentleman of Hugh's standing. Members of the gentry went horse rid-ing, shooting and fishing in their spare time.

Hugh did menial work and some particularly dirty jobs were singled out by the witnesses. He mucked out stables, even on the Sabbath and wearing his best clothes. A servant could stop him only with great diffi-culty. Hugh was also reported to have done other distasteful jobs, such as raking dirt, fetching peat and water and taking out slops in the morning. The last in particular was odd since he did it even when he was observed by visitors to the house. From the witnesses' remarks we can infer that they considered Hugh to have a singular lack of embarrassment. They might have added a lack of discernment which he showed in bringing home dried cow dung for fuel 'like the poorest people'. It was never used in a household like his.

Outdoor activities appealed to Hugh. He was seen 'delving in the fields among the clay and dirt by himself for his own diversion'. More than one witness said that Hugh tried flailing with unsuitable sticks (ash wands). Sometimes he pulled wool off sheepskins and threw it away. In the opinion of one witness Hugh 'never did any pieces of working to any purpose'. Yet he was commended by some witnesses on his stacking of sheaves.

It is unlikely that the Blair family would have forced Hugh into drudgery, either as a punishment or as a way of distancing themselves from him. Perhaps they considered it a kind of occupational therapy, or perhaps they condoned what they could not prevent Hugh from doing. From the examples it is clear that they allowed him space for his chosen activities with freedom to roam about. Hugh's family also sent him to school, where he learned to read and write. It is possible that reading and writing were activities that gave Hugh pleasure and allowed him to excel.

Hugh mended his clothes and shoes – clumsily and without regard for materials. Scandalously, he cut a prized swan skin blanket of his mother's to mend his clothes. Apart from the undesirable outcome, mending was an odd activity for a gentleman in a house where a tailor worked. Similarly, it was peculiar that he helped a weaver who came to the house: he 'handled in the threads, and turned the beam on occasion at his mother's desire'. After his marriage, a servant reported that he helped her with her spinning: giving her a new rowan [roll] of wool, and warming it at the fire. Once he tried to put a new latch on the kitchen door.

Hugh worked on sticks of wood, making them into what he called 'spintles'. Perhaps they were in some way related to spindles used in spinning or weaving, and perhaps they had some special meaning for him. Hugh gave such spintles as gifts to others. One wonders how politely they responded, and what they did with their unwanted gifts. However, it is likely that the needs or opinions of others were of little concern to Hugh.

Preliminary conclusions   Hugh had a wide range of occupations in and out of the house, which demonstrate that he had diverse skills. These were not of much practical use but included manual work as well as reading and writing. Hugh's interest in artisan work was mentioned by the witnesses because it was considered unsuited to his station and confirmed his lack of sensitivity to the general social order. Hugh's occupations suggest a liking for repetitive work with attention to detail rather than purpose. This tendency is characteristic of people with autism.

The pursuit of strange interests

Hugh's garret was filled with odd bits and pieces, feathers and sticks. These piles included purloined materials, which further suggests the obsessive nature of his urge to collect. Some of the objects he hoarded were sticks and bits of wood or furniture. He locked his door presumably because he had good reason to protect his collections from being disturbed or even thrown out.

One of Hugh's odd activities was building stone walls where none were needed. He built such walls in an unusual way. One witness describes how Hugh went to a quarry at night to throw stones out of it, then made a heap of stones, then carried them to make another pile until he had brought them to the chosen site. As mentioned in chapters 2 and 3, in the early part of the eighteenth century dry stone walls, or dykes, were built all over Galloway, a consequence of enclosures. Even today they can still be seen criss-crossing the landscape. However, Hugh's constructions were quite separate from this effort, and normally stones for walls were moved in carts or sledges by labourers.

Perhaps the strangest of Hugh's obsessions was his interest in funerals. Many witnesses commented on this pastime, stressing that he appeared uninvited and without wearing mourning. Hugh went to most parish burials and helped carry the dead. Is this evidence of a fascination with death? Perhaps. An interest in morbid themes is not uncommon in present-day accounts of special interests in autism. A young boy with such an interest was reported to have been thrilled by two deaths in the family which gave him the opportunity to attend two funerals in one year.

Some of the behaviour reported hints at a fascination with dripping water. Hugh frequently went out in the rain, filling a jar with water that was running from the roof. He was said to gaze for a long time at the running rainwater even after the jar was full. Consider also how Hugh washed his wig frequently and hung it up for drying on a tree. Was he watching the drips? One witness speaks of Hugh's interest in the preparation of sheep skins and his desolation at having missed seeing them being washed. It is possible, of course, to read too much in these scant observations, but absorbing interest in drops of water or grains of sand is also mentioned in some modern cases of autism.

We hear that Hugh Blair had the habit of claiming the same place at the head of the family pew even when this meant displacing someone else. This behaviour may be an example of insistence on sameness, one of the features of autism that Kanner emphasized. In line with this idea is that Hugh was very careful to 'set everything right that was any way out of order in the house'.

Preliminary conclusions   One of the most characteristic features of autism is the presence of special interests, which are unusually narrow, and border on obsessions. They often include collecting and hoarding unusual objects. Much of Hugh's work and leisure activities revolved around such interests.

Special talents

It was generally agreed that Hugh Blair was good at reading and accurate at writing. This stood in contrast to his evidently poor understanding of what he read, and his inability to 'compose' writing, coupled with his excellent copying ability. Such a form of literacy is sometimes referred to as hyperlexia and is found quite frequently in autism. It made little difference to Hugh whether he read from the Bible or some odd piece of print: in one curious incident he read out an industrial advertisement[1] for no purpose except that it was there. This incident was in fact related by a witness for the defence to demonstrate that Hugh could read. In addition to reading, Hugh was often seen to copy out the Lord's Prayer; he copied text very exactly, but to no particular purpose. A present-day example of copying – in this case from memory and using a word processor – to no particular purpose is shown in Plate 28.

According to his former schoolmaster, John Gordon, Hugh's memory was better than his own. Hugh had an excellent rote memory for the catechism. By coincidence, Kanner's first and defining case of autism, Donald T., was a child who could recite the 25 questions and answers of the Presbyterian catechism, but had otherwise little ability to communicate.

It remains a mystery how Hugh knew the time of the funerals which he attended, whether invited or not. Perhaps they were announced at church. If so, Hugh must have had more acute perception of speech than he was credited with. This does not mean that the deponents underestimated his ability; rather that Hugh's special interest mobilized attention, which would not be apparent in other situations. Alternatively, it is possible that, like some people with autism, Hugh had excellent knowledge of the calendar, allowing him to derive the day of the week from a given date and vice versa. This could have allowed him to work out by himself when to turn up at a funeral. In most cases, calendar savants are entirely self-taught and their skill may remain unnoticed by others.

Severn Valley Railway

The Severn Valley Railway was one of the first railways to be preserved by enthusiasts, and now boasts sixteen and a quarter miles of skilfully restored railway, offering the visitor a great variety of railway interest. We begin our visit with a classic scene of locomotive 6960 Raveningham Hall, 4-6-0 built in 1944 departing Bridgnorth. Bridgnorth is the northern terminus which houses the locomotive maintenance and running shed. At Hampton Loade 2968, an ex-LMS 2-6-0 built in 1933, drifts past Raveningham Hall. Later we again see 2968 calling at the beautifully preserved Highley Station. Arley, another award winning station plays host to locomotive No 7819 Hinton Manor built in 1939. In the busy summer season, trains often pass at Bewdley. Kidderminster Town Station, adjacement to the British Rail station is the southern terminus of the railway with an impressive building and passenger facility. This new platform was added in 1990. Locomotive No 2968 runs round its train in preparation for its departure to Bridgnorth.

Plate 28: Text typed from memory by a young man with autism. Copying text and faithfully producing text from memory can be a special talent in cases of autism. While Hugh Blair used a quill pen, his modern equivalent is likely to use a word processor. Oliver will often read a book, pamphlet or manual, typically about trains, and memorize the words of a paragraph. He will then type the text entirely from memory and print it out, as in this example.
By kind permission of Oliver Street and his parents and with thanks to Pilar Martin.

On several occasions witness statements implied that Hugh Blair had little sensitivity to temperature. He went out in the rain without a hat; he continued to sleep in his garret when the servants refused to stay there because it was too cold. He stayed on in a quarry after others left on account of the cold. People with autism often show signs of insensitivity to temperature and even to pain. In a present-day case, a boy broke a bone while sledding, but said nothing to anybody about pain. Later his parents noticed one limp arm.

Preliminary conclusions   Special talents, such as prodigious memory, and hyperlexia are not uncommon in autism. Hugh had such talents. Hugh also showed some sensory and perceptual peculiarities that do not currently form part of the essential criteria for autism, yet bear a striking resemblance to modern case reports. In addition, some of Hugh's behaviour already described is suggestive of a narrow preoccupation with unusual things. These diverse behavioural signs may be explained as a result of a cognitive style typical in autism which favours attention to surface detail at the cost of overall meaning.

Social relations

From many examples, Hugh Blair comes across as a gregarious individual. Only some of his pastimes were of the solitary kind, more so in his earlier life when he preferred eating alone. He sought out social occasions such as funerals; he visited people in their houses. Despite his gregariousness Hugh lacked the social insight to know whether his presence on these occasions was wanted. Hugh did not seem to realize that his visits to neighbours at all times of day or night were inappropriate. He also did not seem to be aware of his own status in relation to the servants and to other members of the community. While he knew about social customs, such as wearing a hat and a wig, he did not necessarily follow these customs. He knew how to bow and take off his hat, but he had to watch others for clues and depended on signs from his mother. He wore the correct clothes to church, yet he sometimes wore the same clothes for stable work.

Some of the most impressive evidence of socialization is contained in Hugh's observance of religious rites. Religion had a central place in the everyday life of the community. While Hugh was an outsider as regards most of his family's activities, he was certainly included in their religious life. He regularly attended and 'behaved decently in church'. He claimed the seat at the head of the family pew. When at home Hugh's observance of family worship was less strictly enforced. He did not always join in when prayers were said at home. Sometimes he paced up and down and 'trifled' with candlesticks, or left before prayers were finished. The witnesses were uncertain whether he spontaneously asked for a blessing. He could recite the Lord's Prayer, however.

Hugh Blair appears to have been gentle and good-natured. Acts of helpfulness towards his mother, his wife and servants were mentioned. At the same time the examples of helping his mother and his wife to get dressed, helping with weaving and spinning, and trying to mend a door latch, all strike an odd note. They are unlikely things to be done by a gentleman in a household run by servants. In fact, Hugh was biddable by anyone including servants and schoolboys. He was often a source of crude amusement for others who provoked him into bad behaviour. Even in later years he was laughed at for sitting next to a common 'apple wife'. It is extremely doubtful that the apple wife would have welcomed him as a friend. All this reveals a lack of social discrimination rather than social aloofness.

Another sign of Hugh's lack of social insight are the various references to his occasional stealing. He took clothes that did not belong to him from his own or neighbours' houses. He took away others' good shoes and prized pieces of material and cut them to pieces to mend his own things. All this suggests that he had an inadequate understanding of personal property, difficult for others to understand. More importantly, he did not conceal his thefts. The art of concealment is dependent on being able to understand that the contents of the mind of one person are different from those of another. Poor understanding of deception and lying has been experimentally demonstrated in autism.[2] This trait is one of the many engaging signs of natural innocence in autism. During normal development this natural innocence seems to be lost when children acquire a full-fledged theory of mind. Hugh's lack of deception and embarrassment at nudity are signs of the innocence that attends extreme social naivety.

It follows that Hugh would have been incapable of dishonesty. Therefore, it was fitting that the publican served drinks to Hugh without worrying about repayment. We can presume that his mother would have seen to it that local tradesmen were paid, and that clothes were returned to their proper owners. Examples of contrary evidence would have been statements that Hugh hid the things he stole, that he misled others deliberately, told lies about people, or played tricks on people. No such examples are in the records of the Blair trial. Hugh's innocence contrasts with the frequent examples of delusions, trickery and cunning given in the cases of some of the madmen in Rab Houston's study.[3]

Preliminary conclusions   Hugh Blair did not conform to the image of the aloof and withdrawn individual as described by Kanner. He took part in many social activities and knew the rudiments of customary behaviour. However, he did not understand his social position in relation to others. His poor social insight is revealed in many examples. After his marriage Hugh appears to have retained his social naivety, but expanded his limited set of social rules. He became more amenable to normal standards of hygiene and clothing. The distinctive feature of Hugh's social interactions is the same as that seen today in people with autistic disorder. He lacked the intuitive awareness of mental states necessary either to deceive or impress.

Speech, language and communication

'Though deafish hears when loud spoke to and can speak though not quite so distinct as other people': so one deponent described Hugh. Hugh's speech may have been indistinct, but the main characteristic of his reported speech is that it consisted of repeated one- or two-word utterances. He talked of himself in the third person and did not use pronouns. He was in the habit of repeating simple phrases.

Examples of speech echoing are especially significant since echoing is a well-documented and characteristic feature of autism. Hugh insisted on repeating the questions of the catechism when asked, rather than giving only the answers as anyone else would. The court interrogation gives some direct evidence of Hugh's peculiar use of language. Hugh usually answered the questions of the court with a single word. More often than not this was a repetition of the last word of the question, an example of speech echoing. This evidence also suggests that he could hear what was said.

At the interrogation, Hugh was given Bible sections to read as a reading test. He passed. In fact Hugh could write and read aloud from the Bible from at least the age of 14 years. It used to be rare for deaf children without the benefit of specialist education to learn to read. Likewise it would be difficult for children with specific speech and language problems (as opposed to autism) to learn to read as well as Hugh did. On the other hand, good reading skill is commonly found in cases of autism.

According to one witness, Hugh 'never connected an entire proposition together with its verb and person'. Concrete examples show that Hugh gave stereotyped or nonsensical responses to questions. For instance, he said 'yes' every time when asked whether he was going to marry a certain person, regardless of which name was mentioned. Other examples indicate perseveration (being fixed in a response set): Hugh kept saying 'five' and 'dyke' to several questions when different answers were required. Apparently his speech problems were not compensated for by enhanced use of gesture and facial expression. Hugh was reported never to initiate a conversation. Furthermore, he never 'gave any reasonable answer even in many attempts to make conversation with him', only 'a foolish smiling stare'. By all evidence, a real conversation with Hugh was impossible.

The most striking example of communication failure is shown in the interrogation. Hugh copied out questions instead of writing down the answer as requested. When he was then requested explicitly not to copy out the question, he copied this request as well! After this demonstration of his inability to comprehend even the most basic assumptions of an interrogation, the court had little doubt as to Hugh's mental incapacity. The meaning of the whole court procedure had obviously eluded him. Hugh's hearing and speech impairments were not to blame.

Hugh's own writing is shown in Plate 15. The handwritten letters are formed very evenly and fluidly. They are a sign of a skilled copyist with excellent fine motor co-ordination. The occasional discrepancies in spelling – Hugh consistently wrote 'Edinbrugh' when the original was 'Edinburgh' – indicate that Hugh copied word by word and not letter by letter. His own spelling knowledge guided his writing.

Preliminary conclusions Hugh's comprehension was extremely limited. His short utterances were highly stereotyped. He showed echoing of speech. A confounding factor in evaluating Hugh's problems is his generally assumed hearing impairment coupled with an articulation impairment. Hugh was literate, yet this accomplishment did not help him to overcome his difficulties. Hugh had the communication and language problems that are typical of autism.

Discussion of the Clinical Evidence for Autism

The extensive information gleaned from the court papers is as rich a source of data as many present-day case studies. Hence it is possible to use present-day criteria to arrive at a diagnosis of Hugh's condition, even though the condition itself was not identified or labelled for another 200 years.

With reference to the three main criteria listed in the current diagnostic manuals[4] the following conclusions can be drawn:

> Hugh Blair showed 'qualitative impairment in social interaction'.
> Hugh Blair had 'severe verbal and non-verbal communication impairments'.
> Hugh Blair demonstrated 'restricted, repetitive and stereotyped patterns of behaviour, interests and activities'.

Since Hugh Blair's condition in early childhood is unknown, no evidence for the criterion of early onset is available. This missing evidence is offset by the assumption of all the witnesses that Hugh Blair was a 'natural' fool, that is, from birth. The importance of the early onset criterion is the need to distinguish progressive conditions, either of known neurological origin, or psychosis of later onset. While an improvement in Hugh's behaviour was mentioned quite frequently, there was never a hint at deterioration.

Could Hugh's condition have been due to a different disorder?

Because a diagnosis made purely on the basis of behaviour is never unequivocal, the diagnostic manuals also list exclusion criteria. They demand that the diagnosis of autism only be used when the symptoms are not attributable to another recognized disorder. The disorders which need to be considered as alternatives to autism include schizophrenia, schizotypal disorder, and obsessive-compulsive disorder of childhood. None of these seem to be appropriate in Hugh's case. For a diagnosis of schizophrenia, some significant and consistent change in overall quality of personal behaviour must have been observed, including acute social withdrawal. The available evidence shows the opposite. Hugh did not so much show social withdrawal as indiscriminate social approach.

For the diagnosis of schizotypal disorder Hugh would have had to manifest at least four of the following: 'inappropriate affect; eccentric behaviour; poor rapport with tendency to withdrawal; odd beliefs; paranoid ideas; excessive and unquestioned ruminations; illusions and depersonalization; stereotyped thinking; delusion-like ideas'.[5] Hugh was not described as cold, aloof or suspicious. On the contrary he seems to have been an exceptionally trusting person. There is no evidence of illusions or delusion-like ideas.

It is unlikely that Hugh suffered from obsessive-compulsive disorder. In most cases, this disorder occurs in individuals with normal personality and intelligence. Obsessions (thoughts, ideas, images) and compulsions (irresistible acts) may have been present, but there is no reason to think that Hugh tried to resist them or was distressed by them. Evidence for such resistance is required for the diagnosis of obsessive-compulsive disorder. As far as we know, Hugh enjoyed indulging his special interests.

Did Hugh have Asperger syndrome? It is unlikely that he would receive a diagnosis of Asperger syndrome, because of his lifelong impairment in both spoken and receptive language. Hugh's utterances were rarely more than two nouns strung together. In Asperger syndrome it is also typical for acute self-awareness and social insight to emerge with increasing age, sometimes accompanied by feelings of depression. The witnesses who knew Hugh Blair for the longest time did not hint in their statements at such increased self-awareness. Hugh seemed to cut a more respectable figure after he was married without an increase in problems. It is likely that he steadily learned more acceptable behaviour.

Did Hugh have a primary hearing disability? At first glance it is conceivable that many of Hugh's difficulties were secondary to precisely such a problem. On closer inspection, his behaviour and lack of communication went far beyond that of a person with a hearing problem. This has also been discussed in chapter 3 where a comparison is made with Hugh's sister, Jean, who was said to be 'both deaf and dumb yet by signs she showed a great deal of sagacity and intelligence'. Is it a strange coincidence that Hugh's sister was deaf and dumb? Could there have been a common cause? We do not know. There are several reasons why deafness cannot have been a major causal factor of Hugh's overall condition. In particular, he showed no compensatory signing of the kind his sister used, and no normal social learning. Neither the deponents, nor the advocates for the defence seriously proposed that Hugh's deafness was the source of his weak understanding. After the interrogation by the court, where both spoken and written language was used, it was clear that one mode of communication was as poorly understood as the other.

A final possibility is that Hugh's disorder was a non-specific learning disability without autism. The evidence suggests that his general intellectual abilities were poor, and it is possible to conclude that his social facility was limited by this general disability. We can surmise, however, that Hugh's performance on various intelligence tests would not have been poor throughout. For instance, he mastered reading and writing, and he had excellent rote memory. We can assume that his spatial skills were not bad. They were at least good enough to wander around without getting lost, and to visit other houses at night, with no difficulties in finding his way home. We can also assume that he had relatively good perceptual and motor skills, as he could ride a horse and do all sorts of odd jobs, including those that demanded fine motor co-ordination, such as handwriting, carving, and sewing. On the other hand, Hugh would probably have performed poorly on language tests. The unevenness of intellectual abilities, and especially Hugh's attested memory capacity, makes a diagnosis of non-specific learning disability inappropriate.

Both autism and non-specific mental retardation are due to brain pathology. One way of contrasting autism and mental retardation is to think of autism as primarily due to a circumscribed cognitive deficit, while mental retardation implies primarily a restricted capacity to process information in general. In the case of general mental retardation, certain dedicated cognitive mechanisms may be intact and working well. Individuals with general mental retardation have been found to be much better at understanding communication and insightful social behaviour than individuals with autism, even though their intellectual ability is lower. True enough, mental retardation is a handicapping condition and limits the life of the affected individual. However, as far as social integration is concerned, autism is even more handicapping. Many of Hugh's unusual behaviours fall into place if seen in the light of a specific deficit in social communication accompanied by a restricted repertoire of interests. This is not to say that Hugh may not have suffered from mental retardation as well. The association of mental retardation and autism is so strong that some three-quarters of people with autism also suffer from some degree of mental retardation.

Finally, we can say that descriptions of mentally incapacitated people in other court cases of the same era differed markedly from the way Hugh was described. Let us take a specific example. David Smith was the son of a deceased Glasgow merchant, cognosced as an idiot before Stirling Sheriff Court in 1715. Two men who had lodged him recently gave evidence in his case. Thomas Adam, aged 48, had known David since he was six years old; David was now 28. He had been 'fatuous and naturally an idiot' for as long as Thomas had known him. David 'was two or three years boarded with the deponent and that ever since he has been his near neighbour . . . that he is so much an idiot that he cannot put on his own clothes nor know east or west'. Andrew Paul in Craigannet had known David since he was four: 'and that all that time he has known him to be fatuous and a natural idiot and could not put on his own clothes and did tear his clothes when on'.[6] In both cases self-care was impossible. In contrast, Hugh could dress himself and help to dress others and was keen to mend his clothes.

There are other differences between Hugh's case and that of other people cognosced as idiotic or 'fatuous'. Crucially, witnesses who were called to endorse the view that a man (rarely a woman) was profoundly stupid tended to focus on the look of their face. They spoke of lack of memory, an absence of awareness of geographical location, an ignorance of the names of father and mother and whether they were alive or dead. Sometimes they likened the person's understanding to that of a child. But, while Hugh sometimes played with children a fraction of his age, nobody ever made that comparison, presumably because he had a number of significant skills not found in a young child.

The Clinical Conclusion

The available evidence is rich enough and unambiguous enough to demonstrate that Hugh Blair would be given an unequivocal diagnosis of autism today. This diagnosis rests not just on the necessary criteria for autism, but also on additional features which are found in many modern cases and appear to be highly characteristic. The clinical picture suggests that Hugh showed the classic signs of islets of ability and insistence on sameness. He showed a conspicuous lack of social insight and communication. He had the speech and language peculiarities typical of autism. He had repetitive behaviour and narrow preoccupations. Even his most obscure and puzzling behaviour (attending funerals, watching rainwater, and hoarding junk) has a familiar ring. It is strongly reminiscent in form, and sometimes in content, of behaviour described in cases today.

The autism spectrum accommodates a wide range of degrees of severity. Hugh's pattern of symptoms fits well with Kanner's ideas on autism except that he was not socially withdrawn. Hugh's intellectual ability is difficult to guess at, and was likely to have been patchy. He had an excellent rote memory. He did well learning to read and write and acquiring a range of work skills. Overall, the evidence suggests that Hugh had autism to a severe degree.

Clinical reports usually finish up with recommendations for education and treatment. Although we have few details and must make inferences, some comments are appropriate in Hugh Blair's case. Hugh received an extended education lasting well into his adulthood. He was sent to school, integrated with other children. He was included in religious life, which required conforming to a number of strictly held customs. Hugh learned to participate in family and community activities. His occupations in and out of the house suggest that his talents and skills were allowed to flourish. He was given the freedom to indulge in work that was considered unfit for a gentleman. He was not confined to the house, nor was he sent away into somebody else's care. Instead he was given the freedom to roam about at his pleasure. All this suggests that the treatment which Hugh received was remarkably enlightened. Hugh was relatively well adapted despite his quite severe communication difficulties. According to the witnesses, his appearance, and by implication his social adaptation, was improved after his marriage. It may not be too fanciful to give credit for this to Hugh's wife and to his mother who lived with them. Hugh showed many examples of admirable behaviour. Good management, and patient gradual socialization showed their beneficial effect in later life.

Observations of Hugh Blair's Behaviour Based on a Transliteration of the Depositions of the Witnesses

The observations below are abbreviated quotations from the witnesses' statements. The content is as complete as possible while avoiding repetition. The earlier chapters of this book contain many references to the majority of the statements, placing them in their proper context.

Aspects of appearance and everyday life suggesting problems in social relations

- 'ate often by himself in the kitchen with the servants'
- 'stalked about [while eating] with his [bowl] in his arm'

- [at mealtimes with family] 'either sat down or not as he thought proper'
- [at mealtimes] 'never asked for a blessing or gave thanks'
- 'seldom stayed at table until thanks'
- 'continued supping [with] cats putting their feet in the sups'
- 'was shunned by servants as ill smelling'
- 'did drudgery things of his own accord, foul or fair weather, daytime or night'
- 'mucked the stables on a Sabbath when he had his best clothes on'
- 'carried a [discarded] blue livery coat to his room . . . seemed very fond to wear it'
- 'he ordinarily wore old cast-off clothes'
- 'it was his custom to mend his own clothes . . . with shapings of any sort of cloth and any sort of colour, however unlike to his clothes'
- 'generally went without his hat up and down the streets'
- 'upon his mother giving a sign with her hand, he would take his hat off'
- 'when he got a drink . . . he bowed to those next to him but to no one else of the company'
- 'frequently stalked through the room with the back of his wig forward'
- [at family worship] 'walked up and down and played with anything on the chimney piece'
- 'nor did he seem to take any notice of strangers'
- 'the servants treated him as a fool and paid him no manner of respect'
- 'danced . . . as often as desired . . . in a foolish and ridiculous manner'
- 'bid to uncover his nakedness . . . he did without seeming to know that there was any indecency therein'
- 'the bairns would have made diversion with him'
- 'seen him playing with children and exchanging flowers with them . . . ignoring the religious occasion'
- 'let even young boys [at school] lead him about and command him to do whatever they bid'
- 'made so great a noise and disturbance [with children mostly under five years old] that the town officer thought proper to disperse them'
- 'the boys for their diversion passing and repassing him and taking off their bonnets . . . by way of mock salutation . . . and he returning these salutations by taking off his hat to them'

- 'the bairns bowed to him and he to them ever so long'

Aspects of communication suggesting difficulties

- 'though deafish hears when loud spoke to and can speak though not quite so distinct as other people'
- 'answered [questions] very absurdly and sometimes made a foolish smiling stare'
- 'just came in [to house of minister] without speaking anything'
- 'gazed and stared without saying anything'
- 'in many attempts to make conversation with him, never took part'
- never connected an 'entire proposition with its verb and person'
- 'answered "very well" even when ill'(gave stereotyped responses)
- 'if asked whether he was going to marry a certain person he always answered yes, regardless of who they were'(gave repetitive answers)
- 'spoke in a very muttering way'
- 'gave nonsensical answers to questions'
- said 'Hugh Blair, bonny coat', 'Hugh Blair, no die' (talked of himself in third person)
- 'spintle, spintle' [used mainly one- or two-word utterances which he repeated]
- 'counted one, two, three, four skins' [when more than four sheep skins were hanging up]
- [when examined on catechism] 'began with the question and went on with the answer until stopped'
- chalked upon the wall words 'without any manner of connection'
- 'has often seen him write out the Lord's Prayer and found it to be exact'
- 'turned leaves [of book] from place to place without settling as people ordinarily do when they read'
- 'can read very well but speaks indistinctly'

Activities and interests of peculiar content

- 'went to all the burials whether rich or poor . . . invited or not'
- 'assisted to carry the corpse as other persons at the burial'
- 'upon his appearing [at burials] they showed no regard to him but let him stay outside among the common people'

- 'went about to gentlemen ministers' and other houses'
- 'one morning came in with a coat under his arm . . . when asked where he got it, he answered "Rusco coat", "Rusco coat"'
- 'stuck up bed curtains with sticks, without taking off the bark'
- 'gazed for a long time at rain water running from the roof even after the jar was full'
- 'frequently washed his wig and hung it to dry on the branch of a tree'
- [having missed seeing sheep skins being washed] 'moaned for the want of them'
- 'diverted himself by cutting and shaping small sticks which were of no use to anybody'
- 'made a sort of bonnet' [from odd bits of cloth] and gave bonnets as gifts to children
- 'mended his own clothes [using] any sort of cloth and colour however unlike his own'
- 'would sometimes steal away shaped work or new cloth'
- 'cut up a prized swan skin blanket belonging to Lady Borgue to mend his clothes'
- 'tried to mend wheelbarrows' [with unsuitable materials]
- 'frequently brought in ash wands to use as flails on the corn sheaves . . . but they were unfit for the purpose'
- 'made ready a rowan of wool [for spinning] by warming it at the fire'
- 'sought childish diversion' with toy windmills and scarecrows
- 'helped to stouck the corn . . . any stoucks he put up appeared at the distance as well set as [witness's] own'
- 'pulled wool off sheep skins and threw the wool away'
- 'went to the quarry at night to throw stones out of it'
- 'carried the stones some little distance from the quarry where he made a heap of them and then from that heap he carried them a little further and made another heap and went on carrying them this way until he brought them to a dyke'
- 'has frequently seen him build dykes to no manner or purpose as they were within a very few ells of other dykes and could form no enclosure'
- 'sometimes he worked in the quarry after the workmen had stopped working on account of the cold'
- 'was very careful to set everything right that was any way out of order in the house'

- insisted on the same place in church, 'never rested till he got that particular place'
- 'gazed and played with his hands like a fool'
- 'stalked up and down, gazing foolishly at everything he saw'
- 'stared and gazed about him like a fool in such a way that nobody who saw him would take him for anything else'

Normal or admirable behaviour emphasized by witnesses for the defence

- 'showed very great regard for his mother'
- 'warmed [his mother's] clothes and helped her on with them'
- 'behaved affectionately towards mother; helping her to dress' [when her arm was broken]
- 'behaved affectionately towards wife . . . when indisposed helped her to take off her clothes'
- defended mother when she was allegedly attacked by John Blair 'he interposed and gripped the person and held him til others came to his assistance'
- 'used to call for a bottle of ale in public houses, paying for it'
- 'carved meat at table and served it about'
- 'kept himself neat and clean in his clothes'
- showed 'never more regard [to his wife] than to others in company'
- 'never remained angry for more than half an hour'
- 'he would not kiss any lady but . . . his wife'
- 'when the company [at burials] lifted their hats he lifted his hat to them'

Deponents appearing for the pursuer John Blair

Name	Age	Occupation	Length of acquaintance	Context of familiarity
William Taggart	37	tailor	24 years	since school and frequently at the House of Borgue
Samuel Taggart	34	tailor	20 years	since school and frequently at the House of Borgue
Rachel Courtney	22	servant	7 years	servant to family twice for a total of three years
John McEwan	39	land labourer	13 years	servant in family
Samuel Gordon	36	land labourer	15 years	since school and 4 years as a servant
Betty Monteith	30	minister's daughter	since infancy	neighbour
Hugh Gordon	36	farmer	since childhood	at school and as a neighbour
Mr William Jamieson	40	minister	10–12 years	as clergyman and visited by Hugh
Mr Robert Walker	31	minister	4 years in 1730s	knew family well
Mr Thomas McCourtie	20+	schoolmaster	14 years	as a schoolboy
Mr Robert Monteith	40	minister	since infancy to 1730s	since they were infants until 13 years before
Mr Andrew Boyd	48	minister	22 years	frequently at Borgue
Robert McMillan	50	landowner's brother	25 years	neighbour and visited by Hugh
Margaret Veitch	20+	minister's daughter	14 years	neighbour and frequent house guest

Deponents appearing for the defender Hugh Blair

Name	Age	Occupation	Length of acquaintance	Context of familiarity
John Porter	56	tenant farmer	30 years	tenant
John Porter	26	son of tenant farmer		
Andrew Taggart	50+	weaver	20 years	
James Brown	34	weaver		
John McWhae	30+	shoemaker		casual
John Carsan	50+	tenant farmer	30+ years	at school and as a servant at Borgue
Jean Shennan	20+	servant		servant to Lady Borgue
Mr John Gordon	40+	residenter	24 years	former schoolmaster at Borgue
Isobel Farquharson	52	wife of portioner	3 months	landlady
Margaret Cowie	18	servant	3 months	servant to Tudhopes
Katherine Watson	17	former servant	3 months	servant to Tudhopes
John Tudhope	21	portioner's son	3 months	son of landlord
John Tudhope	50+	portioner	3 months	landlord
Barbara Balfour	59	widow	a few weeks?	lodger with Tudhopes
John Welsh	57	minister	since infancy	in youth

Chapter 6

The Historical-clinical Approach to the Case of Hugh Blair

The historical-clinical approach that we have followed is capable of revealing underlying commonalities in the human condition. It can also tell us about changes in our self-understanding and understanding of others. Mental disorder too reflects these changes even if the biological origin of the disorder remains the same. If it is possible to recognize autism despite vast differences in culture, then this allows us to see more clearly the common and enduring, as well as the local and transient, features of the condition. In this effort to distil the essence of autism a number of key questions have to be posed. Some of these relate to general certainties and uncertainties of the diagnosis. For instance, what are the limitations of our data and what missing information would have made a difference? Other questions relate to the impact of the particular social context. For instance, what questions did the judges think most relevant in deciding about Hugh's mental capacity? How was Hugh's condition reflected by the attitudes of others?

Uncertainties and Certainties in the Diagnosis

We proceeded in our project to treat the case of Hugh Blair as if he had visited a research institute. This is possible because he did in fact visit an institution which had a procedure to record behavioural evidence. The Commissary Court excelled in this respect: 29 different witnesses answered detailed questions about events and incidents that they had observed first hand. Yet with limited information, whether historical or contemporary, the temptation is great to read too much into it.

Hugh's life, work and leisure provided dozens of examples which are typical of autism, and hardly any which are inconsistent with the diagnosis. The clinical evidence that Hugh Blair had autism is strong. It follows that autism is not a new phenomenon, but existed at least three hundred ago. Given the cautionary notes above, just how unequivocal is this conclusion? Was Hugh's autism exactly the same kind of disorder that we meet today?

If we had a time machine

If, with the aid of a time machine, we were allowed to be present in the Edinburgh Court on 16 July 1747, what questions would we most like to have asked? There are many tantalizing questions for which it would have been possible to get an answer then – but which are unanswerable now. For instance, did Hugh have unexplored special talents? Did he have the ability to calculate days and dates of the calendar which allowed him to keep track of funerals? How would he have performed on neuropsychological tests and intelligence tests? We have plenty of evidence to expect that he would have performed dismally on some of them. However, such tests might have baffled Hugh's contemporaries too, and their value would be extremely doubtful without appropriate norms. More profitable would have been the opportunity to talk to Hugh's mother. What was Hugh like as a child? When did he first talk? Did he play like other children? How had he changed? What did she think were the main reasons for the improvements in Hugh's behaviour when he was an adult? We would also have had questions for Hugh's wife, his brother John and any other family members who were not allowed to appear as witnesses. Were there perhaps relatives who had autistic features?

If we had more data

We know a great deal more about Hugh Blair than we do about the vast majority of Scotland's people in the eighteenth century. Nevertheless, we would ideally like more documents to have survived. Letters about Hugh from family or friends would probably give more intimate evidence about the difficulties his family members had in living with him.

Another type of court case could have thrown different light on his be-haviour and attitudes towards it. He might have been prosecuted for theft in one of his kleptomaniac phases; he might have offended the Kirk Session by his behaviour in church; someone might have tried to enter into a business contract with him, which was later subject to question. A medical report on Hugh might have told us whether he had suffered any physical trauma as a child; whether he had any obvious neurological signs; whether he had any oddities in his appearance. Any evidence about the background of the Mitchell family, and especially about Nicholas, would also have been invaluable for our understanding of the survival of the marriage after its official annulment.

It is right to be doubtful about a diagnosis made three hundred years after Hugh was born. But how unequivocal is the diagnosis of present-day cases of autism, with the most up-to-date tools at our disposal? Clini-cians currently make a diagnosis of autism from behaviour, not from biological tests. In the same way, the lawyers and judges in the case of Hugh Blair made their decision on the basis of reported behaviour. This procedure is open to arbitrary whims and subjective biases. Behaviour is what an observer reports, and such a report is permeated by contempo-rary cultural values. We can assume that observers in different cultures would remark on different features in an individual with mental disorder. Each culture has its own way of defining behaviour patterns that fall outside the boundaries of acceptable conduct. Thus, we have to remind ourselves that normative behaviour for Hugh would have been the pur-suit of leisure, not work.

Would a definition on the basis of biology avoid the problems of a behavioural definition and be untouched by historical change? Imagine a diagnostic test for the genes that predispose towards autism. This test would give only a probability estimate to indicate how likely it would be that this person did in fact develop autism. Imagine now a brain scan which reveals abnormalities that are characteristic of autism. This would still not be a definitive indication that the individual has autism. A person may have none of the behavioural signs of autism despite having the genetic predisposition, and despite showing characteristic brain abnor-malities. This could be the case if healthy neural systems have taken over the function of faulty ones. The brain test, just like the DNA test, would not be a reliable predictor of behaviour and hence would not by itself constitute proof of autism.

All in all, it is unlikely that the additional evidence that we might have gained through using a time machine or through newly discovered historical documents would change our conclusions in a major way. Nevertheless, the incompleteness of the data reminds us to be cautious about these conclusions.

Distilling the Essence of Autism

Using either behavioural or biological criteria, the definitive diagnosis appears to be an ever-receding problem. The historical-clinical approach requires a different solution. This is achieved by using explanations at an intermediate level, the cognitive level. Cognitive theories weigh evidence from both behavioural and biological sources but focus on abnormalities in mental functions; they go beyond observation and description by trying to explain the causes of odd or impaired behaviour. Thus, they allow us to strip away those surface differences in behavioural signs and symptoms that are subject to observer bias and are not a universal part of the syndrome. For instance, historical analysis tells us that wearing a hat was part of near-obligatory social convention for a gentleman in the eighteenth century. The fact that Hugh Blair often did not wear a hat suggests that he was indifferent to social conventions. The reason for this indifference is given by the hypothesis of a theory of mind deficit. Three cognitive hypotheses, one concerning a theory of mind deficit and two others concerning peculiarities in non-social information processing, have been particularly useful in interpreting the bulk of the behavioural evidence and relating it to modern cases.

How well does the theory of mind explanation fit the evidence of the case? To recap, the idea is that the social and communication impairments of autism result from a fault in the mechanism that facilitates learning about intentions, thoughts and feelings. Hugh was not asocial but he had characteristic social impairments. These include such disparate examples as wearing strange garb, kleptomania, unwanted gift giving, inability to enter conversations, not taking a full part in family life and being unaware when teased. All of these impairments could be explained by an insensitivity to other people's mental states. He did not understand that people would feel affronted by his lack of social conventions, and by his inability to gauge what they valued. Likewise, Hugh Blair's lack of

160

resentment of others, and his inability to understand mocking, could have all stemmed from this single cognitive fault.

What aspects of Hugh's social and communicative behaviour are out of line with this theory? A mentalizing deficit would make it almost impossible to develop a satisfying relationship, such as one would expect of a lasting marriage. In present day cases of autism, marriage partners are a rarity. Children are an even greater rarity. Yet Hugh's marriage lasted – even after it was officially annulled. Furthermore, two children were born to Nickie, one immediately after the court case, another four years later. This is surprising and suggests some exceptional conditions which made it possible for Hugh's social adaptation to improve markedly after the age of 30 years. We can infer such improvements from the differences in the accounts of servants who knew him as a child and those who knew him only as a married man. Hugh initially was insensitive to other people's attitudes to his appearance. He seems to have learned gradually to improve in his habits of hygiene and dress. Possibly he was guided by his wife. Given these facts, it may be too strong to claim that Hugh completely lacked insight into other people's minds. Present-day cases suggest that people with a milder form of autism and a certain degree of ability can eventually learn to mentalize even though mind reading never becomes the natural and intuitive process that it normally is.

How well do peculiarities of information processing fit the evidence? To recap, the 'executive function impairment' theory tries to explain a predominance of routine at the cost of novel actions; the 'weak central coherence' theory tries to explain a tendency to process information piecemeal at the cost of meaning. Hugh's repetitive behaviour fits with poor executive functioning. His good rote memory, his odd interests and mechanical skills, his collection of sticks and feathers, fit strikingly with weak coherence theory. To be sure, the content of the interests and activities was set by what was available in his particular environment. To use the trainspotting stereotype, Hugh was a 'funeral-spotter'.

What is inconsistent with these hypotheses? Nothing obvious can be pointed to, but this could be due to the limited information that is represented in the depositions. Speculation on how Hugh saw the world, whether or not it resembled a patchwork of details, might simply not have seemed pertinent to the witnesses. Would other hypotheses fare better in accounting for the odd behaviour that was reported? Alterna-

tive accounts that attempt to explain the different way people with autism look at the world, and why they have special interests and talents,
are as yet under-developed.

We believe that the cognitive perspective has been remarkably successful in making sense of the wide range of descriptions of Hugh's behaviour. This underlines one major finding of this case study. The
similarities in the clinical picture of autism across time are greater than
the differences. The impact of the social and cultural environment on the
disorder is subtle rather than overwhelming. This is true for the observed
behaviours that are part of the current diagnostic criteria. It is true also
for some observations which, though highly characteristic, are at present
disregarded in the diagnosis. The historical analysis of the case brings the
non-social features of autism into the spotlight just as much as the social
features. Both underpin the constancy of the clinical picture. This conclusion could be premature. It is necessary to probe in some more detail
just why differences in the clinical picture seem small.

Echoes Across Time – Theory of Mind and Cultural Learning

The apparent constancy of the clinical picture leads us to consider whether
individuals with autism are less subject to the effects of cultural pressures
than other people. However, we know that Hugh Blair absorbed a vast
amount of culturally transmitted knowledge. He learned to read and write;
he knew the Lord's Prayer and the catechism, he read the Bible; he attended church, wore appropriate clothes and did appropriate things on
the Sabbath day. Still, with improvements reported in his middle age, it
appears to have taken many years for Hugh to learn all this, much longer
than other people. Why?

The same mechanism that underpins our human desire to share thoughts
and feelings is also likely to be a vector for cultural values in human
groupings. Evidence that this mechanism does not work properly in the
case of autism is plentiful. A diminished intuitive awareness of mental
states may also imply a diminished awareness of cultural values. Of course,
this would not preclude cultural learning, merely delay it. It follows that
the benefits of cultural learning are not delivered as directly and effort-
lessly as they are to other children. As Hans Asperger maintained, chil-

dren with autism learn after their own fashion and in their own time. While such children may not be quick at picking up culturally pre-screened information, they will learn many things that other children don't learn, and that others don't wish them to learn.

The presumption is that what the child with autism learns about the world is set first and foremost by the child. The opposite is the case when the predominant mode is cultural learning: the goals of learning are largely set by others who have filtered the information they provide through their own knowledge and experience. Parents in particular, and social communities in general, are determined that their children should not have to start from scratch, but benefit from what they and others have learned already. Cultural learning links different generations and is guided by a substantial body of beliefs about the world. If cultural learning is indeed a less dominant mode of learning for children with autism, then this would explain a number of phenomena. It would explain why some of them acquire extraordinary skills without being taught. It would also explain why, on the whole, they do not follow the fads and fashions of their peers, but their own idiosyncratic tastes and fascinations.

Hugh Blair demonstrates the problems that would have arisen from slow cultural learning in his earlier years, making him something of a misfit in the family home. At the same time he also demonstrates the benefits that resulted from the slow and steady increase of cultural learning through his school years and well into his adulthood. Hugh's achievements in reading and writing, his accomplishments in various crafts, all bear witness to the power of cultural learning to ameliorate the effects of autism. The benefits go beyond the acquisition of cultural knowledge. For instance, in several cases, a child with autism has learned to communicate by speech, after having been taught the rudiments of literacy. Efforts to promote cultural learning could therefore be particularly important in the education of children with autism. Hugh Blair's family made such efforts.

Theory of mind and a 'sense of God'

An example of how the mentalizing hypothesis can be applied to phenomena that have so far not been analysed in modern cases is the issue of religious awareness. Indeed, questions about religious awareness simply do not enter into clinical debates and are not seen as relevant to the diagnostic process. In contrast, much weight was given by the Commissary Court – and other tribunals studied by Rab Houston – to the question of the defendant's religious sense. This was not to probe into the nature of the defendant's faith. The court was a secular one, and not responsible for judging questions of faith or heresy. As far as we are concerned, Hugh's faith was just as valid as that of his contemporaries, and for that matter as valid as that of people today. The question was important because the judges held it to be a key element of normal mental capacity. As discussed in earlier chapters, a sense of the divine was considered a major factor that separated man from beast. In many ways this opinion is reminiscent of arguments put forward in present-day debates about theory of mind. Mentalizing capacity too, is considered by some to be a major factor that separates human from non-human species. The question whether non-human species have the ability to mentalize is by no means settled.

If Hugh had diminished awareness of mental states due to autism, what would this imply for his sense of God? There are many ways of conceptualizing God's mind, and not all are based on analogy to human minds. However, in a Calvinist society, we can assume that children were taught that God sees inside their hearts and knows their intentions. Further, they were taught that God has intentions for his creation and that his plans are made plain in the Bible. If this argument approximates the sense of God that prevailed in the local community, then that sense is inextricably linked to a well-functioning theory of mind. It follows that a lack of theory of mind restricts a religious sense of this type. For this reason the question posed by the judges: 'Did Hugh Blair have a sense of God?' can be interpreted as analogous to the question posed by modern psychologists: 'Did Hugh Blair have a theory of mind?'.

How did the expert witnesses, who were ministers themselves, answer the judges' question? Like psychologists today they distinguished between outward behaviour and inner thoughts. It was not enough that Hugh knew the whole of the catechism and attended church regularly. Thus, Mr Gordon succinctly stated that he could not see Hugh's heart. Mr John Welsh, whose statement was recorded among the defence depositions, testified 'that he has seen Hugh Blair at church on Sabbath days, and that he behaved decently as to outward appearance; and at burials has seen him behave decently, as other men, except as to keeping up of conversation'. He thought Hugh Blair had:

some notions of religion, but could not tell how far; he has seen him distinguish between a Sabbath day and a week-day; particularly, he has seen him at the house of Borgue go to a room or keep himself within the house, and not divert himself by play or otherwise upon a Sunday as he used to do on other days.

Clearly, the behavioural signs suggested that Hugh appreciated religious feelings and participated in the proper religious activities. Nevertheless, the final verdict of the court implies that the judges did not believe that Hugh had the same sense of God as other members of his community. This matches our interpretation of Hugh having a diminished awareness of mental states.

A silent madness

Hugh Blair's lawyer described idiocy as 'a silent madness', continuing, 'such men are, as it were, asleep all their life'.[1] This evocative description has echoes in present-day theories of autism and also strikes a chord with ideas that are just beginning to be explored. Sleep-walking is an analogy for diminished self-awareness. Self-awareness and awareness of other people appear to depend on the same mechanism: where there are difficulties in understanding other minds, there are also difficulties in understanding one's own mind. If it is difficult to attribute beliefs to others, it is also difficult to reflect on one's own beliefs. Autobiographies of individuals with autism hint at disturbances of self-consciousness.[2] Just as sleep-walkers can carry out many complex actions without being fully conscious of carrying them out, so children with autism may go about their daily routines without full awareness of their own feelings and thoughts.

Remarkably, in some cases the sleeper awakes. One particularly gifted and insightful writer with autism, Gunilla Gerland,[3] was able to look back on her own childhood and describe experiences which suggest dimmed self-awareness. At the time of her writing, however, she demonstrates an acute degree of self-consciousness, so sharp that it may well exceed ordinary experience. One of the strange symptoms found in severe cases of autism seems to be an altered perception of pain. This appears to be true too in cases of dimmed self-awareness. In Hugh Blair's case, a concrete example is his apparent lack of sensitivity to cold, and the statement, that when he had dysentery, he said he was well. He was apparently unaware of the fact that he was ill, let alone how life-threatening was the condition which had killed one of his sisters.

Comparison with Cases from other Cultures

Our claim that the clinical picture of autism is essentially similar over different cultural contexts can be tested. Here we pick out two other examples of presumed autism in different cultures, although they offer only scant detail. The first case is provided by Challis and Dewey[4] who first suggested a relationship between 'holy fools' of sixteenth-century Russia and modern cases of autism. They concluded that the recorded conduct of the blessed fool Pelagija Serebrenikova resembles a case history of autism in many ways. Pelagija was put in chains during long periods of her life, a not uncommon practice at the time, and on occasion was left free to wander round the town, rattling her chains. She continued to wear her chains even after she was housed in a convent, when they were no longer needed. Indeed she kept them at the head of her bed when sleeping. One of her recorded activities was to collect loose bricks or stones, carry them to a flooded pit and throw them in, one by one. When all had disappeared in the water, she would lower herself into the pit, soaking herself in the process, and pull out all the bricks tossing then back, one by one, 'and for many years did she toil thus'. Her tendency for repetitive activity is reminiscent of Hugh Blair's.

A second case comes from contemporary Japan, described in a letter by a woman, Mrs O., who came to the conclusion that her 75–year-old mother-in-law suffered from autism. She first recognized this after having seen the film *Rainman* and then confirmed her suspicion by reading books on autism. The story she told in a letter to Uta Frith is transcribed below. One aspect of this case that is particularly interesting, and that makes it potentially relevant to the case of Hugh Blair, is that she too was married and had children.

> About 60 years ago, at the age of 19, my future mother-in-law arrived at her future husband's house and repeated several times that her brother had commanded her to accept the place as her home. She had lost her parents when very young and was brought up by her eldest brother and his wife.

She went to school where she learned to sew and to read. When she was grown up, she was sent away as a bride. At first, she was not welcomed by her new family and treated badly. She was forced to work and was constantly accused of being selfish and spoiled. Her self-centredness and inability to make social contact were obvious to all. Eventually her husband took pity on her. He allowed her to do as she pleased. In this way she settled into a lifestyle that she carried on ever since.

She gave birth to four children and looked after them physically, while her husband took charge of their upbringing and education. When I was first introduced to Mrs O. by her son my future husband, he spoke of her as someone who prefers the lifestyle of the old days and who gets upset when her normal routine is changed. He asked me to leave her alone and that she would in any case be able to accept me as a neighbour rather than as a new member of the family.

The farmhouse that my mother-in-law lived in was very traditional. When anything was moved, she immediately put it back where it was. She cooked on a traditional stove with ancient implements, even though there was also a gas stove available, and never ate modern dishes. She always ate alone. She made her own clothes, all in the old Japanese style, and never wore shoes. Instead she made her own straw sandals. She kept everything very clean with a broom and a cloth. Every day she collected firewood from a nearby mountain, always at the same place. She tended an area of farmland on her own and grew a variety of vegetables. She never rode in a motor car, refusing steadfastly even to enter one with a member of her family.

Every day she rose with the sun, cooked breakfast, worked in the field, did the housework and went to the mountains for firewood. She read the newspaper or did sewing if there was any spare time. She also took a nap every day after which she heated the bath water. She took her time while bathing, had a meal and then went to bed. This pattern was the same, every day. While her husband was still alive she went about on her own as if he was not there. Real conversation was not possible. When she spoke she gave the kind of answers that immediately ended any exchange. She seemed unable to understand questions correctly and took other people's remarks very literally. For instance, when one of her daughters was drinking coffee and said casually 'coffee can be bad for you if you drink it every day', she simply threw away all the coffee in the house.

Eventually, in his old age, my father-in-law became ill, was hospitalized, and died. Throughout this period she carried on her life as if nothing had happened. It was at this point that I became involved. I saw that someone had to look after the old lady and see that she had food to eat. I walked up to my mother-in-law when she was burning firewood for the bath water and said 'mother'. She mumbled something to herself. She was probably uneasy because a neighbour, not her own daughter, had called her so. After that I decided to call her 'oba-chan', which is similar to the term grandma, but can be used for someone who is not a relative. She looked into a mirror as if questioning whether she had become that old. However, she soon took to the name and looked up when called. She is over seventy years old. She does not expect or ask for anything. She never speaks badly of others and is not jealous of others. She likes cats, and expresses her interest by saying 'You brought a cat. A big cat'. She remains a stranger in the family. We think of her as someone who has an extremely rare illness, but that it is all right, since it allows for a healthy long life.

There is an enormous historical and cultural gulf between these cases and that of Hugh, but there are also similarities. Neither was diagnosed at the time, although both were recognized as suffering from mental incapacity. Although they clearly experienced hardship, they also experienced kindness from those around them who tolerated them. In each case the essential features of autism, the social impairments as well as the non-social features, are recognizable. In each case, family members treated them badly at times, but in the long run, they did look after them.

A key feature of the relatively successful adaptation of each individual to their very different environments might well have been the freedom they were given to do what they liked to do. Even though the differences between a twentieth-century Japanese lady and an eighteenth-century Scottish laird are large, some of the descriptions and comments seem equally apt when applied to both. Hugh Blair too preferred to eat alone, mended his own clothes and insisted on certain traditions, such as attending funerals and keeping his place at church. The Japanese case allows us to imagine what might have happened in Hugh's married life, and what his relationship to his wife and his two children might have been like. Although it is very rare for people with autism to have children, and little is known about them, the Japanese case demonstrates that such children may not only be entirely normal, but loving and understanding towards their afflicted parent.

Our conclusion remains that autism is a condition that can be recognized in different cultural contexts, and indeed as a condition is little

influenced by cultural context. Thus individual cases show more similarities than differences when compared across historical time, geographical
space and social hierarchy.

The Impact of Autism on Society

Autism, with its indifference to cultural values, implies an existential
critique of society. It questions some of its most valued concepts. For
instance, Hugh Blair did not have the same attitude to personal property
as his family; he stole the things he liked, regardless of their worth. He
broke many social conventions, to the horror and disgust of his peers. It
is obvious that he did not share their socially conditioned emotions,
such as respect, embarrassment and pride. Neither did he show disre-
spect, mistrust or envy. Like other people with autism, Hugh Blair was
not aware of the social position he was born into. It must have been
galling to some that he was content to be in the company of people who
were well below him in status. Society is challenged and humbled by the
sheer existence of people who are unmoved by values that it takes for
granted.

Scientific theories that address the underlying features of autism have
paid little attention to the impact of the condition on others. Yet it is
clear that the members of the family of the affected individual all carry
the burden of the handicap. Hugh Blair appears before us in such vivid
detail only because his immediate family fell out. This has been a story of
family life as much as it has about one individual.

What of the wider community? The nature of autism always implies a
degree of exclusion. This is because the disorder compromises the ability
to reflect on one's own feelings and to share these feelings with others.
On the other hand, the special talents of autism enrich and help define
what a community values as originality, art and order. If we think of the
impact of society on the person with autism, the situation is rather different. Thus it is very clear that the participation of Hugh Blair in local
funerals was at once an expression of his interest in taking part in social
events, and of his inability to understand his role in such events. Possibly,
the ritual of funerals itself was irrelevant to Hugh, and any ritual might
have done as well. However, the structured and predictable nature of the
solemn event must have provided some form of pleasure. Hugh's liking

for funerals can serve as a valid example for the influence of socio–cultural factors on the management of mental disorder.

The treatment of Hugh Blair in the historical context

In modern developed countries, the state plays a much greater role in caring for the mentally impaired than was the case in the eighteenth century. Those found insane by a criminal court at that date might have been incarcerated to protect society from them until someone else came along to fulfil that function. The expectation was that the family would stand surety against further outrages by a criminally insane relative. Those who locked up a 'furious criminal' were, according to the early jurist Sir James Balfour, acting in place of kinsmen. If nobody came to claim the criminal insane, they might remain for years in jail or in a madhouse.[5]

Sending the criminal insane to an institution to be cared for 'in loco amicorum' only later became the norm. In the 1800s and beyond, the criminal insane might be sent straight to Edinburgh Bedlam or to one of the public asylums, rather than languishing in a jail.[6] The Sheriff-Depute's report on Aberdeen Asylum of 1816 noted how 'The court of justiciary have been of late years in the practice of ordering lunatic convicts to be confined for life'.[7] The eighteenth-century Justiciary Court (approximately equivalent to an English Assize) had no legal right to order the committal of convict lunatics to public madhouses. Not until the early nineteenth century was the state beginning to accept direct responsibility for certain types of insane poor, rather than simply passing prescriptive or proscriptive legislation.[8] The family context in which Hugh was cared for characterized the treatment of almost all mentally disabled people prior to the nineteenth century.

As a landowner's eldest son, there was no question of Hugh Blair doing anything other than be a landlord and farmer or live a life of leisure. The family's social capital, which in other circumstances would have been used to make alliances and promote the well-being of its members, was deployed by the Blair family to protect Hugh rather than seek him advancement. The extensive social support that Hugh obtained is impressive. It might well be similar in comparable social strata and in similar circumscribed communities, even today. The legal obligations enshrined in law in most advanced societies would now guarantee any child with special needs the right to education and life-long assistance. Hugh Blair today might by preference have continued to live with his ageing mother for as long as possible. However, he would not have had to rely entirely on his close kin. He may have been offered some form of sheltered housing. He might have lived in a small-group home with some supervision. A generation ago he might have been offered a place at a large institution, where he would have stayed all his life, possibly from quite a young age. All these solutions to the serious problem of mental retardation and autism vary according to the carers and their ethos and the society they live in.

Whether long ago or today, efforts at teaching and modelling social behaviour can be very successful, even if learning is very slow.[9] The success, however, does not imply a cure. Well-adapted adults with autism tend to be eager to please and may appear to be more 'normal' than they actually are. They may have absorbed the surface characteristics of social behaviour but not necessarily its deeper meaning. For example, Hugh Blair visited neighbours but did not take into account whether he was welcome at a particular time. He was able to change his behaviour when given clear evidence of disapproval. Thus he stopped working in the stables on the Sabbath day when given remonstrations in the strongest possible terms. Hugh may have wanted to please others without understanding how best to do this. His unsuitable occupations could be seen as examples of helpfulness. A more striking sign of the desire to please was his habit of giving presents, albeit inappropriate ones.

John Welsh, a witness for the defence, was asked whether he thought Hugh Blair was capable of becoming a mechanic, a word which in this period meant someone who worked with their hands. His perceptive answer was: 'that from his knowledge and experience, as Hugh Blair was more capable of being taught by the eye than by the ear, he might have been taught some mechanical employment, and accordingly advised his friends to try him that way'. This reasoning anticipates modern attempts at maximizing the potential for useful work irrespective of social class.

Attitudes to Hugh Blair

Attitudes towards mental disorder are shaped by culture. The attitudes prevalent in a community have a considerable impact on the quality of life of its handicapped members. Indeed it has often been said that the degree of civilization of a society can be judged by its concern for its most vulnerable and needy members.

Many of the witnesses not only reported examples of behaviour but also expressed their attitudes to Hugh Blair and commented on the attitudes of others. Some witnesses said that Hugh was not treated like the other children in the family. He spent much of his time with servants. The question of deliberate and cruel neglect has been raised at several points already. However, comparative contemporary examples of cases of acute neglect suggest that Hugh was not badly treated. At worst we can allege that his mother condoned abuse by not stopping it. An alternative view is that she was resigned to not being able to do anything about it, and accepted what she could not change. We know that Hugh's mother occasionally turned him out of the room when visitors called. Visitors tended to take no notice of him, perhaps trying to be tactful.

The family members did not insist that Hugh join in prayers, but they included him as long as he was content to stay. This suggests a certain degree of tolerance. Or, had they given up on coercion and persuasion? The classic methods of social learning through habit-forming repetition seem to have worked well with Hugh, especially in view of his evidently severe impairments. However, in matters of eating, sleeping, work and leisure, Hugh seems to have set his own standards. Others probably came to accept that it was useless to expect otherwise. In modern cases, parents complain that strangers tend to censor them when they see their child misbehave in public. People who judge them as lax or abusively strict have no idea how difficult it is to bring up a child with autism.

Household servants were inclined to make fun of Hugh. At best, they showed him no respect. No one was afraid of him, neither children nor adults. This is one of the main reasons that we can infer that he was of a gentle disposition. Even little urchins could order Hugh around. An incident of taunting was recorded in detail. John Tudhope made to threaten Hugh with iron tongs. Hugh held him by the wrist and shook him but soon forgot to be angry. Several times we hear that a boy aged three or four led the grown-up Hugh about and made him do his bidding. Hugh's mother was reported to have commented on this, showing that she was aware of such mocking. Yet not everyone was unkind to Hugh. Neighbours who Hugh visited unannounced treated him civilly and gave him hospitality. Social status was too robust to be overturned by mere personal weakness. Hugh was given credit that had been earned by his forebears figuratively and literally. For instance, he was served at public houses like any paying customer and the publican could rely on repayment even if Hugh did not carry money on him. Neighbours from whom he took clothes made special allowances for his kleptomaniac tendencies. His presence at the parish funerals was tolerated and perhaps even appreciated.

Hugh's condition meant severe restrictions of civic rights and duties. He depended on others to act on his behalf in any matter of public concern. Besides his mother, he could rely on staunch family friends. Significantly, John Gordon, whose statement is transcribed in chapter 3, said that he never knew Hugh Blair to make any bargains. Nevertheless he did not want to exclude the possibility that Hugh could be made to understand the matrimonial contract if people talked to him in a language he could understand.

What was Nickie Mitchell's attitude to Hugh? She was initially reluctant to enter the marriage, but she stayed with Hugh even after the marriage was annulled, and had two children by him. By the time of the trial Nickie must have known the extent of Hugh's handicap. She must also have realized that any children would be disinherited. Perhaps she got on well with Grizell who lived with them. Perhaps Grizell gave her money to Nickie. Perhaps she had no better alternatives. In any case, she did not return to her father, who, as we have been told, was comfortably off as a surgeon and merchant. We might speculate that Nickie was adept at managing Hugh's problems. Perhaps this explains the improvement in Hugh's appearance and behaviour after his marriage. We might imagine that she found a measure of freedom and achieved some happiness with her children. What were the children like? We have no idea. But it is possible that they were charming. Autism in a parent does not rule out perfectly normal and well-brought-up children, as for example, in the case of the Japanese mother-in-law.

What did Hugh's contemporaries say that illuminates the extent and quality of his suffering? Did he suffer at all? Some of the witnesses certainly assumed so. Some witnesses did not even consider what it might feel like being teased, shamed and bullied, and instead told of their own cruel pranks on Hugh Blair. This suggests that they either regarded Hugh as incapable of noticing the cruelty, or that they did not care even if he did. Today things are little changed at the street level. Autistic people are still mocked and bullied. In polite society people still pretend not to notice foolish behaviour, just as visitors to the Blairs. Yet there has been progress. Autistic people have entered public awareness in thoughtful books and films. The programmes which integrate autistic children into society include education for social tolerance. In school, classmates are challenged to understand and help their odd new friend. On the job, co-workers are trained to sympathise and assist, rather than using a naïve employee to relieve the tedium of work by baiting him.

In some ways society's attitudes to autism are wide-ranging and appear as similar across time as the condition itself. Hugh Blair was considered by his contemporaries a curiosity, an entertainment and a source of abhorrence. The gentle, civilized, and considered depositions of some of the witnesses contrast with the cruelly revealing statements of others. People living in 1750 in Kirkcudbright were in many respects not so different from people today. Just as we can read and understand eighteenth-century commentators' views on their time, so we can read and understand the witnesses' attitudes to mental disorder and see our own attitudes reflected in them.

Links across Disciplines and Links across Time

Cognitive science suggests that self-understanding and understanding of others is not exclusively determined by historical context, but that insights into one's own and other people's minds have a neurological basis. Social history addresses the question of whether this has been constant throughout human history or whether there have been profound changes in self-understanding. Just as in the discovery of biological functions and human health the study of disease has been most instructive, it may be that in history the study of the atypical individual reveals things about the typical individual that would never otherwise come to light. Even simple issues, such as the ability to copy and repeat rote-learned passages, which are taken for granted in a literate person, are not as straightforward as they seem. The difference between a literate and illiterate person can be smaller than that between a literate person who understands the act of copying and one who does not. Examples such as Hugh Blair's curious behaviours throw light on what it means to be able to think as an individual and to be part of a social group.

His social naivety made Hugh Blair as vulnerable in the Kirkcudbrightshire community as it would have made him in other societies. The high status of his family gave him a modicum of protection. However, for the most part, his own status in ordinary people's eyes was extremely low, lower than that of a child. Similar attitudes to handicapped individuals prevail today. Just as Grizell Blair fought with every means at her disposal to see her son settled and looked after, so present-day parents fight, often ferociously, for their handicapped children's future. Some would surely consider an arranged marriage, if only they could. We have to conclude that in many ways the treatment and management of Hugh Blair was as good as he would get today: he was taught at school well into adulthood, he learned some language despite a hearing impairment, he learned to read and write, he was given occupations suited to his temperament and he had freedom enough to go about his own harmless pursuits. Thus we can see many similarities, not only in the perception of the handicap, but also in its treatment.

Has there then been no improvement in the management of autism since Hugh Blair's time? Of course there has. Fortunately, the treatment of children from less privileged backgrounds has very much improved since the eighteenth century. Increased knowledge of mental disorder and increased social welfare has benefited large sections of the population. It is only in the case of a person from a high social stratum, such as Hugh, that the modern advantages may seem small. Even in these cases the tailored educational approaches that are now available certainly constitute an improvement.

The recurring verdict of the deponents that Hugh Blair lacked 'common sense' can still hardly be bettered as a concise description of the autistic handicap. Of course, such intuitive judgement, succinct and useful as it is, does not inform us about the mechanisms that are responsible for 'common sense', nor about the nature of the mind that lacks such mechanisms. We suggest that it is here that some progress has been made, but mainly this has occurred very recently, over the last 20 years. During this relatively short time period, which saw the rise of cognitive neuroscience, a better understanding about the underlying neurocognitive deficit in autism has been gained. Autism implicates the very mechanism that makes it easy for people to communicate with each other effectively over many generations to create culture. In a sense, this piece of evolutionary mental engineering is what allows us to benefit from the detailed and careful observations of Hugh Blair's contemporaries about his condition.

Notes

Chapter 1   The Background to the Study

1   P. H. McKerlie, *History of the lands and their owners in Galloway*, 5 vols. (Edinburgh: Paterson, 1877), vol. 3, p. 181.

2   R. J. Barrett, *The psychiatric team and the social definition of schizophrenia* (New York: Cambridge University Press, 1995); T. H. Turner, 'Schizophrenia as a permanent problem. Some aspects of historical evidence in the recency (new disease) hypothesis', *History of Psychiatry*, 3 (1992), pp. 413–29.

3   C. Ginzburg, *The cheese and the worms* (London: Routledge and Kegan Paul, 1980), is a notable exception.

4   M. Jackson, *New-born child murder. Women, illegitimacy and the courts in eighteenth-century England* (Manchester University Press: Manchester, 1996).

5   G. B. Risse, *Hospital life in Enlightenment Scotland* (Cambridge: Cambridge University Press, 1986).

6   Greater Glasgow Health Board, HB13/7/1.

7   Royal College of Physicians of Edinburgh.

8   G. M. Carstairs and R. L. Kapur, *The great universe of Kota. Stress, change and mental disorder in an Indian village* (London: Hogarth Press, 1976), pp. 14–15.

9   L. Wing, *The autistic spectrum* (London: Constable, 1997)

10   For a recent review see F. Volkmar and C. Lord 'Diagnosis and definition of autism and other pervasive developmental disorders', in F. Volkmar (ed.) *Autism and pervasive developmental disorders* (Cambridge: Cambridge University Press, 1998), pp. 1–31. A well-known instrument for diagnosis is described by C. Lord, M. Rutter, A. LeCouteur in 'Autism Diagnostic Interview-Revised: A revised version of a diagnostic interview for caregivers

of individuals with possible pervasive developmental disorder', *Journal of Autism and Developmental Disorders*, 24 (1994), pp. 659–85.

11 ICD-10 is published by the WHO (1992) and DSM-IV by the American Psychiatric Association (1994). The criteria for autism and related disorders in both publications are discussed in the review by Volkmar and Lord (1998).

Chapter 2   The Life and Times of Hugh Blair

1 National Archives of Scotland (NAS), CC13/6/60, item 9 (1734).

2 Ibid., C22/64, f. 168: 29 March 1737, registered 5 May 1737. Hugh and Jean. The jury were: David Telfer, merchant and provost of Kirkcudbright; Robert Carmont, merchant and present bailie in Kirkcudbright; Alexander Fisher, bailie in Kirkcudbright; Thomas Mirrie, merchant in Kirkcudbright; Samuel McCoskrie, gardener in Kirkcudbright; Thomas Bean, merchant in Kirkcudbright; James Afleck of Edingham; David Corrie, merchant burgess of Kirkcudbright; Thomas McCartney, surgeon or apothecary in Kirkcudbright; Andrew McKeun, shoemaker in Kirkcudbright; William Hunter, former customs officer in Kirkcudbright; John Ewart, wright in Kirkcudbright; John Thomson, merchant in Kirkcudbright; Alexander Murray, dyer in Kirkcudbright; William Cowpar, shopkeeper in Kirkcudbright.

3 It should be noted that Nicholas or Nicolas was a rather common girl's name in eighteenth-century Scotland.

4 R. A. Houston, *Social change in the age of Enlightenment: Edinburgh, 1660–1760* (Oxford: Oxford University Press, 1994), pp. 24, 58–9.

5 NAS CC8/6/15, Blair v Blair (1748). Signet Library (SL) Session Papers, vol. 7, case 12; vol. 580, case 17.

6 James B. Henderson, *Borgue: its parish churches, pastors, and people* (Castle-Douglas: A. Rae, 1890); J. R. Hume (ed.), *The statistical account of Scotland, 1791–1799, edited by Sir John Sinclair. Volume V: Stewartry of Kirkcudbright and Wigtownshire* (Wakefield: EP Publishing, 1983), pp. 35–48; R. Heron, *Observations made in a journey thro' the western counties of Scotland in the autumn of 1792* (Edinburgh: R. Morison, 1793); I. Donnachie and I. MacLeod, *Old Galloway* (Newton Abbot: David and Charles, 1974).

7 A. Mitchell (ed.), *Geographical collections relating to Scotland made by Walter Macfarlane*, 3 vols. (Edinburgh: Scottish History Society, 1906–8), vol. 2, p. 65.

8 C. M. Armet (ed.), *Kirkcudbright sheriff court deeds, 1676–1700* (Kirkcudbright: Oliver & Boyd 1953), pp. 733–7.

9 Mitchell, *Geographical collections*, 2, p. 78.

10 M. Young (ed.), *The parliaments of Scotland: burgh and shire commissioners*, 2 vols (Edinburgh: Scottish Academic Press, 1992–3), vol. 1, p. 208, vol. 2, p. 453; NAS SP4/11, 224. I owe this information to Dr John Shaw.

11 W. Bell, *Dictionary and digest of the law of Scotland* (Edinburgh: Bell & Bradfute, 1838), pp. 112–13.

12 D. M. Walker (ed.), *The institutions of the law of Scotland . . . by James, Viscount of Stair . . . 1693* (Edinburgh: University Presses of Edinburgh and Glasgow, 1981), p. 705. (Hereafter *Stair's institutions*).

13 The post-1815 qualification was £100 a year of valued rent or a house worth £30 a year if rented. Bell, *Dictionary*, p. 546.

14 The following discussion is based largely on *Stair's institutions*, pp. 702–11; P. G. B. McNeill (ed.), *The practicks of Sir James Balfour of Pittendreich, reproduced from the printed edition of 1754* (Edinburgh: Stair Society, 1962–3), vol.2, p. 434. For an example of the form of such a brieve see Ibid., pp. 648–9.

15 *The practicks of Sir James Balfour*, vol. 2, p. 433. Balfour also suggested that there should be two or three curators drawn from the father and mother's side (vol. 1, pp. 122–3). In practice only one person is ever named in the retour.

16 'deaf and dumb, and the sort of people who are prevented by law from administering or alienating their goods, and who should be supported by a curator in case their shortcomings leave them defective in judgement'

17 NAS C22/64, f. 168.

18 R. A. Houston, *Madness and society in eighteenth-century Scotland* (Oxford: Oxford University Press, 2000).

19 J. Erskine, *The principles of the law of Scotland* (Edinburgh: Elphingston Balfour, 1809 edn), p. 83.

20 Ibid., p. 88.

21 *Acts of the Parliaments of Scotland,* vol. 8, pp. 59–60 (c. 2), vol. 8, p. 352 (c. 85). These stringent requirements were later relaxed somewhat. *APS* vol. 10, p. 35 (c. 9) placed a 10–year limitation period on actions against tutors by minors come of age, *The decisions of the court of session, from its institution till the year 1764,* 5 vols (London: Printed for the editor Henry Home, Lord Kames, 1774), vol. 4, pp. 393–5. No such document has been traced for any of the Blair children in any state of dependency. Even if they were routinely kept, few survive for anywhere in Scotland.

22 NAS C22/58, pp. 303–4: 1 February 1722, registered 9 February 1722. This document, a retoured service of heirship, states that the marriage contract between David Blair and Grizell Blair was signed on 18 and 21 July 1705, and registered on 25 July 1712. A later document has the marriage contract being signed in May 1706, NAS CS234/B/1/5.

23 NAS CC13/6/60, item 9 (1734) P. H. McKerlie, *History of the lands and their owners in Galloway* (Edinburgh: Paterson, 1877), vol. 3, p. 181.

24 For example, NAS RD4/1–295, Register of Deeds, Second Series, Mackenzie, 1661–1811; RH15/14/28. RH9/7.

25 C. Dolan, 'The artisans of Aix-en-Provence in the sixteenth century: A micro-analysis of social relationships', in P. Benedict (ed.), *Cities and social change in early modern France* (London: Unwin Hyman, 1989), p. 176.

26 NAS CS234/B/1/5.

27 Ibid., CC13/6/60, item 9 (1734).

28 Ibid., RS23/20, f. 206. The pound sterling was increasingly the standard for payments and accounting during the eighteenth century. The Scottish pound was worth approximately one-twelfth of its English equivalent following savage devaluations in the sixteenth century. The 'merk' was worth two-thirds of a Scottish pound or thirteen shillings and four pence in pre-decimal money. If we offer an equivalent in modern coinage, 13/4 would be 67 pence.

29 Stewartry Museum, Kirkcudbright, Blair of Borgue, Miscellaneous documents, 1978/25/03.

30 NAS CC13/6/65, item 1 (1740).

31 R. A. Houston, 'Women in the economy and society of Scotland, 1500–1800', in R. A. Houston and I. D. Whyte (eds), *Scottish society, 1500–1800* (Cambridge: Cambridge University Press, 1989), pp. 118–47.

32 NAS CC13/6/65, item 1 (1740). Margaret Dunbar died in February 1724.

33 Armet, *Kirkcudbright sheriff court deeds*, pp. 573–4. The contract was registered on 14 July 1696.

34 'The old house on the Borgue estate, looks in its roofless and delapidated state like a castle, but comparatively it is a modern building and was occupied in the present century, the late Dr Blair of Kirkcudbright having been born in it.' McKerlie, *History*, vol. 3, p. 183.

35 J. Gifford, *The buildings of Scotland: Dumfries and Galloway* (Harmondsworth: Penguin, 1996), p. 133. See also *Buildings of special architectural or historical interest* (Dumfries and Galloway Council, 1990); *Royal Commission on Ancient and Historical Monuments and Constructions of Scotland*, fifth report, vol. 2 (London, 1914), pp. 40–1. Plans and elevations of the house are available from RCAHMCS: accession numbers C22301 and C22302.

36 NAS CS229/B/2/16.

37 The lands of Low Borgue had been farmed directly by the laird from at least the late seventeenth century. Armet, *Kirkcudbright sheriff court deeds*, pp. 717–18.

38 NAS SC16/58/10, 9 March 1742.

39 NAS CH2/526/5, pp. 186–7.

40 SL Session Papers, vol. 7, case 12, 'Information for Hugh Blair . . . ', p. 9.

41 NAS CH2/526/5, p. 192.

42 *Stair's institutions*, p. 107. See also J. C. Barry (ed.), *William Hay's lectures on marriage*, vol. 24 (Edinburgh: Stair Society, 1967), p. 111.

43 *Stair's institutions*, p. 206.

44 For example, NAS CC8/5/29/1, Walker v Macadam (1806). I owe this reference to Leah Leneman.

45 *Decennial indexes to the services of heirs in Scotland, 1700–1859*, 4 vols. (Edinburgh: Murray and Gibb, 1863–91), vols 1 and 2.

46 NAS C22/64, f. 3: 15 June 1736, registered 30 June 1736.

47 *APS* vol. 2, p. 106 (c. 6).

48 NAS CC13/6/60, item 9 (1734).

49 SL Session Papers, vol. 7, case 12, 'Bill of Advocation . . . ', p. 4.

50 Ibid., 'Information for Hugh Blair . . . ', p. 1.

51 Ibid., vol. 69, case 11. 'The petition of David Blair younger of Borgue, factor *loco tutoris* for Hugh and John Blairs of Borgue, and of Patrick Brown of Gategill or Barharrow [against Andrew Hunter, writer in Edinburgh], 25 January 1763'.

52 NAS C22/76, ff. 290v-291v: both 1 November 1765, registered 3 December 1765.

53 See R. A. Houston, *The population history of Britain and Ireland, 1500–1750* (London: Macmillan, 1991) on nuptiality and other demographic parameters in this society.

54 Some contemporaries argued that marriage could be a cure for madness. See G. S. Rousseau, 'Psychology', in G. S. Rousseau and R. Porter (eds), *The ferment of knowledge. Studies in the historiography of eighteenth-century science* (Cambridge: Cambridge University Press, 1980), pp. 181–2.

55 R. A. Houston, '"Not simple boarding": Care of the mentally incapacitated in Scotland during the long eighteenth century', in P. Bartlett and D. Wright (eds), *Outside the walls of the asylum: The history of care in the community, 1750–2000* (London: Athlone, 1999), 19–44.

56 J. E. Gibson, *A medical sketch of Dumfriesshire* (Dumfries, 1827), pp. 53–5; C. C. Easterbrook, *The chronicle of Crichton Royal (1833–1936)* (Dumfries: Courier Press, 1940), pp. 14–15; M. Williams, *History of Crichton Royal Hospital, 1839–1939* (Dumfries: Crichton Royal Infirmary, 1989), p. 7. For part of the 1790s only four cells were available because a gentleman murderer called Douglas of Luce lived in one and his servant in the other. Crichton Royal Hospital, Dumfries and Galloway Royal Infirmary, Minutes of the Weekly Meeting, 12 September 1795.

57 Dumfries and Galloway Archives (DGA), GG2/1, 2 March 1775. GG2/2, 12 June 1782. J. Andrews, 'Identifying and providing for the mentally disa-

bled in early modern London', in D. Wright and A. Digby (eds), *From idiocy to mental deficiency: Historical perspectives on people with learning disabilities* (London: Routledge, 1996), pp. 72–4 shows that London poor relief records are similarly sparse in mentions.

58 DGA GG2/1, 60. Her destination is unclear.

59 Even at reduced rates, Bedlam was twice the price of care in a workhouse, Edinburgh City Archives, St Cuthbert's Charity Workhouse Minutes, vol. 3, 2 July 1782.

60 R. A. Cage, *The Scottish poor law, 1745–1845* (Edinburgh: Scottish Academic Press, 1981); R. Mitchison, 'The making of the old Scottish poor law', *Past & Present*, 63 (1974), pp. 58–93; A. M'Neel-Caird, *The poor-law manual for Scotland* (Edinburgh, 1851), pp. 17, 20, 66; A. M. Dunlop, *The law of Scotland regarding the poor* (Edinburgh: Blackwood, 1854), pp. 45–6.

61 National Register of Archives for Scotland, 3503/1/21/1–15 [Tyninghame Estate Office, Dunbar: TD73/130/ bundle 21, unnumbered].

62 DGA RB2/1/14. Quoted in M. M. Stewart, '"In durance vile": crime and punishment in seventeenth and eighteenth century records of Dumfries', *Scottish Archives,* 1 (1995), p. 67.

63 DGA RB2/2/92/9 and 11 (1728). GF4/19, 13 August 1728.

64 Broughton House, Kirkcudbright: K1/20, Blair v Blair: 'Information for John Blair . . . 21 March 1748', 10, 14.

65 J. Galt, *The entail, or the lairds of Grippy* ([1822] London: Oxford University Press, 1970), p. 188.

66 Ibid., p. 189.

67 SL Session Papers, vol. 7, case 12, 'Information for Hugh Blair . . . ', p. 12.

68 NAS CS234/B/1/5.

69 SL Session Papers, vol. 53, case 47, 'Answers for Fawside's trustees . . . [to the petition of John Ballantyne of Corehouse], 6 January 1756', p. 1.

70 Ibid., p. 4.

71 Ibid., vol. 117, case 45, 'State of the process . . . ', p. 29.

72 NAS SC49/57/8, Ann Blair (1812). See also SL Session Papers, vol. 284, case 17.

73 L. Rosner, *Medical education in the age of improvement. Edinburgh students and apprentices, 1760–1826* (Edinburgh: Edinburgh University Press, 1991), p. 12.

74 Stewartry Museum, Kirkcudbright, Town Council Minutes, vol. 3 (1714–29), p. 136.

75 Ibid., p. 299.

76 NAS SC16/58/6.

77 Stewartry Museum, Kirkcudbright, Town Council Minutes, vol. 5 (1743–59). p. 76.

78 Ibid., p. 94.
79 NAS E106/20/3. The valuation roll is reproduced in L. R. Timperley (ed.), *A directory of landownership in Scotland, c.1770* (Edinburgh: Scottish Record Society, 1976), pp. 191–2. It is worth noting that a landowners' assessment for the parish of Borgue in 1681 contains no mention of either Blairs or McGuffogs. NAS GD10/567.
80 SC16/58/10, 9 March 1742.
81 NAS SC16/58/3. Hugh McGuffog died in February 1706. NAS CC13/6/ 58, item 17 (1732).
82 NAS CC13/6/60, item 9 (1734).
83 James Webster, *General view of the agriculture of Galloway, comprehending the Stewartry of Kirkcudbright and shire of Wigton* . . . (Edinburgh: John Paterson, 1794), pp. 16–20.
84 R. A. Houston, 'Geographical mobility in Scotland, 1652–1811: The evidence of testimonials', *Journal of Historical Geography*, 11 (1985), pp. 379–94.
85 Webster, *General view*, p. 16.
86 NAS SC39/47/2, Alexander Goldie (1765).
87 L. E. Schmidt, *Holy fairs. Scottish communions and American revivals in the early modern period* (Princeton: Princeton University Press, 1989), pp. 81, 92–3, 102–4, 159–60.
88 A. F. Mitchell, *Catechisms of the second reformation* (London: James Nesbit, 1886).
89 On the work of Borgue Kirk Session see Henderson, *Borgue*, pp. 67–72.
90 R. A. Houston, *Scottish literacy and the Scottish identity* (Cambridge: Cambridge University Press, 1985), pp. 111–30.
91 Donnachie and MacLeod, *Old Galloway*, p. 41.
92 NAS CH2/526/5, p. 184.
93 Ibid., pp. 186–7.
94 L. Leneman and R. Mitchison, *Sexuality and social control. Scotland, 1660–1780* (Oxford: Blackwell, 1989); A. Blaikie, *Illegitimacy, sex and society. North-east Scotland, 1750–1900* (Oxford: Oxford University Press, 1993).
95 T. C. Smout, 'Scottish marriage, regular and irregular, 1500–1940', in R. B. Outhwaite (ed.), *Marriage and society. Studies in the social history of marriage* (London: Europa, 1981), pp. 204–36 ; N. Smith, 'Sexual mores and attitudes in Enlightenment Scotland', in P-G. Boucé (ed.), *Sexuality in eighteenth-century Britain* (Manchester: Manchester University Press, 1982), pp. 47–73; L. Leneman and R. Mitchison, 'Clandestine marriage in the Scottish cities, 1660–1780', *Journal of Social History*, 26, 4 (1993), pp. 845–61.
96 As Smith notes, 'habit and repute' did not constitute marriage but only gave grounds for believing that a couple might be married ('Sexual mores',

p. 49); see also R. D. Ireland, 'Husband and wife: post-Reformation canon law of marriage . . . ', in *An introduction to Scottish legal history*, vol. 20 (Edinburgh: Stair Society, 1958), pp. 82–9; W. D. H. Sellar, 'Marriage, divorce and the forbidden degrees: Canon law and Scots law', in W. N. Osborough (ed.), *Explorations in law and history. Irish legal history society discourses, 1988–1994* (Dublin: Irish Academic Press, 1995), pp. 59–82.

97 Houston, 'Women . . . 1500–1800', pp. 118–47.

98 Quoted in Smout, 'Scottish marriage', p. 216; Ireland, 'Husband and wife', pp. 84–5.

99 SL Session Papers, vol. 7, case 12, 'Answers for John Blair . . . ', p. 3.

100 Smout, 'Scottish marriage', p. 234

101 Smith, 'Sexual mores', p. 50. On the earlier law see J. D. Scanlan, 'Husband and wife: pre-Reformation canon law of marriage . . . ', in *An introduction to Scottish legal history*, vol. 20 (Edinburgh: Stair Society, 1958), pp. 69–81; C. J. Guthrie, 'The history of divorce in Scotland', *Scottish Historical Review*, 8 (1910), pp. 39–52.

102 R. Marshall, *Virgins and viragos. A history of women in Scotland from 1080 to 1980* (London: Collins, 1983), p. 196.

103 In the civil court cognitions used by Houston for his study of madness in eighteenth-century Scotland, male deponents outnumbered female by more than six to one. In a sample of 3,215 witnesses before the High Court of Justiciary (Scotland's supreme criminal court) between 1650 and 1760 the sex ratio was only slightly more balanced at 454 males per 100 females (Houston, *Scottish literacy*, pp. 57–70). For the reasons see George Mackenzie 'The laws and customs of Scotland in matters criminal', in *The works of that eminent and learned lawyer, Sir George Mackenzie of Rosehaugh, advocate* . . . , 2 vols. (Edinburgh: James Watson, 1716, 1722), vol. 2, pp. 255–6. See also Houston, 'Women . . . 1500–1800', pp. 128–34.

104 H. Scott, *Fasti ecclesiae Scoticanae* (new edition, 7 vols, Edinburgh: Oliver & Boyd, 1915–28), vol. 2, p. 424.

105 On the composition of Scottish society in this period see R. A. Houston and I. D. Whyte, 'Introduction. Scottish society in perspective, 1500–1800', in R. A. Houston and I. D. Whyte (eds.), *Scottish Society, 1500–1800* (Cambridge: Cambridge University Press, 1988) pp. 1–36. On rural domestic industry see R. A. Houston and K. D. M. Snell, 'Proto-industrialization? Cottage industry, social change and industrial revolution', *Historical Journal*, 27, 2 (1984), pp. 473–92.

106 The only person of that name who appears in listings of householders from 1752 is a Mrs Tudhope, who lived in Kinloch Close North. J. Gilhooley, *A directory of Edinburgh in 1752* (Edinburgh: Edinburgh University Press, 1989).

107 Scott, *Fasti*.
108 Ibid., vol. 1, pp. 60, 164, 167. On Walker's career after leaving Kirk-cudbrightshire see R. A. Houston, '"Bustling artisans". Patronage disputes in South Leith during the 1740s and 1750s', *Albion* 26, 1 (1994), pp. 55–77.
109 R. A. Houston, *Literacy in early modern Europe: Culture and education, 1500–1800* (London: Longman,1989).
110 Scott, *Fasti*, vol. 1, p. 251.
111 NAS CC13/6/65, item 1 (1740).

Chapter 3   Understanding Mental Incapacity

1 R. Porter, 'The patient in England, c. 1660 – c. 1800', in A. Wear (ed.), *Medicine in society: Historical essays* (Cambridge: Cambridge University Press, 1992), pp. 91–118.
2 In its eighteenth-century meaning, this phrase is usually associated with Thomas Reid, *Essays on the intellectual powers of man* (Edinburgh: T. Cadell, J. Bell and W. Creech, 1785).
3 NAS CC8/6/15, Blair v Blair (1748).
4 D. Defoe, An essay upon projects. Quoted in R. Hunter and I. Macalpine (eds), *Three hundred years of psychiatry, 1535–1860* (London: Oxford University Press, 1963), p. 266.
5 SL Session Papers, vol. 18, case 24, 'Information for Alexander Wedderburn . . . ', p. 10.
6 Ibid., vol. 7, case 12, 'Bill of Advocation for Hugh Blair', pp. 3–4.
7 Ibid., 'Information for Hugh Blair . . . ', p. 6.
8 Ibid., 'Bill of advocation . . . ', 17 June 1748.
9 Ibid., 'Information for Hugh Blair . . . ', p. 2.
10 NAS SC39/37/9, Cecilia Stevenson (1783). For comparison see the fourteenth-century English case quoted by R. Neugebauer 'Mental handicap in medieval and early modern England. Criteria, measurement and care', in D. Wright and A. Digby (eds), *From idiocy to mental deficiency: Historical perspectives on people with learning disabilities* (London: Routledge, 1996), p. 29.
11 SL Session Papers, vol. 7, case 12, 'Answers for John Blair . . . ', p. 2.
12 Ibid., 'Answers for John Blair . . . ', p. 3.
13 Ibid., 'Information for Hugh Blair . . . ', p. 6.
14 A. Digby, *Madness, morality and medicine: A study of the York Retreat, 1796–1914* (Cambridge: Cambridge University Press, 1985), p. 3. See also R. Porter, 'Being mad in Georgian England', *History Today* 31 (December

1981), p. 43. A. T. Scull, *The most solitary of afflictions. Madness and society in Britain, 1700–1900* (London: Yale University Press, 1993), p. 61 suggests contemporaries drew 'the conclusion that in losing his reason, the essence of his humanity, the madman had lost his claim to be treated as a human being'. A. Suzuki, 'Dualism and the transformation of psychiatric language in the seventeenth and eighteenth centuries', *History of Science*, 33 (1995), p. 437, offers a better analysis.

15   SL Session Papers, vol. 7, case 12, 'Bill of Advocation . . . ', p. 7.

16   NAS CC8/6/15, Blair v Blair (1748).

17   E. Muir, *Ritual in early modern Europe* (Cambridge: Cambridge University Press, 1997), pp. 128–9.

18   SL Session Papers, vol. 7, case 12, 'Bill of Advocation . . . ', p. 12.

19   NAS CC8/6/15, Blair v Blair (1748). Jamie Duff, one of John Kay's 'characters', had a similar passion. J. Kay, *A series of original portraits and caricature etchings, by the late John Kay, miniature painter, Edinburgh; with biographical sketches and illustrative anecdotes*, 2 vols (Edinburgh, 1838), vol. 1, p. 7.

20   See for example J. Andrews, 'Begging the question of idiocy: The definition and socio-cultural meaning of idiocy in early modern Britain: part 2', *History of Psychiatry*, 9 (1998), pp. 182–95.

21   C. Bell, *The anatomy and philosophy of expression as connected with the fine arts* (London: John Murray, 1806. 3rd edition [of *Essays on the anatomy of expression in painting*, 1806], 1844), p. 121; pp. 179–81 describe the physiognomy of the madman. Ludmilla Jordanova describes Bell's work as the culmination of a physiognomic tradition (L. Jordanova, 'The art and science of seeing in medicine: Physiognomy, 1780–1820', in W. F. Bynum and R. Porter (eds), *Medicine and the senses* (Cambridge: Cambridge University Press, 1993), p. 123). See also J. Browne, 'Darwin and the face of madness', in W. F. Bynum, R. Porter and M. Shepherd (eds), *The anatomy of madness. Essays in the history of psychiatry* (London: Tavistock, 1985), vol. 1, pp. 151–65.

22   See, for example, R. Bartlett, 'Symbolic meanings of hair in the middle ages', *Transactions of the Royal Historical Society*, 6th series, 4 (1994), pp. 43–60; M. Pointon, *Hanging the head. Portraiture and social formation in eighteenth-century England* (London: Yale University Press, 1993), esp. pp. 107–33.

23   Pointon, *Hanging the head*, p. 112. See also E. Sitwell, *English eccentrics* ([1933] London: Folio Society, 1994), pp. 29–37.

24   John Gregory, *A comparative view of the state and faculties of man with those of the natural world*, 2 vols. (London: J. Dodsley, 6th edition, 1774), vol. 1, p. 25.

25   S. Maxwell and R. Hutchison, *Scottish costume, 1550–1850* (London: Black, 1958), pp. 72, 130–1.

26 F. Heal, *Hospitality in early modern England* (Oxford: Oxford University Press, 1990), p. 399.

27 Broughton House, Kirkcudbright: K1/20, Blair v Blair: 'Information for John Blair . . . 21 March 1748', p. 11.

28 For context see R. A. Houston, 'Literacy, education and the culture of print in Enlightenment Edinburgh', *History*, 78, 254 (1993), pp. 373–92.

29 See James Webster, *General view of the agriculture of Galloway, comprehending the Stewartry of Kirkcudbright and shire of Wigton* . . . (Edinburgh: John Paterson, 1794), pp. 19–20, for details of regional wall-building styles.

30 Some psychologists, linguists, and ethnographers tell us that in all human societies individuals will on average have about 150 people whom they know well enough to talk to, and to ask a favour of without embarrassment. The evidence is summarized in R. Dunbar, *Grooming, gossip and the evolution of language* (London: Faber, 1996). S. D'Cruze, 'The middling sort in eighteenth-century Colchester: Independence, social relations and the community broker', in J. Barry and C. Brooks (eds), *The middling sort of people. Culture, society and politics in England, 1550–1800* (London: Macmillan, 1994), pp. 181–207, offers a historical analysis of this topic for an English town.

31 E. Muir, *Ritual in early modern Europe* (Cambridge: Cambridge University Press, 1997), p. 125.

32 J. Bremmer and H. Roodenburg (eds), *A cultural history of gesture from antiquity to the present day* (Cambridge: Cambridge University Press, 1991).

33 Quoted in E. C. Sanderson, *Women and work in eighteenth-century Edinburgh* (London: Macmillan, 1996), p. 65. See also the chapter on burial in W. McMillan, *The worship of the Scottish reformed church, 1550–1638* (London: Clarke, 1931), pp. 283–98.

34 K. Cameron, 'Humour and history', in K. Cameron (ed.), *Humour and history* (Oxford: Intellect, 1993), p. 5, summarizing the standpoint of Bergson and Hobbes. See also B. Sanders, 'Lie it as it plays: Chaucer becomes an author', in D. R. Olson and N. Torrance (eds), *Literacy and orality* (Cambridge: Cambridge University Press, 1991), pp. 121–2.

35 Thomas Hobbes, *Leviathan* ed. and intro. C. B. Macpherson (Harmondsworth: Penguin, 1968), p. 125. Francis Hutcheson, *Thoughts on laughter . . .* (Glasgow: Robert and Andrew Foulis, 1758), devotes pp. 1–18 to a biting critique of Hobbes.

36 It was pointed out in a legal submission that the boy's mother was a cousin of Hugh Blair. SL Session Papers, vol. 7, case 12, 'Information for Hugh Blair . . . ', 7. Hugh's lawyer continued: 'Alexander Telfer, a boy about three years of age, led the defender, with his hat off, up and down the town of Kirkcudbright for his diversion. Now this is a most improbable story,

that a mere infant was capable to have done any such thing . . . unless this boy of three years old had had the sense of one of thirteen, he was incapable of such imperious behaviour towards the defender, nor could it have entered his thoughts.'

37 J. Erskine, *The principles of the law of Scotland* (Edinburgh: Elphingston Balfour, 1809 edn), p. 102.

38 Ibid., p. 103.

39 NAS SC67/57/14, Catherine Leny (1798).

40 SL Session Papers, vol. 7, case 12, 'Bill of Advocation . . . ', pp. 2–3.

41 Ibid., 'Answers for John Blair . . . ', p. 18.

42 Ibid., vol. 580, case 17, p. 3.

43 P. Rushton, 'Lunatics and idiots: Mental disability, the community, and the poor law in north-east England, 1600–1800', *Medical History*, 32 (1988), pp. 51–2, outlines the simple tests of reason and knowledge applied by English courts.

44 J. Erskine, *An institute of the law of Scotland* (Edinburgh: Bell & Bradfute, 5th edition, 1812), vol. 1, p. 158.

45 SL Session Papers, vol. 7, case 12, 'Bill of Advocation . . . ', p. 5.

46 Ibid, 'Information for Hugh Blair . . . ', p. 10.

47 Broughton House, Kirkcudbright: K1/20, Blair v Blair: 'Memorial for Hugh Blair . . . 22 July 1747', p. 1.

48 Old Parochial Register 871/1.

49 H. E. Bell, *An introduction to the history and records of the court of wards and liveries* (Cambridge: Cambridge University Press, 1953), p. 128.

50 Broughton House, Kirkcudbright: K1/20, Blair v Blair: 'Memorial for Hugh Blair . . . 22 July 1747, p. 2: 'an idiot is supposed incapable of issue'.

51 NAS CS229/B/2/16.

52 Ibid. CS234/B/1/5.

53 Ibid. SC16/58/12, 31 December 1741, registered on 2 May 1747. It is possible that David Blair had mortgaged the estate since William McGuffog, eldest son of William McGuffog of Rusco had a title to it in 1713 (McKerlie, *History*, vol. 3, p. 181. The definition of usury did not simply depend on the rate charged. Strictly speaking, usury was lending where the risk was not shared by both parties, but was loaded against the borrower.

54 NAS CS234/B/1/5.

55 SL Session papers, vol. 69, case 11, p. 2. 'The petition of David Blair younger of Borgue . . . 25 January 1763'.

56 Ibid, p. 7.

57 NAS SC16/58/12, 15 April 1748.

58 A. Mitchell, *Pre-1855 gravestone inscriptions: An index for the stewartry of Kirkcudbright*, 2 vols (Edinburgh: Scottish Genealogy Society, 1990).

59 *Decennial indexes to the services of heirs in Scotland, 1700–1859*, 4 vols (Edinburgh, 1863–91). Volumes 1 and 2. NAS RS23/20, f. 186. NAS C22/78, f. 285–285v: 10 February 1769, registered 25 February 1769. Soon after, David had himself served heir to his grandfather, David Blair. NAS C22/79, ff. 338–9: 10 September 1769, registered 7 July 1770.

60 NAS RS23/20, f. 206. The contract was dated 1 March 1737 and is referred to in the document cited, which is a 'sasine' of 22 February 1769. Stewartry Museum, Kirkcudbright, Blair of Borgue, Miscellaneous documents, 1978/25/03.

Chapter 4   Autism and its Relevance to the Case of Hugh Blair

1   L. Kanner, 'Autistic disturbances of affective contact', *Nervous Child*, 2 (1943), pp. 217–50.

2   J. Haslam, *Observations on madness and melancholy* (London: G. Hayden, 1809).

3   N. Challis and H. W. Dewey, 'The blessed fools of old Russia', *Jahrbücher für die Geschichte Osteuropas*, 22 (1974), pp. 1–11.

4   H. Lane, *The wild boy of Aveyron* (Cambridge, Mass.: Harvard University Press, 1977).

5   E. M. Itard, *De l'education d'un homme sauvage, ou des premiers dévelopements physiques et moraux du jeune sauvage de l'Aveyron* (Paris: Goujon Fils, 1801).

6   H. Asperger, 'Die autistischen Psychopathen im Kindesalter', *Archiv für Psychiatrie und Nervenkrankheiten*, 117 (1944), pp. 76–136. Translated by U. Frith in U. Frith (ed.) *Autism and Asperger syndrome* (Cambridge: Cambridge University Press, 1991), pp. 37–92.

7   A. R. Damasio and R. G. Maurer, 'A neurological model for childhood autism', *Archives of Neurology*, 35 (1978), pp. 777–86.

8   A. Bailey, A. LeCouteur, I. Gottesmann et al., 'Autism as a strongly genetic disorder: Evidence from a British twin study', *Psychological Medicine*, 25 (1995), pp. 63–77.

9   A. Bailey, P. Bolton and M. Rutter, 'A full genome screen for autism with evidence for linkage to a region on chromosome 7q', *Human Molecular Genetics*, 7 (1998), pp. 571–8.

10 E. Fombonne, 'Epidemiological surveys of autism', in F. R. Volkmar (ed.), *Autism and pervasive developmental disorders* (Cambridge: Cambridge University Press, 1988), pp. 32–63.

11 A. Bailey, W. Phillips and M. Rutter, 'Autism: Towards an integration of clinical, genetic, neuropsychological and neurobiological perspectives', *Journal of Child Psychology and Psychiatry*, 37 (1996), pp. 89–126.

12 L. Wing and J. Gould, 'Severe impairments in social interaction and associ-

ated abnormalities in children: Epidemiology and classification', *Journal of Autism and Developmental Disorders*, 9 (1979), pp. 11–30.

13　L. Wing , *The autistic spectrum* (London: Constable, 1996).

14　See chapters in Volkmar, *Autism. See note 10, p. 176.*

15　E. Schopler and G. B. Mesibov (eds), *Autism in adolescents and adults* (New York: Plenum, 1983).

16　M. Frankland, *Freddie the weaver: The boy who fought to join the world* (London: Sinclair-Stevenson, 1995).

17　C. Hart, *Without reason: A family copes with two generations of autism* (NewYork: Penguin, 1989).

18　D. Williams, *Nobody nowhere* (London: Corgi, 1992); T. Grandin, 'An inside view of autism', in E. Schopler and G. Mesibov (eds) *High-functioning individuals with autism* (New York: Plenum, 1992), pp. 105–26; G. Gerland, *A real person. Life on the outside* (London: Souvenir Press, 1997); for an insightful account of Temple Grandin, see also O. Sacks, *An anthropologist on Mars* (London; Picador, 1995).

19　S. Baron-Cohen, A. Cox, G. Baird et al. (1996) 'Psychological markers of autism at 18 months of age in a large population', *British Journal of Psychiatry*, 168 (1996), pp. 59–163.

20　B. Hermelin and N. O'Connor, *Psychological experiments with autistic children* (Oxford: Pergamon Press, 1971).

21　For a review see F. Happé and U. Frith 'The neuropsychology of autism', *Brain*, 119 (1996), pp. 1377–1400

22　M. Bauman and T. L. Kemper 'Neuroanatomic observations of the brain in autism', in M. Bauman and T. L. Kemper (eds) *The neurobiology of autism* (Baltimore: Johns Hopkins University Press, 1994), pp. 119–45.

23　F. Abell, M. Krams, J. Ashburner, R. Passingham, K. J. Friston, R. Frackowiak, F. Happé, C. Frith and U. Frith 'The neuroanatomy of autism: A voxel based whole brain analysis of structural MRI scans in high functioning individuals', *Neuroreport*, 10 (1999), pp. 1647–51.

24　For up-to-date reviews see S. Baron-Cohen, H. Tager-Flusberg and D. Cohen *Understanding other minds II: Perspectives from autism and cognitive neuroscience* (Oxford: Oxford University Press, 2000).

25　A. Leslie, 'Pretence and representation: The origins of "theory of mind"', *Psychological Review*, 94 (1987), pp. 412–26

26　This paradigm was developed by H. Wimmer and J. Perner, 'Beliefs about beliefs: Representation and the constraining function of wrong beliefs in young children's understanding of deception', *Cognition*, 13 (1983), pp. 103–28. It was applied to autism by S. Baron-Cohen, A. Leslie and U. Frith, 'Does the autistic child have a "theory of mind"?' *Cognition*, 21 (1985), pp. 37–46.

27   C. D. Frith and U. Frith 'Interacting minds – A biological basis', *Science,* 286 (1999), pp. 1692–5.

28   M. Sigman and L. Capps, *Children with autism: A developmental perspective* (Cambridge, Mass: Harvard University Press, 1997); P. Hobson 'Understanding persons: The role of affect', in S. Baron-Cohen, H. Tager-Flusberg and D. Cohen (eds), *Understanding other minds: Perspectives from autism* (Oxford: Oxford University Press, 1993), pp. 204–27.

29   R. J. R. Blair, 'Physiological responsiveness to the distress of others in children with autism', *Personality and Individual Differences,* 26 (1999), pp. 477–85.

30   J. Russell, *Autism as an executive disorder* (Oxford: Oxford University Press, 1997); M. Turner, 'Repetitive behaviour in autism', *Journal of Child Psychology and Psychiatry,* 40 (1999), pp. 839–49.

31   T. Shallice, *From neuropsychology to mental structure* (Cambridge: Cambridge University Press, 1988); for details of the Tower of London test see T. Shallice, 'Specific impairments of planning', *Philosophical Transactions of the Royal Society of London* B, 298 (1982), pp. 199–208.

32   C. L. Gerstadt, Y. H. Hong and A. Diamond, 'The relationship between cognition and action: Performance of children 3-7 years old on a Stroop-like day–night test', *Cognition,* 53 (1994), pp. 129–53.

33   For a recent review see F. Happé, 'Autism: Cognitive deficit or cognitive style', *Trends in Cognitive Sciences,* 3 (1999), pp. 216–22 ; the Titchener illusion shown in Plate 27 was included in the study by F. Happé, 'Studying weak central coherence at low levels: Children with autism do not succumb to visual illusions: A research note', *Journal of Child Psychology and Psychiatry,* 37 (1996), pp. 873–77.

34   A. Shah and U. Frith, 'An islet of ability in autistic children: A research note', *Journal of Child Psychology and Psychiatry,* 24 (1983), pp. 613–20. This study used the embedded figures task, while the following study used the block design task shown in Plate 27: A. Shah and U. Frith, 'Why do autistic individuals show superior performance on the block design task?', *Journal of Child Psychology and Psychiatry,* 34 (1993), pp. 1351–64.

Chapter 5   *Reading the Court Case as a Clinical Case*

1   The advertisement concerned the bleach field at Ormiston. This was a topical subject, but unlikely to be of interest to Hugh. Ormiston in East Lothian was the project of the celebrated landowner and 'improver' John Cockburn, who planned and built the village in the 1730s as a farming and linen-making community. The enterprise was a financial failure and the

village was sold to the Earl of Hopetoun in 1747.

2   B. Sodian and U. Frith, 'Deception and sabotage in children with autism', *Journal of Child Psychology and Psychiatry*, 33 (1992), pp. 591–605.

3   R. A. Houston, *Madness and society in eighteenth-century Scotland* (Oxford: Oxford University Press, 2000). Three years after John Blair began his suit, Mary Kerr sought a separation from her husband of 11 years, John Rutherford of Knowsouth. Suffering what others thought were pathological jealousies and delusions that he was being poisoned, Rutherford was said to 'maltreat her in a most barbarous and cruel manner frequently reviled, beat, bruised and wounded the complainer to the effusion of her blood and thrust her out of his house of Knowsouth'. At least once in every year between 1743 and 1750 Mary was so seriously injured that she had to seek refuge with relatives. Rutherford was cognosced in January 1763, by which time he was firmly locked in Edinburgh's Bedlam where he remained fatuous and furious for 20 years – nearly as long as he had been married. The keeper described Rutherford as a dangerous and devious man and singled him out as the only one of 40 inmates who was too violent for him to handle alone.

4   The latest edition of the *Diagnostic and statistical manual of mental disorders*, 4th edn (DSM-IV, Washington, DC: American Psychiatric Association,1994, p. 66) lists four criteria for autistic disorder. The same criteria are specified in *ICD-10 Classification of mental and behavioural disorders: Clinical descriptions and guidelines* (Geneva:World Health Organization, 1992), pp. 253–5 and *ICD-10 Classification of mental and behavioural disorders: Diagnostic criteria for research* (Geneva:World Health Organization, 1993), pp. 147–50: qualitative impairment in social interaction; qualitative abnormalities in communication; restricted, repetitive, and stereotyped patterns of behaviour, interests and activities. The fourth criterion, as listed in both DSM-IV and ICD-10, requires evidence for abnormal development before the age of three years in language, in the development of social attachments or of reciprocal social interaction, and in functional or symbolic play.

5   *ICD-10* 1993, p. 69.

6   NAS SC67/42/1, David Smith (1715).

Chapter 6   The Historical-clinical Approach to the Case of Hugh Blair

1   SL Session Papers, vol. 7, case 12, 'Information for Hugh Blair . . . ', pp. 3, 11.

2   U.Frith and F. Happé, 'Self-consciousness and autism. What it is like to be autistic?', *Mind and Language*, 14 (1999), pp. 1–22 .

3 G. Gerland, *A real person: Life on the outside* (London, Souvenir Press,1997).

4 N. Challis and H. W. Dewey, 'The blessed fools of old Russia", *Jahrbücher für die Geschichte Osteuropas,* 22 (1974), 1–11.

5 P. G. B. McNeill (ed), *The practicks of Sir James Balfour of Pittendreich, reproduced from the printed edition of 1754,* 2 vols. (Edinburgh, Stair Society,1962–3), vol. 2, p. 514. See also George Mackenzie 'The laws and customs of Scotland in matters criminal', in *The works of that eminent and learned lawyer, Sir George Mackenzie of Rosehaugh, advocate* . . . , 2 vols. (Edinburgh: James Watson, 1716, 1722), vol. 2, p. 59.

6 This had earlier happened to Jean Blair. SRO JC3/41, 13 March 1781.

7 SRO SC1/18/1, 16.

8 The development should not be seen as a simple indicator of 'progress'. The Scottish poor law was being reinterpreted around this time to exclude parish responsibility for the able-bodied poor, making some form of central provision for the criminal insane increasingly necessary. R. Mitchison, 'The making of the old Scottish poor law', *Past & Present,* 63 (1974), pp. 88–92.

9 P. Howlin, 'Outcome in adult life for people with autism and Asperger syndrome', in: F. R. Volkmar (ed.), *Autism and pervasive developmental disorders* (Cambridge, Cambridge University Press,1998), pp. 209–241.

Glossary of Historical Terms

Advocate   An élite lawyer, member of the Faculty of Advocates.

Bailie   A magistrate (alderman) in towns, or a steward in rural areas.

Barony   Jurisdiction with limited civil and criminal powers.

Brieve   A brief or writ.

Cognosce   To judicially investigate (here pronounce a person insane after judicial investigation).

Cognition   A process of law to ascertain facts (here concerning a person's sanity).

Curator   An administrator or guardian of the estate of a minor (q.v.) or mentally incapable person, but sometimes used interchangeably with tutor (q.v.).

Dative   Someone (here a tutor or curator) appointed by a court in default of a tutor-nominate.

Decreet   A judgement.

Deponent   A witness; one who gives evidence in a court case.

Friends   Kin (beyond the nuclear family) and patrons whose advice and opinion was valued.

Heritor   An owner of heritable property, usually land or buildings.

Kirk Session   A parish body comprising clergyman, clerk or 'precentor', and lay elders who policed poor relief, and moral and religious life.

Laird   A landed proprietor described as 'of' rather than 'in' his place of residence (usually a rural estate).

Minor   A boy aged 14–20 years, or a girl aged 12–20 years.

Portioner   An owner by inheritance of part of a heritable property.

Pound (£) Scots   Approximately one twelfth of a pound (£) sterling.

Presbytery   An association of parish clergy and selected kirk session (q.v.) elders dealing with ecclesiastical administration and with difficult cases of moral or religious deviance sent from kirk sessions; part of the Presbyterian form of church government.

Procurator   A legal representative or pleader; member of a society of that name in Glasgow and Aberdeen.

Pupil   A boy aged less than 14 years, or a girl aged less than 12 years .

Reduction   A legal process to suspend or overturn a previous judgement or contract.

Residenter   An inhabitant or resident of a burgh.

Retour   To extract or return to Chancery for recording of the verdict of an inquest; the record itself.

Sasine   An act or document transferring legal ownership of heritable property such as land.

Subject   The person named in a brieve.

Tack   A lease.

Testament   A will.

Tolbooth   A prison or guardhouse.

Tutor   An administrator or guardian of the person and estate of a pupil (q.v.) or mentally incapable person, but sometimes used interchangeably with curator (q.v.).

Writer   A legal clerk.

Writer to the Signet (WS)   A specialist legal clerk or notary, part of a 'society' or professional association of the same name. Of higher status than a 'writer' (q.v.) but below advocate (q.v.)

Glossary and Topics in Autism

Asperger syndrome Label used for a high-functioning variant of autism with predominantly good language and intelligence and better social insight. The present consensus is that Asperger syndrome falls within the autistic spectrum, but deserves its own label because the course of the disorder, and consequently prognosis and management, diverge from nuclear autism. People with Asperger syndrome tend to be less aloof, more socially interested, more verbal in a pedantic style. They tend to have special interests to the point of obsession.

Autism – spectrum The spectrum of manifestations of autism covers a wide range of severity from silent and aloof to overfriendly and verbose. The term pervasive developmental disorder is similar in its range.

Autism – prevalence Estimated at 5 per 10,000 with four males to every female, and intellectual impairment in 75 per cent. If the wider autism spectrum is considered, including Asperger syndrome, the prevalence is considerably higher, 1 to 3 in 1,000, but precise estimates are lacking.

Autism – developmental course During the second and third year the characteristic signs of autism are most strongly apparent in poverty of imaginative play, lack of joint attention with others, and lack of social rapport with others. Behaviour problems are very common, including sleeping and eating problems, temper tantrums and general inflexibility. Improvements often occur during later childhood. Puberty is often troublesome and set-backs are possible. Social learning and adaptation continue well into adulthood. Sheltered employment and some degree of supervision of daily living arrangements are likely to be needed. Life span studies of autism covering middle and old age are as yet lacking.

Autism – Intelligence and mental retardation   Autism can occur at all IQ levels, but 75 per cent of individuals with autism also have some degree of mental retardation (i.e. IQ below 70). Associated medical conditions (q.v.) often imply severe degrees of general learning disability. The profile of performance across different parts of the Wechsler IQ scales has peaks and troughs regardless of overall level of IQ scores.

Cognition, cognitive   Terms referring to the mind and mental processes, in distinction to brain and behaviour. The cognitive level of description occupies a space in between brain and behaviour. It includes emotions as well as other types of thought, memory and perception. Cognitive mechanisms are mental mechanisms that can potentially be mapped onto brain mechanisms. Cognitive processes must be carefully distinguished from descriptions of behavioural facts, such as scores on psychological tests.

Executive function   Umbrella term covering a wide array of higher cognitive processes typically impaired in patients with frontal lobe damage, and also in individuals suffering from autism. The frontal lobes are thought to be responsible for generating new ideas, disengaging from context, inhibiting inappropriate responses, and planning novel sequences of actions. It is likely that brain abnormality in autism involves the frontal lobes, or else a system that has strong interconnections to the frontal lobes.

Executive function tests   These tests include a variety of tasks that involve working memory, planning, inhibition, and fluency. For instance, in the 'Tower of London' test, you are presented with a starting arrangement with balls on three pegs and an end state.   By moving the balls one at a time you have to get from the starting to the end state.   Advance planning is needed to do this in the minimum number of moves. Another example is generating as many uses as possible for a handkerchief or a brick. People with autism have been shown to be impaired on these and similar tasks.

Genetic factors   Concordance for autism in identical twins is high (90 per cent) as opposed to fraternal twins (10 per cent). Research so far suggests the effects of several genes (estimated between three and ten), all contributing to the autism phenotype. Family members (in particular, fathers) may have traits that are reminiscent of certain features of autism (including assets such as attention to detail and specialist interests) without being clinically affected themselves.

Hyperlexia   The opposite of dyslexia. The ability to decode from print to sound is superior to the ability to comprehend text meaning. Hyperlexia is not infrequent in cases of autism, though dyslexia has also been reported.

Islets of ability   Often found when testing children with autism. Performance on certain tasks will stand out in comparison with otherwise poor perform-ance. Peaks and troughs in the profile of IQ sub-tests are common at all levels of ability. Performance peaks often include good rote memory, skill at completing jigsaw puzzles, and reading aloud and spelling.

Joint attention   Refers to the sharing of a focus of attention through eye gaze, pointing and showing. At 18 months the normally developing child will sponta-neously show things to others, and point to objects purely for the sake of sharing attention, rather than to obtain the object. These can be considered as examples of true two-way communication, facilitating word learning. Children with au-tism lack this type of joint attention.

Language and communication   Impairments in verbal and non-verbal com-munication form an important part of the diagnostic criteria for autism at all ages. One of the commonest signs in young children suspected of autism is a worry over their language development. Muteness and lack of speech until about age five are common problems. Even if speech is present, problems in compre-hension are noted, in particular over-literal comprehension. Children with au-tism typically use idiosyncratic and stereotyped language. Repetition and echoing is common.

Medical conditions and autism   A number of medical disorders have been reported to be associated with autism in 10 per cent of cases, based on existing epidemiological studies. The disorders most frequently mentioned are fragile-X syndrome, neurofibromatosis and tuberous sclerosis. In all these cases autism may be linked via mental retardation and widespread brain damage, rather than autism-specific neurological abnormality. Autism can co-exist with almost all known neurodevelopmental disorders, and furthermore appears to have signifi-cantly raised incidence in conditions such as Williams syndrome, Turner syn-drome and phenylketonuria. Acquired illnesses, such as viral encephalopathy in childhood, can also lead to autism in the presence of severe mental retardation.

Mentalizing   A novel term coined to refer to the automatic tendency to at-tribute mental states (e.g. beliefs, desires) to self and others. Mentalizing under-lies the ability to develop an intuitive theory of mind and is also a shorthand for referring to the application of theory of mind, on-line, in social situations. If mentalizing is impaired, as is hypothesised for autism, other abilities may be used to compensate. For instance, strategies can be developed to infer consequences and causes of behaviour based on repeated experience. See also Theory of mind.

Mentalizing mechanism   Individuals with autism can understand physical cause and effect in the world around them, but are less good at understanding cause and effect in the behaviour of other people. This suggests that a separate cognitive mechanism is needed for mentalizing, thought to be faulty in autism.

The underlying brain system, which may be structurally and functionally abnormal, has not yet been identified, but is thought to involve parts of the frontal and temporal lobes of the brain. See also Theory of mind: brain basis.

Neurological abnormalities and autism   Epilepsy affects about a third of individuals with autism with seizures beginning in puberty in about half of these cases. Other neurological signs include tiptoe walking, nystagmus, motor posturing, hypotonia and spasticity, and abnormal persistence of infantile reflexes. Raised incidence of left handedness or mixed handedness is found, similar to the incidence in other mentally handicapped groups.

Pervasive developmental disorder (PDD)   DSM–IV currently places autistic disorder within the category of pervasive developmental disorders (PDD): disorders characterized by severe impairments in more than one area of development. PDD includes Asperger syndrome, Rett syndrome, childhood disintegrative disorder, and PDD–not otherwise specified. This last category is a catch-all for somewhat atypical cases and cases where the severity of symptoms is considered below a clinically significant threshold. The term autism spectrum covers approximately the same ground but is specifically anchored in the triad of impairments in socialization, communication and imagination.

Savant abilities   Superior functioning in certain domains against a background of low general ability. They typically occur in art, music, and calculation. Approximately one in ten people with autism are 'savants'.

Stereotypies   Apparently pointless repetitive behaviour, less complex than mannerisms or rituals. Stereotypies are characteristic features of autism but are of variable frequency and intensity. Common examples are hand-flapping or body-rocking.

Theory of mind   Tendency to attribute mental states to others and self. Lack of theory of mind is assumed to be typical in autism. In contrast to their inability to understand psychological motivation, individuals with autism can understand physical cause and effect in the world around them. This suggests that a separate cognitive mechanism is needed for 'mentalizing' that is faulty in autism, while other cognitive processes are not.

Theory of mind – brain basis   Some initial data suggest that a circumscribed area of the cortex may be 'dedicated' to mentalizing. Brain scanning experiments, using Positron Emission Tomography (PET), have shown that special areas in the brain (including the paracingulate sulcus, para-amygdaloid cortex and temporal-parietal junction) are highly active during mentalizing tasks. Interestingly, these areas appear to be less active in individuals with autism. Although very preliminary, these results are consistent with the idea that the brain system that underpins mentalizing is not functioning normally in autism.

Trainspotting   Nickname for tendencies common in people with autism that the theory of weak central coherence (q.v.) attempts to explain, e.g. narrow interests; emphasis on surface features of objects, which may be collected obsessively.

Triad of impairments   Specific impairments in socialization, communication and imagination. These may manifest as aloofness as well as odd social approaches; lack of speech as well as fluent but stilted speech; absence of make-believe play as well as repetitive acting out of characters and situations seen on TV.

Weak central coherence   One extreme of a cognitive style which implies greater attention to detail at the cost of global meaning. Evidence exists that people with autism process information in an unusually piecemeal fashion. Weak central coherence is not a deficit but an information processing preference associated with skills as well as difficulties.

Weak central coherence tests   People with autism and others with weak central coherence do exceptionally well on tasks which demand a focus on detail. They tend to find hidden figures easily and can quickly construct a block design where others might fail to see the pieces in the whole design. They perceive visual illusions (generated by context effects) more veridically. They remember the surface form of text extremely well, better than its gist. However, despite good reading skills, they may fail to use context to disambiguate words: in a homograph reading task, for example, reading 'lead' in 'The dog was on a lead' as if it were 'lead' as in the metal.

Further Historical Reading

Donnachie, I. and MacLeod, I. (1974) *Old Galloway*. London: David and Charles.

Houston, R. A. (1985) *Scottish literacy and the Scottish identity*. Cambridge: Cambridge University Press.

Houston, R. A. (1991) *The population history of Britain and Ireland, 1500–1750*. London: Macmillan.

Houston, R. A. (1994) *Social change in the age of Enlightenment. Edinburgh, 1660–1760*. Oxford: Oxford University Press.

Houston, R. A. (2000) *Madness and society in eighteenth-century Scotland*. Oxford: Oxford University Press.

Houston, R. A. and Knox, W. W. (eds) (2001) *The Penguin history of Scotland*. Harmondsworth: Penguin.

Houston, R. A. and Whyte, I. D. (eds) (1989) *Scottish society, 1500–1800*. Cambridge: Cambridge University Press.

Further Reading on Autism

There are now dozens of books on autism and hundreds of scientific articles. Updated information, reviews and recommendations can be obtained from internet sites that specialize in autism. In the footnotes to chapters 4 to 6 a number of references have been given to document some important facts that have emerged from empirical studies. Below are some books published in the last few years on a variety of topics which contain further useful references.

Baron-Cohen, S., Tager-Flusberg, H. and Cohen, D. (2000) *Understanding other minds Second edition: Perspectives from developmental cognitive neuroscience.* Oxford: Oxford University Press.

Bauman, M. L. and Kemper, T. L. (1994) *The neurobiology of autism.* Baltimore: The Johns Hopkins University Press.

Frith, U. (2000) *Autism, explaining the enigma,* 2nd edn., Oxford: Blackwell.

Happé, F. (1994) *Autism: An introduction to psychological theory.* London: Psychology Press and Cambridge, Mass: Harvard University Press (1995).

Russell, J. (ed.) (1998) *Autism as an executive disorder.* Oxford: Oxford University Press.

Sigman, M. and Capps, L. (1997) *Children with autism: A developmental perspective.* Cambridge, Mass: Harvard University Press.

Schopler, E. and Mesibov, G. B. (eds) (1983 onwards) *Current issues in autism* series. (NewYork: Plenum).

Tager-Flusberg, H. (ed.) (1999) *Developmental neuropsychology.* Cambridge, Mass: MIT Press.

Volkmar, F. R. (ed.) (1998) *Autism and pervasive developmental disorders.* Cambridge: Cambridge University Press.

Wing, L. (1996) *The autistic spectrum.* London: Constable.

Index